W9-BUX-280

# [the nest]

## newlywed

## HANDBOOK

DISCARD

Carley Roney
& the Editors of
TheNest.com

# [the nest]

## newlywed

## HANDBOOK

An Owner's Manual for Modern Married Life

Clarkson Potter/Publishers
New York

Copyright © 2006 by The Knot, Inc.

All rights reserved.
Published in the United States by Clarkson Potter Publishers,
an imprint of the Crown Publishing Group,
a division of Random House, Inc., New York.
www.crownpublishing.com
www.clarksonpotter.com

Clarkson N. Potter is a trademark and Potter and colophon are registered trademarks of Random House, Inc.

Library of Congress Cataloging-in-Publication Data
Roney, Carley.
    The Nest newlywed handbook : an owner's manual for modern
married life / Carley Roney and the editors of The nest.—1st ed.
    Includes bibliographical references and index.
    1. Marriage.   2. Married people—Life skills guides.   I. Nest
(Online).   II. Title.
HQ734.R725   2006
646.7'8—dc22          2006003965

ISBN-13: 978-0-307-34022-1
ISBN-10: 0-307-34022-8

Printed in the United States of America

Design by Laura Palese
Illustrations by Jason O'Malley


10   9   8   7   6   5   4   3   2   1

First Edition

# [contents]

# [introduction]

## Project Marriage

**You found your soul mate. You pulled off the perfect wedding. You said the vows and signed on the dotted line. . . . That's it, you're done. Happily ever after, here we come!**

**If only it were that simple.**

Here's what we've learned in the few years we've all been married and since we started TheNest.com: *Being* married is twice the undertaking of *getting* married! First of all, most people don't know how to do half the things that are required of married people—from figuring out what to call their in-laws to deciding which neighborhood to live in for the next twenty years. Second, most couples assume this marriage thing runs itself. Big surprise—it actually requires major work (fun work, but work nonetheless). Third, being married today is just *different.* Everyone has different expectations of the roles they are supposed to play, or worse yet, the roles they expect *you* to play, and this all needs to be sorted out pretty early to get things off on the right foot.

Why do we think the world needs an owner's manual for marriage? Because learning how to do "the grown-up marriage thing" is a big project. It turns out you don't just say "I do" and find yourself magically imbued with the collective knowledge of everyone who's gotten married before you. No, it turns out that you—yes, you, the fun-loving, reality-TV-addicted couple who still feel like two college kids—have to figure out how to buy insurance, split trash duty, and time your first baby all by yourselves. Eek!

The good news? You're not completely alone. You've got us! And *we've* got thousands of married couples who shared their hard-won knowledge to help us develop this book. Inside, you'll find seven of the most challenging, hardest-to-tackle issues that face newlyweds. Not only will we give you a preview of what's ahead, we'll actually give you tools for dealing with these

# Postwedding Checklist

### Your Last Wedding To-Do List

[ ] Send thank-you notes for all the wedding gifts you received. Split up the list by who knows whom better. Remember: The note should be sent within two weeks of receiving the gift.

[ ] Send thank yous to your vendors, particularly if they went above and beyond the call of duty. Sending a photograph of their work is always a nice addition.

[ ] Take care of any remaining invoices.

[ ] Return doubles or other registry items you no longer want or need.

[ ] Order prints of photos you want to send to family members and friends.

[ ] Finalize your wedding DVD and select the photographs you want in your wedding album.

[ ] Clean and store your wedding gown by taking it to a dry cleaner that specializes in fine garments. Don't delay—"invisible" stains like body oils and Champagne can discolor your dress over time.

[ ] Let people know of your new name, address, and/or e-mail address.

[ ] Change health care if one of you is switching to the other's coverage—many times, you are required to within a month of the qualifying event (aka your marriage) or you'll have to wait until the annual reenrollment time to add someone to a policy.

[ ] Update your wedding website with photos from the wedding day and a thank you to guests.

Need to know the details of changing your name? Turn to page 8.

issues, whether you're already overwhelmed by them or won't stumble across them for a few years. We'll also provide some talking points to get the conversational ball rolling about these important topics.

The first big challenge? Money. It's the biggest stressor for Americans, and becoming a twosome doesn't make things any easier. You've got to consider your financial goals, your actual capabilities, and your attitudes toward spending and saving—not just as an individual, but as a couple. When you've got different approaches in one or more categories (and you will), tensions can flare. It sounds like nitty-gritty, emotionally unimportant stuff, but many people's senses of identity and self-worth are wrapped up in their finances, so leaving these problems unresolved can actually eat away at your new, otherwise-perfect marriage. That doesn't make cents! (Sorry.) But no matter your situation, Chapter One will help you get organized, make the best choices for saving and investing, and work as a unit to reach your goals. We'll also help you deal with the downright boring stuff, like taxes and insurance.

Whether you lived together for years before you got married or are sharing a mailing address for the first time, moving in is a huge rite of passage . . . and adjustment . . . for couples. Even for those who cohabitated, the process of moving in mentally marks the start of the real partnership. In Chapter Two, we give you a primer on living together: as roommates, lovers, and spouses. From choosing a decorating scheme that defines your home, to working out a schedule for actually cleaning the darn thing, we've got worksheets and ideas to make even the most abstract concepts seem simple. And we'll walk you through the myriad milestones of being a grown-up couple: buying a home, having houseguests, hosting a party.

Something strange happens when you become half of a married couple (besides having to share your TiVo, we mean). Your swinging social life—the network of friends, interests, and activities that makes you you—becomes "our" social life. Learning to balance dates with each other, time alone with friends, and your spouse's obligations that you don't necessarily care for can be tough, but you don't have to take the "fun" out of "social functions." Chapter

Three will help you adapt to this shift by addressing the unique phenomenon of socializing as a couple. From family vacations to precious alone time, office events to lunches with exes, we'll give you a primer on what works and what backfires as you set up a new routine as Mr. and Mrs.

Now to in-laws. Some in-laws are amazing; other in-laws are amazingly difficult. What makes in-law relations such a tricky part of marriage is that they haven't evolved the way our relations with our own parents have. Some of us are "best friends" with our parents, speaking our minds on everything from pulled pork recipes to political power plays, others have perfected the art of tiptoeing around our repressed parents' hot buttons or minimizing nonstop dramas. Whatever the case, it's natural to expect the same kind of relationship with the in-laws. Here's a hard cold fact: They are not your parents. They never will be. Whatever your parents' style, you've had decades to learn how best to deal with them—an advantage you simply don't have during high-tension times with the in-laws. Our best advice here is to go ultra-traditional. Your key to success is being the world's best (read: most diplomatic) daughter- or son-in-law—and simply dealing. We don't mean that you can't create some boundaries or have to go over every time they ask (and we have lots of tips for creatively handling just these types of situations). But we do mean that you need to welcome them with open arms on Sunday afternoon even if you were waiting all week to watch the game. You need to bite your tongue when your MIL gives you more tips on improving your cooking. You need to learn not to take these things personally. Every family has its own quirks and ideas of the only right way to cut carrots/load the dishwasher/cure the common cold—no matter how hard you try

IN CASE OF
M.I.L. OVERDOSE
TAKE 2

you are not going to change these things. You need to learn how to love . . . or at least lovingly respect them. We'll teach you all that in Chapter Four.

In Chapter Five, we tiptoe into your bedroom. For something so essential, sex certainly is hard to talk about—and unfortunately that is the key to success on that front. So we're going to go at it straight. Your job is to become obsessed with figuring out what makes your partner in crime "happy." And—here's another important bit—helping them figure out how to make you happy. For some people, maintaining heat under the sheets is easy. For most of us, it is a bit more of a struggle. Different libidos. Weird baggage. Stressful work schedules. But all of it can be overcome with commitment, talking, a sense of humor, and a standing sex appointment (we're not kidding).

The natural follow-up to our sex talk, bookwise and biologically, is the baby discussion. Even if you and your future co-parent haven't talked it out, your in-laws and family friends have probably already started nosing around for news on when they can expect your family to grow to three. In case you weren't paying attention the last dozen years or so, baby-making isn't as simple as it always seemed growing up: You get married, the baby shows up, everyone's happy. Chapter Six will prep you for the various challenges (physical *and* emotional) that you'll face when discussing future munchkins: when to get pregnant, how to get pregnant, how often to get pregnant, where to get pregnant (seriously, school districts are a factor—we told you there's a lot more to think about than you realized!), and what to do if you're not into the whole getting pregnant thing at all. Of course there's more than a chapter . . . or a library . . . that we could write about the art of creating a family, but we like to think we've got the bare-bones, straight-shooting basics to help you start thinking about it without a lot of stork talk.

Lastly, since this book is essentially about the two of *you,* we're going to leave you with a discussion of how to nurture your relationship. Just because your union is now legal doesn't mean it's suddenly going to be easy. You'll still struggle with the same issues you had before you tied the knot, plus a whole new range of tensions that are intensified by the unique circumstances of marriage (see: money, home, friends, in-laws, sex, babies, etc.). Chapter Seven reminds you how important it is to stay *friends* with your partner, and gives you some ways to do that. We'll also help you figure out the best way to resolve arguments when they come up—if you're healthy, they will—and then move on to the more pleasant parts of being a unit, like second honeymoons.

Anniversaries, dates, vacations, childbirth—these are the high points of being married. With enough smarts about both love and the gritty stuff (like budgeting, paying down debt, and paint chips), you can cruise easily through everything in between. Read on for driving directions, and have a fabulous trip!

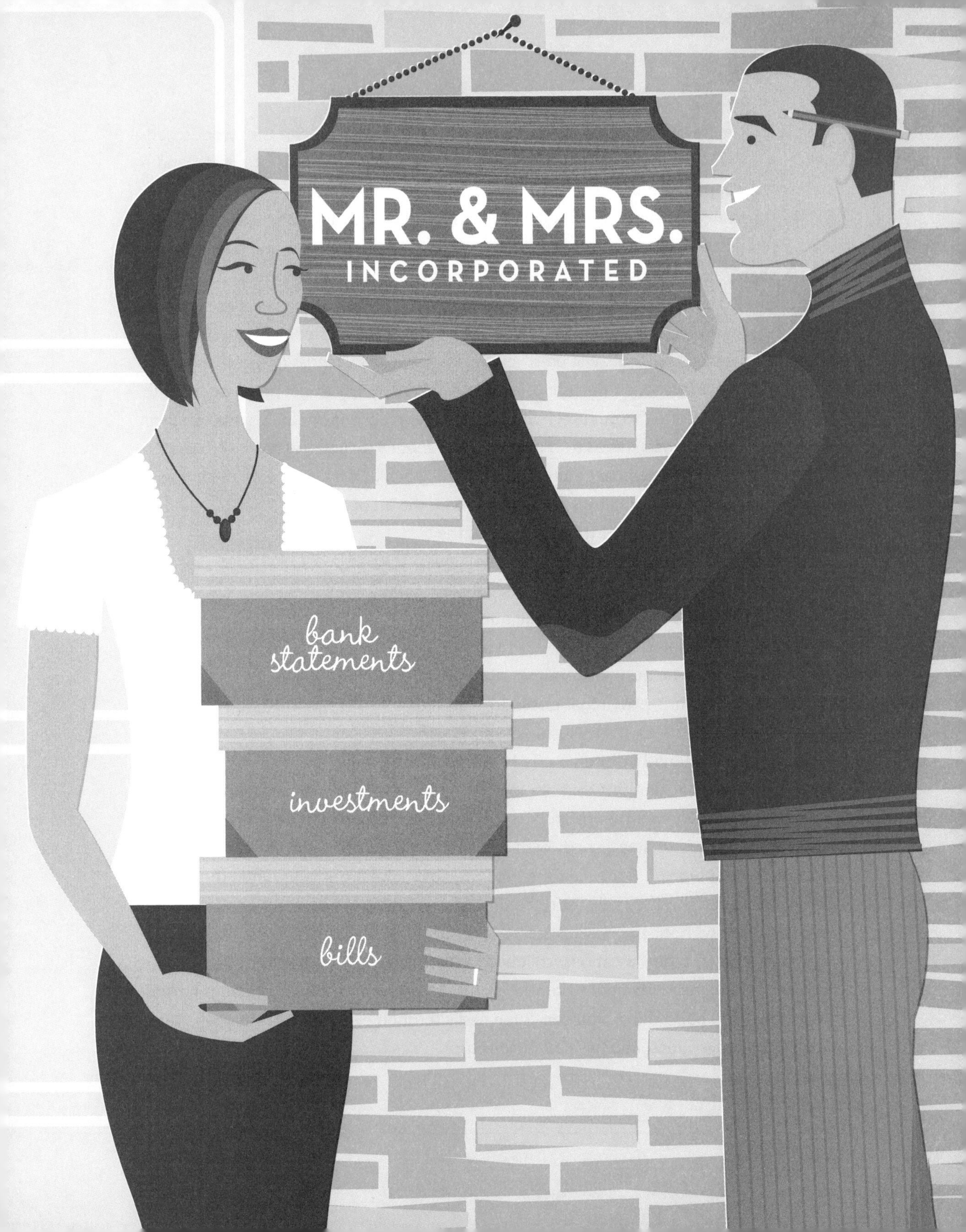
MR. & MRS.
INCORPORATED
bank statements
investments
bills

# [ money ]

We know what you're thinking: "How could they start with money— so unromantic?" Well, you can't live on love alone, but you can live well with stable finances (and lots of love, of course). If you can get on the same financial page from day one, your new venture, Couple, Inc., will profit both literally and figuratively.

# the nest test:
## your financial compatibility

Quiz each other with these money questions *before* you get into the nitty-gritty of this chapter. Answer honestly; the time to know your differences (dollar-wise) is now.

1. How much cash do you need in the bank to feel secure?

2. What do you think should be our financial priority?

3. Say I get a surprise bonus . . . do we splurge on something big or do we put it away for a rainy day?

4. On a scale of 1 to 5, how much do you worry about our finances?

5. How do you feel about merging all our money?

6. Do my money habits ever make you want to scream?

7. Do I need to explain every $20 I spend?

8. How much credit-card debt do you have?

# merging your money

"We had a hard time figuring out how much money to put where because **we hadn't been sharing money** or living together before. It took us at least two to four months to figure it out."
—Cinderin

Many couples avoid exploring the subject of money before marriage, trusting that someone they have enough in common with to choose as a spouse will naturally make fiscally sound decisions and share the same financial goals or styles. Sadly, that is not always the case, a fact that becomes all too apparent when he wants to give his sister $200 for a housewarming gift and you balk at the amount (which may be better saved for a new kitchen), leading to a fight. Here's what you missed: the married money talk. You think you know your counterpart really well, but it's amazing what you'll find out when you break out the checkbooks.

## MONEY STYLES MATTER

Money is a tough subject for a lot of reasons, but perhaps the most basic one is that it simply means something different to everyone. For some, cash is just a means to an end; for others, it represents security or independence. For a few more, it's equated with happiness. Money can also contribute to self-worth, social standing, and style. Whatever your views are they directly relate to how you deal with money. This is not to say that one way is better than another, but determining what attitudes guide your personal financial life will help you figure out the best plan for you as a couple. Plus, it will help you better understand (and accept) if one person is a saver and the other a paycheck-to-paycheck spender. There are four factors that can help you establish your money outlook.

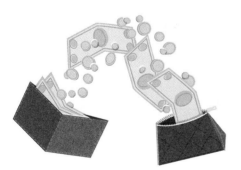

**1. Your Economic Background:** This one is pretty self-explanatory. If one of you is more accustomed to working for your money and the other got slipped a $20 bill just for smiling, there may be some inherent issues with setting spending limits and understanding the need to save for the future.

# Private Funds

**Q.** Sometimes friends ask us about our finances and it makes me uneasy. How do I deal?

**A.** The subject of money will always come up between friends. They are curious—admit it, so are you. People like to see where they stand among their peers and it's not always just to be nosy, but also to see if they are earning enough or taking control of their finances in the best way possible. The best strategy is to be vague. You might indicate that your salary is at the top of the normal range but you don't have to give a number. Tell them if you have a diversified portfolio but don't name stocks or how much you have invested. There's always the straight up, "I'd rather not talk about it" route, which works just fine. Sounds too harsh? Feign ignorance and give them the name of your financial adviser.

**2. Your family's money culture:** This isn't how *much* money your respective parents had, but how they *managed* it (aka the generosity factor). For instance, it may seem natural to accept financial help from your family, whereas your partner may feel uncomfortable with the implications of these gestures (will there be strings attached?). If your mate's mom was always worried about the emergency fund, chances are he will be, too.

**3. Different salaries:** If one of you makes significantly more money than the other, does it mean that he or she should be able to spend significantly more money? Does the lower earner expect the high-roller to pay all the bills *and* pick up the dinner tab? Find out if there are any hidden feelings behind the paychecks.

**4. Money control issues.** Do you need to know exactly how much money is in your bank account, down to the nickel? Do you check your investment portfolio hourly to make sure you're not losing any dough? Or, maybe you have no control: As long as your bank statement isn't in the negative, you think you've successfully balanced your checkbook.

## COMBINING APPROACHES

There's a good chance you won't feel exactly the same about the role of money, but there are ways for all sorts of spenders and savers to operate as a team.

**If you're both savers:** You're probably focused on the future and eager to exceed your nest-egg expectations. But you need to figure out what you're each saving for: a luxury car, a new house, a family, retirement? You must match up your short-term vs. long-term saving goals so one of you is not surprised (or irate) when the other is ready to cash in the kitty for a flat-screen TV.

**If you're both spenders:** The good news is that you're completely compatible, so money fights may be few and far between; the bad news is that living-in-the-money-moment can only last so long. Together, reassess your spending habits, come up with a savings goal, and agree to put away X amount into a joint savings account or a mutual fund every month. Then pick out a problem purchase area for each of you (shoes, gadgets, expensive wine) and agree to cut down.

**If one's a spender, one's a saver:** Remember, you can't change someone's money habits overnight. A spender could regard a saver as cheap, and a saver may see a spender as frivolous. Instead, try to respect the other's style and compromise on a middle ground. The spender should set up an automatic bank transfer to savings every month, but not be faulted for buying one or two splurge items. The saver should happily contribute to something new (possibly unnecessary) for your home, but not be criticized for balking at a spontaneous trip to Paris.

## GETTING ORGANIZED

Once you get a general sense of where the other person stands, it's time to confront reality. We strongly believe that 100 percent disclosure on the money front is essential—from annual salary and student-loan debt to alimony payments and real estate investments. Knowing each others' numbers inside and out is a great way to establish trust, roles, and financial goals.

**tip**

Both of you should order and crosscheck your personal credit report from the top three credit report companies and compare notes. (You get one free per year at www.annualcreditreport.com.) Reports can be ordered from Experian (www.Experian.com), Equifax (www.Equifax.com), or TransUnion (www.True Credit.com). Review them carefully, check for mistakes, and immediately notify the company of any errors.

Before you set aside a time (or several times, as the topic can be too much to tackle in one sitting) for an uninterrupted discussion on where you're at with your money, get all your paperwork in order. Seeing the numbers (and interest rates and service fees) all together will help you figure out how to make this union work for you, i.e., paying off the highest-interest credit card first. Before you can make a solid plan, you've got to get organized. Here's how:

**Order your credit report.** It lists all of your outstanding loans and debts (including credit cards), as well as any information about debt default. You may think your credit rating is in fine standing because you *eventually* pay off your bills, but each time you're late, it appears on your credit report. Having a poor one could affect your ability to get loans or additional credit cards.

**Pull your paperwork.** Gather a copy of both of your latest financial statements (bring to the table everything and anything related to your current and future cash flow).

- Pay stubs
- Benefit packages (bonuses, stock options)
- Retirement statements (401(k))
- Bank statements (both checking and savings)
- Credit card statements
- Investment information
- Loan statements (student, car, etc.)
- Any other large financial payments like alimony or mortgages

**Document your status.** Create a spreadsheet on your computer that lists all the pertinent information from these statements: balances, interest rates, deductions, earnings. This document will be vital to every part of discussing your money matters, from establishing a budget to getting out of debt. Plus, it gives you the opportunity to check your annual progress—to see if your hard work is paying off.

**Create a filing system.** Save hard copies of important financial documents. File them in an easily accessible, well-labeled storing device.

flip

Once you've gathered and organized your financial paperwork, you need to keep a detailed list of where everything is stored and important financial contact info. Get started on page 264 in our resource section.

# managing your money

Once you have a good idea of how much money you both brought to the altar, it's time to devise a realistic and specific plan that takes your state of affairs and goals into account. The most important decision: Are you going to combine your funds?

## JOINT VS. SEPARATE ACCOUNTS

You share CD collections, the Sunday newspaper, and the remote control (sometimes). But where do you draw the line on togetherness? Sometimes all that unity can be a pain, especially when you have seven inactive bank accounts, sixteen credit cards, two warehouse club memberships, and a handful of abandoned 401(k) accounts spread across three states. There is no one perfect bank-account solution that satisfies every couple, so here are three options to choose from.

- Joint checking and savings accounts. (In other words, "What's mine is yours.")
- Separate checking and savings. ("Look at what a cute, independent couple we are!")
- A joint account (checking or savings) as well as separate accounts (either checking or savings). ("My mate and I pay the bills together, but let each other have some space.")

There are pros and cons for each scenario (we list them, don't worry). Read. Discuss. Make up. If you try out one option and it doesn't work, all hope is not lost; just try a different one. They say that couples begin to resemble each other physically over time. Your money views may evolve similarly, too. And after any lifestyle change (having a baby, getting a better-paying job), be sure to revisit the joint vs. separate account issue. Here's how to decide what's right for you.

### Option 1: Joint Checking and Savings Accounts

WHAT IT IS: One shared checking account and one shared savings account.

WHO IT'S RIGHT FOR: Are your finances an open checkbook? Do you and your significant other regularly talk about money matters? Do you both share similar practices when it comes to spending vs. saving? For those who believe in total togetherness, setting up "ours" accounts may be the way to go.

# Changing Your Name Checklist

[ ] Arm yourself with a *certified* marriage license—be sure it has a raised seal, which means it's authentic. If it hasn't automatically been sent to you or if you need duplicate copies, call the county clerk's office where your license was filed.

[ ] Visit the Social Security Administration's website (SocialSecurity.gov) and download the form. Your new card will be *free*—if you're contacted by a company that claims to do this for a fee, don't buy it. These companies have nothing to do with the SSA and should be reported to authorities.

[ ] Visit the Department of Motor Vehicles to change your driver's license. Bring your new SS card, your certified marriage license, and any other paperwork required. Check your state's DMV site (DMV.org will link you there) for what you need before you go as they won't be able to be flexible if you forget something, no matter how long you just waited in line.

[ ] Change the title on any cars you own—another to-do for your trip to the DMV.

[ ] Notify banks and other financial institutions. (Note: The name on your income taxes has to match that on your Social Security card, so make sure you take care of that before April 14.)

[ ] Notify employers/payroll.

[ ] Notify the post office.

[ ] Notify the phone company and other utilities.

[ ] Notify credit card companies.

[ ] Notify schools and alumni associations.

[ ] Notify voter registration.

[ ] Update your passport. (Do not do this before the wedding—your passport name must match the name on your ticket and all other travel documents! It's easier to take your honeymoon with your maiden name.

[ ] Update mortgages and leases.

[ ] Update wills.

[ ] Update insurance policies.

[ ] Update your e-mail address and edit any online accounts where you store credit card information.

[ ] Update magazine subscriptions.

- Less paperwork. One account, one statement—it's a pretty simple setup. A joint account is also likely to involve fewer maintenance fees (depending on your bank's policies) than two separate accounts.
- Everyone knows the score. If you both see the statements, you both know exactly what's being spent, making your overall budget less complicated.
- Joint expenses are easy. Paying for doggy daycare is simpler, since you don't have to coordinate two accounts or figure out who pays for what.
- You're a team. Emotionally, it feels like this is what marriage is about: What's mine is yours and what's yours is mine.

CONS

- Too many cooks. After all, how reliably did you balance the checkbook when it was just your account? Now you have to do it for two and may have to work a bit harder to avoid errors.
- Potential inequality. Are your salaries dramatically different, or does only one of you work outside the house? If so, the partner bringing home most of the money may feel resentful if both have equal access to the funds.
- Less privacy and independence. Since all expenditures are public knowledge, everything—from what you spent on that sleek leather jacket (yeah, we know it was on sale) to what you spent on birthday gifts—will be available for you both to see.

TIPS

- Take turns balancing the checkbook or doing the online banking so neither of you is unfairly burdened by taking on the bulk of the paperwork. Taking turns also ensures that no one loses touch with how money is being

---

**Time Out**

# Cash Break

Money woes got you down? Take yourselves out on a fantastic, free date. Yes, free (you might have to pay for gas). Sounds difficult, but if you look hard enough, you can find events in your town that are free to the public: concerts in the park, book readings, even food and wine tastings. Pick up your local city guide and scour the pages for fun-together activities that won't cost you a dime.

spent and what your actual expenses are. If you never pay a bill, it's easy to overspend.

- If you're in two different salary brackets, consider prorating your spending allowance based on the percentage each is bringing to the overall pot.

- Want a bit more privacy? Buy gifts and other splurge items with your own plastic. Even though you're paying the credit card bill together, you can keep the itemized list of purchases to yourself.

### Option 2: Separate Accounts

WHAT IT IS: Four accounts—checking and savings for each of you.

WHO IT'S RIGHT FOR: Have you mastered a Nobel Prize–worthy system for keeping your checkbook balanced? Would dealing with someone else's register entries (or forgotten decimal points) drive you to drink? Or, is one partner's financial life exceptionally complex? In no way do separate accounts signify lack of commitment between two spouses. Assuming you share financial goals and have agreed how to get there, all it really says about your union is, "We both like to do our own math."

**tip**
Another option is to have separate but jointly accessible accounts. What this means is that you manage your separate accounts but trust each other enough to have total access to the other's accounts by sharing passwords and authorizing your spouse to sign for your credit cards and such. The Pros: It shows that you have nothing to hide from your spouse, while maintaining your financial freedom. The Con: privacy issues (of course).

PROS

- Autonomy. There's no looking over each other's shoulders—and therefore, no need to justify big cell phone bills.

- More accurate accounting for merged households. In cases where one or both of you are remarried or have children from a previous relationship, separate accounts make tracking things like child support much easier.

- Less sticker shock. If you have different ideas about financial priorities, keeping your money in two distinct columns lessens the likelihood for conflict—especially those embarrassing ones in the grocery store checkout line.

- Clashing lifestyles. Again, when salaries are dramatically different, dividing expenses can make one partner feel he or she isn't pulling his or her weight.
- Less communication. If you're solely responsible for balancing your own check-book and putting money in your own IRA, there's little reason to discuss bigger money goals.
- More paperwork. Complicated households (and aren't they all these days with TiVo, cable modems, and the sprinkler-maintenance service?) have dozens of shared expenses. Double the accounts and you double your paperwork—particularly around tax time.

TIPS

- With separate accounts, it may not seem difficult to split fixed bills, but what about variable ones? Similar to creating spending allowances in the joint scenario, consider dividing expenses based on a percentage of income, so you each contribute a similar proportion of your take-home pay to the family bills. If one joint expense clearly benefits one partner more than the other (like a gym membership or dry cleaning), and if that partner is you, be generous and offer to cover that bill, no questions asked.
- Avoid the danger of merely assuming that your partner is taking care of things like retirement savings and vacation funds by making a date to talk money. Serve popcorn and share your best monthly money moves with each other.
- Make bill paying and account balancing an activity that you do together. The lighting may not be romantic, but at least you can play footsie while you're organizing your ATM receipts.

## Option 3: Some Joint, Some Separate Accounts

WHAT IT IS: There are many variations on this popular method. You may decide to pool your funds for one savings account but maintain separate checking accounts to cover all your personal and mutual expenses. You could have one checking account, but separate savings accounts to maintain financial independence. Or, you could have six accounts: a joint checking (from which to pay the big bills) and joint savings (for all that wedding money), and personal checking and savings accounts (to maintain that fee-free minimum balance). In this case, it's advisable to limit debit privileges to the

# Time for a New Bank?

If you currently bank at different institutions, you're going to have to decide where to store your dough. Since we're all about a fresh financial start, why not choose a new bank altogether? The following checklist should help you whittle down the choices:

- Does the bank offer free checking?

- How close is the bank to your home?

- Does the bank have many locations?

- Does it have twenty-four-hour ATMs? How many? Near your home? Office?

- Does the bank charge you to use your ATM card?

- Can you use your ATM card at other banks?

- Are there monthly fees? Do they waive fees with a specified minimum balance? If so, can you meet that balance? Can you link accounts to meet the minimum?

- What is the interest rate offered for their checking and savings accounts?

- Does the bank feature overdraft protection?

- Does the bank try to attract personal accounts, rather than just business accounts?

- Does the bank promote online banking? Is it free?

- Do they have financial advisers?

Pick a bank you feel comfortable with, but make sure it's a member of the Federal Deposit Insurance Corporation (FDIC). This government agency will insure your account up to $100,000 should the bank become insolvent.

personal checking accounts in order to prevent one partner from making a spontaneous and questionable purchase on the joint account. Instead, use checks (yes, those antiquated pieces of paper) from your joint account to pay for big credit card purchases like vacations or mattresses, as well as home repair and car bills.

WHO IT'S RIGHT FOR: Did you drag a lot of your own debt down the aisle? Has money been a source of contention in your relationship? A combo approach to accounts may serve you well. Couples who have distinctly separate expenses (or even ideas about how to handle money) can alleviate some of the stress by going solo on an account or two. This is our preferred method (though the six-account variation is probably too much trouble to maintain).

### PROS

- A little slack in the leash. Everyone has their own spending downfall (records, shoes, vintage tchotchkes, etc.). But if bird-shaped salt and pepper shakers are your passion, don't hold back. A separate account specifically for individual pursuits lets you keep doing those (weird) things that make you you.
- Exposure to other money-management tactics. When you sit down and go over your accounts—both those you have together and those in your own names—you may pick up a few savings tricks from your spouse or discover that you live with a disciple of Suze Orman.
- Opportunity to be generous. Did you get a raise at work or a bonus check from your part-time gig? Go ahead and pitch in more to your joint bills or savings.

### CONS

- More up-front work. What are the "mine," "yours," and "ours" accounts supposed to cover? For example, does your individual account cover gifts for your side of the family? Dinner out together? What about joint money? Is that for childcare, family travel, and utilities? Be really specific. These are decisions you need to make before you start dividing your dough.
- Joint expenses are harder. Coordinating two accounts to pay one bill is simply more complicated. And every time you add a new joint expense to the roster, like weekly cleaning service, you need to decide which fund is going to cover the cost.
- Increased opportunities for clashes. Is he really paying $400 every month toward his student loans? Is she spending too much on groceries that eventually go bad in

# Topic:
# fun money?

"

**WE HAVE A JOINT CHECKING ACCOUNT** and then we each have our own savings accounts. Every two weeks we each get more fun money added into our savings accounts. That way he can buy all the video games and stuff he wants with his fun money and I can buy whatever I want with my share.

—Buttercup16

We each get $100 a week 'fun money.' It's none of my business what he does with it, and vice versa.

—Stumpygrrl

"

**It's an issue for us.** For example, I overpaid for a skirt but it was 'fun' money and I felt like I could spend it any way I want. DH wasn't upset but he says I don't 'need' any more clothes. Well then I can say he didn't 'need' the system for his car.

—babywifey

the fridge? Just because your name isn't on your betrothed's account doesn't mean that you shouldn't worry about it.

TIPS

- Check in regularly to ensure there is no miscommunication or sentiments of inequality regarding how you two are covering family expenses.
- Communicate: Even if you have an only-tell-if-you-spend-more-than-$500 policy, you don't want your spouse feeling like you're sneaky.
- Reevaluate your plan every couple of months to make sure you're both working toward the same financial goals—not just staying afloat for the moment.

## COUPLING YOUR CREDIT CARDS

Despite what you think, credit cards are not completely evil—they help you establish a credit record (if you use them responsibly and make regular payments), shop online, reserve hotel rooms, and let you make big purchases without toting around a wad of cash. But too many cards can be too much to manage. The number of cards you carry should be determined by how much you can actually afford to pay off. We think two per person is a safe bet: Have at least one card that's accepted almost everywhere (American Express, Visa, MasterCard, or Discover Card) and one retail card from a shop you visit frequently.

Now, those two cards can be joint or separate accounts. The same three strategies that apply to banking apply here: You can share the plastic, have your very own accounts, or mingle some while maintaining sole responsibility for others. How you decide to split your bank accounts doesn't necessarily dictate your credit card situation. We like the idea of one shared credit card to use for dinners out, travel, and other daily expenses, and a credit card for each of you for individual splurge purchases like spa days

### Credit Comparison

If you're like the average American, you carry about eight credit and charge cards in your wallet, owe more than $7,500, and are paying around 14 percent in interest on those balances. If you paid off your credit card balance in full last month, take a bow—you're part of the 40 percent minority who did so.

# Hack-free Online Banking

There's no reason not to manage your money online. But to protect your financial information, you need to follow these safety steps.

- Make sure it's secure. Look for the tiny lock on the bottom of your screen. It means you're on a secure website that encrypts your information and stores it securely.

- Protect your passwords. Don't use the same password for your online banking, bill paying, and investing that you do for online shopping, memberships, and e-mailing. And don't keep your list of passwords out in the open (like on a sticky on your desktop). If you want to store the info, be imaginative; create a document with an unappealing title like projectreport2004.

- Don't use public computers. Many sites store your personal information in "cookies," and when you use a public computer in a library or café, this information can be inadvertently left alive for the next customer to uncover. Public spaces are also easy places for thieves to sneak a peek when you enter your passwords.

- Update your software. Were you prompted to install the latest antivirus program? Download it now. Make sure your computer automatically checks for updates.

- Use computer common sense. If a site seems shady, it probably is (especially when someone is asking you for money). It goes without saying, but never provide personal financial information to an unknown source.

and sports tickets. Even if the payment is coming from a joint account, it will still feel like your own rainy-day fund.

The ideal card: 0 percent APR (annual percentage rate), no annual fee, long grace periods, low fees for late payments, and a killer rewards program. In the real world, the best bet for most people is a card with a low, fixed APR and minimal fees. A low APR will keep down the interest you're charged if you are carrying a balance, and a fixed rate means that the card company has to notify you fifteen days in advance if they want to change your rates. (Institutions that offer variable rate cards can up your interest without any prior notification and make it hard to check your statement for errors.) In general, try to avoid cards with

**tip**

When you're combining cards, or shopping for a new one, don't forget to take customer rewards programs into account. Will certain cards add miles to your frequent flier accounts? What about money back for purchases or points that you can cash in later? Think about how you'll use the cards and then choose one that gives you bonuses (either as points or money back) on the things you buy the most.

annual fees unless their rewards programs or other incentives (like a really low APR) make it worth your while. And of course, before you sign up for anything, get the details of the offer in writing. If anything in the fine print confuses you, call the 800 number and ask questions.

## PAYING BILLS

After wading through your financial history, we need to bring you to the immediate future. How are you going to pay (as in fund) the bills? Once again, the joint vs. separate debate comes into play. If you're sharing funds, it's a no-brainer: The money will come from your shared account. But if you favor separate accounts, you must discuss a check-writing strategy that you're both agreeable to: You can split the bills down the middle, each sending a check for half the amount due; split the bills down the middle, but have one person send the full amount and the other write the bill-payer a check; split up the expenses evenly (you pay cable, I pay gas and electric); or alternate covering months of expenses (though this could be a budgeting nightmare). What you decide will probably be determined by how you're divvying up the bill-paying duties.

Your next task: Assign duties based on each person's strengths (the Web-savvy partner should set up and manage your online banking; the financial whiz should

# Topic:
# what was your biggest money mistake?

My biggest money mistake was getting in the **habit of using credit cards.** Because along with that came the overspending, then the balance I could no longer pay off every month, then the higher and higher cc balances. —catali150

I lived at home for a few years after college— **I should have saved more** than I did. —chpmnk1015

**Loose spending in general.** —bicoastalbride

GOING TO A VERY EXPENSIVE GRADUATE SCHOOL just because of its name when I could have gotten a scholarship at a really good school, but not as good.

—sekhmet101

"

Not researching insurance prices. I found out I've been paying way too much for over two years.

—Desde

**nest note:**

Many of us get into trouble with our credit cards. Always pay your balance IN FULL at the end of the month, or use your debit card to make purchases. If those options don't work, stick with cash instead. People are less likely to make an impulse buy when they have an instant visual of how much they're spending.

Honestly spending 2.5K on flowers for my wedding. **WHAT WAS I THINKING ?????**

—gmugrad9

**Cashing out my 401K** when I left my 1st job. Ended up owing the IRS, paying penalty, and having 0 in my retirement fund @ age 28.

—pinkcaddy

# Loaning Dough

**Q.** My friend borrowed money from us. Can we ask for it back?

**A.** You must be a really good friend to have lent out your hard-earned cash. And your pal must have been really hard up to ask this of you. If it's a matter of $20 or paying for his or her fair share at dinner every now and then, it's probably not an issue and you shouldn't request repayment. We're assuming this pal probably does the same for you when you find your wallet empty. But if you've loaned out a significant sum of money (say, more than $500), we hope you have a simple little signed agreement. This makes it easier (and you feel a lot less guilty) to ask for your money at the time agreed to in the document. If not, realize it's your friend's responsibility for having put you in this awkward situation. Don't feel bad, and do ask for your money back in a reasonable time (the following day is unrealistic) or come up with an installment plan. Next time, establish *before* you loan the money that it *will* be repaid and when.

control your investments). Decide who's going to be the bookkeeper—consolidating statements and keeping tabs on your savings. Or, you can split the tasks evenly, swapping months of responsibility. The point is to avoid late fees and blemishes on your credit report by paying bills on time.

Concerned that neither of you are up for the challenge? Consider having some of your bills automatically deducted from your bank accounts. This way you'll never be late with that payment. The downside? You must remember to account for the deduction in your balance.

Be sure to set up a bill-paying system that works for you and your home: While one of you tracks the bills (most financial experts advise paying bills as they come rather than once monthly to avoid late fees), the other can be in charge of financial statements and entering interest earned into the checkbook. Create a place where you can hold the bills until payday and a filing system for paid bills.

Wondering how long to keep what? See our sidebar on page 21.

Electronic options: Many companies now bill and accept payments electronically, eliminating the need to write checks and hunt down stamps. First, sign up for online banking on your bank's website. Typically, you'll need your ATM/debit card, your pin number, and your account number. Then, you can begin adding payees. To do this, you'll need to have a copy of each bill with the account number and payment address information.

To go completely electronic, you can arrange it so that the majority of your bills are e-mailed to you. It's easy and, unlike your monthly statements, always up-to-date. Pay them right away to avoid losing the statement in your in-box.

You should still save at least one month's paper copy of a utility bill (often required to prove residence) and download credit card and bank statements every month, but by going the cyber route, you'll eliminate unnecessary paperwork and save some cash on stamps.

# balancing your budget

Getting married is often a wake-up call for your finances, and it may be tough to tame years of independent spending. The best way to think about money and your lifestyle is to aim to live beneath your means—that way, you don't spend more than you can afford but you still have a comfy existence. Finding the right balance will be a whole lot easier if you have a budget.

It sounds so old-fashioned, but if you want to be able to afford little luxuries in the present and the future (not to mention college, retirement, and that speedboat for your lake house), you need to save. Following your money flow will put you in control of your cash. You may be surprised when you see exactly where your extra money is going: Expensive takeout? Weekly manicures? What if the takeout offender started bringing lunch, and the spa-driven spouse used clear polish to make that manicure last? Over time these small sacrifices could pad your savings account—a feat for any married couple regardless of your financial goals.

flip

Need more ideas on ways to save? Skip ahead to page 29.

Once you both agree to establish—and stick to—a budget, don't expect instant miracles. You can't lose twenty-five pounds in a month and you can't automatically save 25 percent more money. It might even take a few tries before you find the budget that matches your personality as well as your spouse's.

# Bill Collecting

For future budgeting, here's a list of the must-save documents. Keep a year's worth on file as your expenses may vary per month (especially electric and heating costs).

- Electric bill

- Heating bill

- Gas bill

- Water bill

- Home phone bill

- Cell phone bills

- Cable bill

- Internet-provider bill

- Credit card bills

- Bank statements

- Investments (monthly/quarterly statements, to be shredded and replaced by end-of-year statement)

- Mortgage or lease papers

- Renovation and repair bills

- Service agreements

- Car titles, loan agreements, maintenance records, and emissions tests

- Health, homeowner's, life, and auto insurance

- Medical records

# Tax Time for Two

According to the government, if you marry by midnight on December 31, you've been married for the entire year. So you need to decide whether to file together or separately (are you sensing a theme yet?).

Figure out which method will require you to pay the least in taxes. While it's typically in most couples' favor to file jointly, you'll need to run the numbers both ways to see which is to your advantage. IRS.gov can help you figure it out.

### HOW TO FILE

- **Filing jointly** means you report your combined income and deduct all combined allowable deductions from that total. You can file a joint return even if only one spouse works. The benefit: Tax rates for couples are usually lower than for marrieds filing separately, and there are more miscellaneous deductions to take. The downside: You now have a larger combined income and you could be taxed at a higher percentage, depending on where you fall on the scale. The tax rate schedule (the chart that lets you know at what percent your hard-earned dough is being taxed) changes from year to year, so head to IRS.gov to find out where you are.

- **Filing separately** is a better choice if your taxes will be less as individuals or if one spouse has substantial medical or miscellaneous expenses that would allow a large deduction from his or her adjusted gross income, thus lowering his overall tax liability. The downside: not being able to claim certain common credits, like education and childcare. Also, you're subject to a capital loss deduction of $1,500 vs. $3,000 when filing a joint return.

### REWORK YOUR WITHHOLDING

Now that you're married, you may want to increase your withholdings—the deductions or allowances you noted on your W-4 form. That's what you'll need to fill out to change your status. IRS.gov (yes, it's the be-all and end-all for tax info) offers an easy-to-use withholding calculator to help you compute the best allowance for your situation.

### DEDUCTIONS FOR DUOS

- **The marriage "penalty":** The good news is that the standard deduction—the amount you can subtract from your total taxable income—for a married couple can be twice the amount of a standard deduction for a single taxpayer. (It's called a penalty because this was not the case before the marriage penalty relief, when single taxpayers were favored.) But you don't reap this benefit if you are married and filing separately or if you fall into a high tax bracket (the percentage of your total income that you pay in taxes).

**95**%

Tax advisers estimate that about 95 percent of couples are better off filing jointly.

- **Standard deduction:** It's a fixed dollar amount that reduces the amount of income on which you are taxed on your return. The amount of the basic standard deduction depends upon your tax return filing status (i.e., married filing jointly, married filing separately, single, blind, etc.). If you choose the standard deduction, then you would subtract this set sum (as dictated by the IRS, for married couples filing together it's about $10,000) from your adjusted gross income to calculate your taxable income.

For our couple's guide to tax prep, go to TheNest.com/taxes.

click

- **Itemized deductions:** These are personal expenses like medical bills, real estate taxes, state and local taxes, and investment interest expenses. To decide if the standard or itemized deductions are better for you, just do the math. If the total of your itemized deductions will be greater than the standard deduction that applies to you, then itemize. If not, take the standard deduction. If you itemize, you can't also claim the standard deduction. And if you're filing separately, whichever option the first spouse chooses (itemized vs. standard), the other has to follow suit.

- **Unexpected deductions:** These include contributions to a SEP (simplified employee pension) IRA, interest paid on student loans, points paid on a mortgage or refinancing, tuition for college education, charitable contributions, subscriptions to professional job-related journals, and even fees paid for tax preparation. Did you know that part of your wedding might be deductible? If you own your own business and invite clients to the wedding, you can take part of those expenses as a business deduction. Ask your tax pro for advice.

**tip**

About 60 million returns were e-filed last year. We say follow this trend. E-filing is more accurate, and if you're getting a refund, the money will be deposited directly into your bank account in about three weeks, compared with eight weeks if you file a paper return. If you owe, you can authorize the funds to be withdrawn from your bank account—or even your credit card—on the tax deadline.

# Topic:
# do you live within your means?

Yup, we both work, live in a small apartment, don't use credit cards **EVER** and have two vehicles that we own outright. We also save my entire paycheck each month and live off of his, which is smaller than mine. —stellasmom

**We're trying!**
—ahjen7

**Mostly. :)**
—KatersVaughan

**We don't—if you consider the insane amounts of loans we took out for my law school education.**

—Mrs.ScottyC

**WE DON'T GO TO NICE RESTAURANTS** and I don't have a lot of new clothes, but we have a beautiful apartment and great furniture :) I'm happy with that.

—NYCNancy

**WE ARE NOW, AFTER YEARS OF NOT LIVING WITHIN OUR MEANS.** And quite frankly, it's killing us, but we are looking towards that goal of being debt free.

—txlady

If I couldn't cut a check for the full amount of something on the spot, **I don't buy it.** —minifalda

**nest note:**

Living within your means doesn't mean you can't live it up! There are plenty of ways to have fun without spending a fortune. A few ideas: Go to a free tasting at the local wine shop, share a few appetizers at a restaurant instead of ordering entrées, and check out videos from the public library instead of paying rental fees.

## YOUR BUDGET FORMULA

There's no one budget that works for everyone, but at its most basic level your budget should take your combined income and subtract your monthly household expenses plus debt payments to see what's left over for everything else (like a weekend getaway or new floor mats for the car).

## Time Out

# Chart Your Progress

Think back to where you both were five years ago and how much money you had to your names. It's probably a lot less than you have now. We bet you'll have big smiles on your faces when you see just how far you have come with the combining of cash, wedding gifts, investments in stocks and maybe a house, raises, and year-end bonuses. Yeah, life is good.

Part of everyone's budget should include setting aside a percentage of your income to go to savings, not spending. A good rule of thumb is to "pay" yourself 10 percent of every paycheck you receive. That means the money goes right to your savings account—not to pay bills, buy dinner, or anything else.

And you'll want to mentally earmark some money for an emergency fund. A good rule of thumb is to have sufficient cash in the bank to live on for three to six months should you lose your job, be temporarily unable to work (as a result of a car accident, for example), or rendered homeless due to fire or natural disaster.

It can be tough to anticipate what you spend your money on as it can fluctuate dramatically from month to month (December's holidays can take a beating on your budget, while in the summertime, AC-crazy electricity bills can break your bank account). Your best bet is to approximate monthly averages for rent, utilities, and car payments and spend and save accordingly. Here are the categories to be mindful of:

- Your nest (rent/mortgage/maintenance, phone, electricity, cable, cell phone, housekeeper, etc.)
- Transportation (car payments, gas, public transportation, taxis, parking, car insurance, etc.)
- Necessities (food and groceries, loan payments, medical, health insurance, new clothes, pet care, etc.)

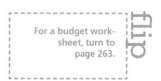

For a budget worksheet, turn to page 263.

- Investments (401[k], CDs, retirement IRA, etc.)
- The Fun Stuff (eating out, travel, music, grooming, gifts, gym membership, etc.)

## SETTING SPENDING RULES

Your budget will only work if you're using with the right numbers: You need to enter what you *really* pay for things, not what you *think* you pay. A can of cola here, an extra taxi there, and some cat food in between all add up. Even impulse buys like funky art from a street vendor need to be accounted for (and a solid budget would have made an allowance for that under "misc. fun purchases").

Once you know how much you spend, and on what, you'll have a better idea of how to cut costs. If two-ply toilet paper is not negotiable, then so be it. But what about your text messaging plan or preference for fine wine? Everyone has their own problem purchases—pricey items that you consistently overbuy like fancy body washes or hardcover books. Together, decide on one type of allowable problem purchase for each of you, and agree to spend a specific amount each month on those items. And set a rule to consult the other person for purchases over, say, $150 (obviously, you need to determine what the do-you-really-need-it amount is).

It's also a good idea to review the budget monthly to see if there have been any changes in income (a bonus!), spending (wedding gifts), and goals (*Hola,* Acapulco!). This will be easy to accomplish if your budget is kept in an orderly fashion.

## DEALING WITH DEBT

You've sealed your commitment with a kiss, and now the Visa bill is due—yikes. And in addition to the complete Led Zeppelin discography on vinyl, your spouse may bring some (or a lot of) debt to the party, too. But debt doesn't have to kill the mood. Being debt-free takes resolve and a little know-how, but it's very possible. Here's how to get it done.

**Separate "bad debt" and "okay debt."** Okay debt has an interest rate well below 10 percent—preferably with some tax advantages to boot. In the best case, the thing you bought with borrowed funds will appreciate in value. (Think mortgage, and even that student loan.) Bad debt is everything else. Your first step: Rank your credit card accounts from lowest to highest interest rate. Identify the one major credit card with the lowest annual interest rate and

**tip**
Do not cancel your other credit cards. Your credit score counts all available credit, so those cards—even if unused—serve the purpose of boosting your credit score.

enough unused credit to allow for a balance transfer. Transfer all your balances to this one card. Your other cards are now dead to you—take them out of commission. Then promise you'll use the one card remaining for emergencies only.

This will be hard if you're used to outspending your income. So you'll need to . . .

**Resolve to spend less than you make.** If you can't pay for it today, then you can't afford it. Period. Getting and staying out of debt boils down to this simple formula: Outflow is less than inflow. In other words, spend less money than you make on a consistent, long-term basis. By making just a few small sacrifices—and paying a little more attention to the bigger money items—you can amass a nice chunk of change in just a few months.

**Take charge of your rates.** If any of your cards are charging you more than 14 percent interest, dial the toll-free number and ask to have your rate lowered. Many companies will at least lower it on a temporary basis, giving you time to find a card with a low fixed rate. Expect to be made very uncomfortable, but stand firm and remember that, to them, you are both a customer and a profit center. If they say no, shop around for a new card with low or no fee on balance transfers.

**Don't pay the minimum balance.** It's cleverly calculated to keep you beholden to The Man for your entire adult life. A $4,500 balance on a card with an 11-percent APR, for instance, will take forty-four years to pay off, even if you don't put another dime on the card. Oh, and the interest you'll pay on that loan? A cool seventeen grand. That's why you're going to pay by *your* rules.

**Keep at it.** Pay your newly determined minimum amount due (on time, every time!) and send every extra dollar, every quarter you find on the street, every dime you earn over time, and that $20 your mother-in-law gave you for cab fare last month to your credit card company. Lather, rinse, and repeat.

**Organize your statements.** Buy a three-ring binder or accordion folder and allocate a section for each credit card. In the very front, place a photocopy of your latest statement, and highlight the current balance and your interest rate. Once you start paying off the debt, create (and print) graphs in Excel to show your progress.

Want someone to give you a script for negotiating a lower rate? Head to BankRate.com

click

# Topic: getting out of debt

**We've paid off $30,000 this year.** I made out spreadsheets of our finances, and seeing the figures really helped us want to deal with the problem. —KateLouise

**Budget, budget, budget.** —NatalieJoy

**WE SET A GOAL** on what we want paid off by the end of the year, and we're taking it one month at a time. —corsicabride04

When we put our money together and opened an account, we wrote down every bill and the amount. Then we divided the rest of the money up between our credit cards, so each gets the same amount put towards it. **The key is to both be on the same page together,** and talk about your financial goals. —Justins_Bride

**nest note:** Trust us, ignoring debt won't make it go away. The first step to getting rid of it is to sit down with your spouse and come up with a realistic plan on how to pay it off. Even if it's going to take you a few years, at least you'll have the satisfaction of knowing that you're both working toward this goal.

**WELL, WE HAVE BEEN SNOWBALLING OUR DEBT.** We are paying off the lowest balance first and moving up from there. —AIDAN

**I always buy everything when it's on sale,** use coupons whenever possible, and throw every possible penny towards our high-interest credit card debt. —italianbride2be

# starting a nest egg

Do you fantasize about traveling the world, going back to school, building a home, buying a car, having babies? When? It's starting to sound like money is the key to your future. Well, it's certainly part of it. You're more likely to have enough money well down the road if you can agree now on goals and saving strategies for achieving them.

No matter how little your stash, it's important to decide together how it should be spent or invested. Knowing that you share similar goals gives you incentive to make the necessary sacrifices to reach them. But if you discover that your goals differ wildly (he dreams of a beach house, she wants to start a college fund), apply a little creativity and a lot of compromise to prioritize goals as a team. And figure out a way to nurture individual—and dueling—dreams at the same time (you could set up two savings accounts, or invest in two different mutual funds, each designated toward one of these goals). Once you've figured out your game plan, start raising the funds.

## SIMPLE WAYS TO SAVE

Every little bit counts when you're trying to save money. Read through our budget-saving ideas and try to incorporate at least two each month.

### Your Nest

**Rent/mortgage/maintenance:** Think about how you can get the greatest financial benefit from your home. Are you taking full advantage of your tax deductions?

**Electricity:** Remember what your mother said and turn off those lights! Turn down your AC/heat when you're not at home, too. During winter months, put on a sweater and dial back the thermostat when you're home; even a few degrees makes a difference.

**Phone:** Call your phone company to make sure you're not paying for any services you don't really need. Consider going completely wireless and using just your cell phone instead of a landline. Look into phone services that use your broadband connection.

**Cable:** Consider all the options in your area. Is it cheaper to go with satellite than with cable? Also, save money by cutting channels you don't need. Do an experiment—go one month without the premium channels to see if you miss them. If you do, you can always sign back up for one or two at a time.

Internet: High-speed Internet companies are always trying to lure customers with specials. If you're in an area where both cable and DSL services are competing, you can often play one off the other. Find out the competitor's best rate and call up your existing service as you approach the end of your contract. Ask them to meet or beat the rival offer—if they don't, consider taking your business elsewhere.

Home repairs: It's always cheaper to do minor repairs yourself. Head to the library to pick up books on the area you're looking to work on, or surf around the Web for streaming video instructions. If you need to call in outside help, make sure you get a job estimate before you hire someone.

Housekeeper: If you need a housekeeper, hire someone to come in once a month or every two weeks to do the heavy cleaning. Try to keep up with the day-to-day stuff yourselves.

## What If We Rent?

Renter's insurance covers your possessions against losses from fire or smoke, lightning, vandalism, explosion, and water damage (not including floods). It also covers your responsibility to other people who are injured at your home or elsewhere by you, a family member, or your pet. It's a good idea to get it, and it's generally pretty inexpensive.

## Transportation

Public transportation: Buy in bulk. If you use public transportation enough to make it worthwhile, buy a weekly or monthly pass instead of an individual fare every time you travel. Also, many companies will allow you to buy your pass pretax. Ask your human resources department if your employer offers this.

Taxis: Keep a map of public transportation in your bag at all times. When you have the choice to take the subway or a taxi, not knowing which line to take won't be an excuse to drop the extra dough on a cab.

Car and homeowners' insurance: Different antitheft devices

**tip**

Just getting a deadbolt lock on your home can bring down your insurance premiums.

can drop your insurance rates drastically. Call your insurance company to see which gadgets will save you cash.

## Necessities

**Food and groceries:** Take advantage of sales. (Butter prices drop around the holidays. Stock up and store it in your freezer until you need it.) Also, shop at club stores—but make sure whatever you're buying is really a bargain.

**Wine/beer:** Find a wine or beer you like and then invest in a case. You'll save 10 to 15 percent in many stores by buying in bulk.

**School loan payments:** Consider consolidation. When interest rates are low, many banks offer great deals on consolidation.

**Health insurance:** Compare your health plans with your partner's. If one is a lot better or a lot cheaper, consider switching. You usually have thirty days after your wedding date to change your insurance without waiting for the enrollment period, but check with your HR department to verify the exact deadline.

**Pet care:** Got a pet that needs tending? Call your friends. Bribe them for pet favors with gifts that are less costly than kennels and dog walkers—a nice bottle of wine

---

**Mr. & Mrs. Manners**

# Down Payment from Daddy?

**Q.** My parents offered to give us money for a down payment on a house. Do we take it?

**A.** As long as you have a healthy and loving relationship with your parents, there is no reason to refuse their generous gift, but make sure it's a gift and not a loan. Not that a loan is bad—it still helps—but you want to make sure everyone is on the same playing field. If they expect you to pay it back, you need to set up a time frame with specific guidelines on the when and how much you give back to them each year. Thank them profusely and treat the loan repayment as a legit financial responsibility. If it's a gift, make sure to show your gratitude by buying them tickets to a show (or even inviting them over for dinner). Giving them free rein over how to decorate the living room or what to plant in the shade garden is a bit much, but let them know they are always welcome at your place.

works wonders. If you need dog walking on a regular basis, consider a neighborhood teen rather than an (adult) pro—the teen will usually charge far less.

## Tax Deductions

Gifts and charity: As you're making room for your new wedding loot, get receipts and keep track of all the charitable contributions you make (including clothes and furniture) to Goodwill or the Salvation Army and deduct them at tax time.

## The Fun Stuff

Eating out: Allow yourself a set number of nights per month to eat out—and stick to it. It's amazing how these costs can add up. Stuck in a takeout rut? Buy prepared meals (like rotisserie chicken at the grocery store) instead of picking up the phone and dialing for delivery.

Clothes: Set a quarterly clothing budget. The urge to splurge typically comes at the start of each season (fall tweeds, summer shorts), when there's still a selection. Later in the season, pad your savings to gear up for next season's spree.

Entertainment: Look into memberships at your favorite venues. Many museums and independent movie theaters offer subscriber discounts, deals, and other benefits like two-for-one tickets. Don't want to make the commitment? Ask about free or discounted nights. And buy concert tickets in advance and at the box office, whenever possible. Those $3 to $5 day-of-purchase surcharges and convenience fees can start to add up.

Travel: Book early and be flexible. These are the two cardinal rules for saving on travel. Participate in any and all frequent-traveler plans and use your accumulated points to score free travel. Don't forget to get mileage for your business travel if your employer allows it.

Grooming: Seek out the good, cheap places and stick to them. Or, if you're daring, go to the top salon in your city on a training night. Your stylist-in-training will be overseen by a senior stylist (if that makes you feel more comfortable), and you'll get a great discount.

Gym membership: Many health plans actually offer incentives for keeping in shape. Make sure you know what your benefits are and take advantage of them. Also, analyze your gym habits. Are you really going regularly? If not, think about

# How to Hire . . .
## an Accountant

If you want to keep using your family CPA, that's cool, but it wouldn't be such a bad idea to get your own accountant—just to preserve that all-important line of privacy. Consult CPADirectory.com or AccountantsWorld.com for referrals. Before you shriek, "You're hired!" ask these questions:

- How many years has the accountant been in business? (The more experience he or she has, the more well-versed the CPA should be with tax laws and loopholes.)

- Does he or she have experience with people in your specific field? (Discuss examples of situations similar to yours and see if the CPA has a quick and satisfactory response as to how he or she would handle it.)

- What is the company's average response time? (Availability during off-hours and good phone etiquette are pluses.)

- What is the size of the firm? (It should be at least three people: You want a network of associates whom he or she can use as a resource to supplement his or her knowledge.)

- What are his or her fees? Discuss the fee structure. Is it time-based or value-based, where the CPA would charge you for the value he or she delivers versus the hours spent? Determine which is better for your needs.

your monthly cost and how much you're actually spending each time you go. Maybe it's more cost-effective to just pay per visit (if your gym allows), or invest in exercise equipment and workout tapes to use at home.

**Other membership dues:** Remember that dues relating to your vocation are often tax deductible.

## INVESTING 102

You don't need an economics degree to invest in your future; you just need to know a few fundamentals for two.

**Decide to invest now.** Don't wait till tomorrow. The quicker you start an investment plan, the more time you have to let your savings grow. If you think you don't have enough cash to spare, relax, there's no minimum. You don't need to be rich, just patient. Sure, there are some mutual funds that require an investment of at least $10,000 to start, but you can open a simple IRA with $2,000 (or allocate just 1 percent of your gross paycheck—check with plan administrator for details). What you need more than wads of cash are goals. Once you have goals, you can develop a savings and investment program to help you meet them.

# Stockbroker vs. a Financial Planner

They both have the same license, they just charge and/or work with you differently. Whereas stockbrokers just buy and sell for you, financial planners help devise a strategy for meeting your goals through a variety of investments, including bonds, stocks, and more, and will want to see your financial records.

Some financial advisers are commission based; others charge an hourly fee or a flat rate. Some planners bill quarterly based on your portfolio. This type of planner offers ideas on what to do with your money; you can buy the plan and go on your own, or work with the planner and he'll do it for you (for a fee). Aside from offering advice on investments, financial planners can help with insurance, wills, taxes, retirement, and mortgages. A stockbroker makes recommendations on where to invest your money and then does all of the buying and selling for you. Of course there's a commission involved: Brokers earn a fee on each transaction they process.

Ask friends and family for names of brokers and planners whom they have used and what they like about those people. Most banks have planners on staff, so check in there, as well as with any other financial companies you do business with. The Financial Planning Association (FPAnet.org) can also make suggestions. Interview the top contenders, and be up front about your concerns. Ask about their qualifications, experience, fee, and how often you will be contacted about new strategies. Then get it in writing. No matter who you go with, he or she needs to be an individual you both feel comfortable with.

**Assess how much you can afford to invest.** Before you start, it's wise to have at least three months' expenses in cash in your savings account, a place to live, food in the fridge, and maybe even a vacuum. (Flat-screen TVs are not required.) If you don't have enough money left over after paying for basic living expenses, begin accumulating cash in a high-yield savings account at your bank. Set up an automatic transfer from your checking account to make sure you stay on top of saving.

**Sign up for your company's 401(k) plan.** It's an investment, not just an annoying deduction from your paycheck. Especially if your company matches all or a portion of your contribution (meaning they kick in a percentage to your fund). Another benefit? Typically, your 401(k) is managed by a professional investment company based on how you've decided to allocate the funds.

Like with any investment, check the returns on your 401(k) every so often to make sure your money is going where it should be. And refrain from borrowing against your 401(k). If you take out a chunk, even temporarily, that money won't be earning interest while you're repaying it. You can take out a loan to pay for college, a car, or a house—but not your retirement.

Also, if you work for a large public company, ask if they have an employee investment program that allows you to buy stock at a discount by having money deducted right from your paycheck. If the stock is profitable, it will be a great addition to your retirement savings.

**Talk to a money manager.** If you have some extra money to play with, visit an investment adviser or custodian to help you get started (see our sidebar, opposite, for help finding a reputable one). It's going to be easier to track your assets and how they fare through a

## Mr. & Mrs. Manners

# Insider Trading

Q. My friend has a moneymaking tip—should I follow it?

A. This sounds like a scene from a bad sitcom. Don't ruin your friendship over a bogus tip. Is it speculation? A bad tip? Something she overheard in line at the grocery store? Even worse, is it insider info that could land you behind bars? Even if the advice is valid, chances are a lot of people already know about it, and you won't be the only one looking to invest. People who try to make quick money often end up losing. Tell your pal you'll pass.

# Glossary of Investing Verbiage

**Actively managed fund:** A mutual fund where the managers make daily decisions about which stocks to keep in the fund portfolio.

**Asset class:** An investment category such as stocks, bonds, cash, or real estate.

**Bond:** A certificate of debt (usually interest-bearing or discounted) that is issued by a government or corporation in order to raise money; the issuer is required to pay a fixed sum annually until maturity and then a fixed sum to repay the principal.

**Company match:** The annual contribution your employer makes into your 401(k) account. It's usually a flat fixed rate or a percentage of your contribution.

**Consolidation:** A student loan or credit card debt repayment move where you pile all your debt into one loan.

**Diversified portfolio:** A group of investments in a range of asset classes.

**Dow Jones industrial average:** An index of the thirty largest industrial companies in the United States based on market capitalization (number of shares outstanding multiplied by the stock price). It acts as a benchmark for the overall condition of the stock market.

**Equity:** A stock.

**Financial planner:** An agent licensed to manage your assets and/or provide investing advice, usually for a fee or for an annual percentage of your wealth that he/she manages.

**401(k):** An investment plan offered through an employer which allows employees to set aside pretax dollars for retirement.

**Index fund:** A mutual fund that invests in stocks listed in a certain index (such as the Dow Jones or S&P 500) in order to mirror its performance. Index funds are easy to track and are more tax efficient than managed mutual funds.

**IRA (traditional):** An individual retirement account where the earnings are tax deferred until withdrawn at retirement and sometimes tax-deductible.

**Mutual fund:** A collection of stocks and/or bonds that individuals or institutions may buy shares in (think co-op vs. condo). The fund is managed by an investment company.

**Stock:** A small percentage of ownership in a company that's usually traded on the public exchange.

**Stockbroker:** An agent licensed to buy and sell stock on your behalf while earning a commission on the trades.

**Stock mutual fund:** A mutual fund that invests primarily in stocks.

**S&P 500:** An index of the five hundred largest U.S. stocks that is used as a benchmark for some mutual funds to compare investment returns.

single source, and this person will help you choose the right type of fund (conservative vs. aggressive) based on your growth goals. Plus, you'll often benefit from improved client services and better pricing.

**Create a diversified portfolio of stocks and/or mutual funds.** Simple rule of thumb: Don't put all your eggs in one basket. Having a diversified portfolio means you have some of everything and not too much of one, i.e., investing in various asset classes: stocks, bonds, cash, real estate, international funds, etc. (Don't worry—we have a glossary of terms on page 36.) There are many classes even just within stocks—U.S. large growth, U.S. small value, international large growth, emerging markets, etc.—but that doesn't mean you need to spread your money across twenty different classes. How you diversify depends on your age, goals, and how much money you have to invest.

**Be patient.** Most people would say to be as risky as you need to be to reach your goals. But since your goals could be constantly changing, you need to reassess and reallocate your money accordingly. If you're investing to save for retirement, you might put 90 to 100 percent of your assets into stock mutual funds. While you might witness a big decline here and there, you've got a lot of time to ride the ups and downs in the market. How you invest also depends on your age and what other risks already exist in your lives. Will you need liquid cash within the next ten years? Can you sit still and leave your money in a fund through economic downswings and upswings? These are all issues an expert can help you hash out.

**Track your progress.** It's going to take a lot of discipline, but don't peek at long-term investments (bonds, 401[k], growth mutual funds) more than twice a year. When you do, it's a good time to see if your portfolio needs to be rebalanced, to make sure you don't have too much or too little money invested in each asset class. (For example, a strong economy will see a rise in corporate profits and an increase in stock prices. Yet bond values often surge when the economy is slowing. Holding both stocks and bonds in a portfolio will help you strike a good balance.) The point is not to get hung up on the day-to-day changes. It can take years to determine if a fund has been successful. But if you intend to buy a house in three years, you'll probably be checking in on your short-term investments (money market accounts, aggressive mutual funds) more often, since you need them to perform well in the short run. Individual stocks, on the other hand, should be monitored daily. You're looking not at performances here but at how news or world events may be affecting that company and its financial health. If a company tanks, the price of the stock will fall, leaving your investment practically worthless.

Aside from rebalancing, it's smart to review your assets every ten years if you are under the age of fifty or to review them in conjunction with a major life change—like having a baby, buying a home, or making a major career shift. You should also make changes when your investments no longer fit the financial model you set for yourselves.

# insurance & legalities

Sure, you were supposed to have those big discussions about important life issues—like insurance and wills—before you tied the knot. But who had the time? To help you out, here's our list of situations that may have changed now that there are two of you. Of course neither of you wants to think about this stuff, but nor do you want to end up in a bad situation made worse by lack of planning. So suck it up, make some decisions, and set your mind at rest that you'll be covered, just in case.

## CHOOSING AN INSURANCE COMPANY

We detail specifics for each type of insurance, but first arm yourself with some general hiring know-how. Ask family members, friends, and coworkers for recommendations. Then start doing your own research. You'll want to look for a company based on the following.

**Price:** Shop around! There are deals to be had. Get quotes from at least three companies and compare them. Many state insurance departments also publish guides showing what various insurers charge.

**Stability:** Be confident that your insurer is financially stable. Various research agencies, such as Standard & Poor's Insurance Ratings Service (StandardandPoors.com), chart this.

**Service:** Make sure an agent you like and trust will be the one to personally handle your claim.

**Deductibles:** Almost all insurance operates with a deductible—which is the set amount that you have to pay before your insurance kicks in. Nab a higher one; the higher the deductible, the lower your rate.

**Consolidation:** See if you can get a lower rate if you buy your homeowner's and car insurance from the same company.

**Incentives:** Ask about discounts (for having home-security devices, or for staying with the same company for a long time). Keep in mind that these offers differ from company to company and from state to state.

## INSURING YOUR STUFF

Here is a directory of detailed information on the types of insurance most newlyweds need.

**Auto insurance** Since you're married, you'll probably qualify for a discount on your auto insurance. If a different company covers each of you, review your policies to see which has the best price for its coverage.

If you're first-time car owners, know the price of your insurance will vary depending on age, where you live, and what kind of car you drive (insurance for a fire-engine-red convertible will run more than a sturdy sedan). Get quotes from at least three companies and compare. Check out websites like Netquote.com or Insure.com that allow you to enter your criteria so multiple companies can e-mail you with their best offers. (Note: These sites also work for the next two types of coverage we touch on.)

**Health insurance** If you both have your own insurance, you should investigate whether it would be more economical to be covered under a single plan and cancel the other. Look at how much it costs on a regular basis, what your copays are for your primary care physician and specialists, and, of course, what's covered (vision, dental, etc.). One factor to consider: Even if you're not planning to have a family for ages, check what sort of coverage each plan has for pregnancy and birth. That may figure into your decision on which plan to retain. Most policies also allow you to change your elections (i.e., pretax health-care spending) after marriage.

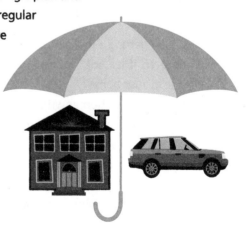

**Pet insurance** Don't forget about your pet's medical bills, which can add up (especially as your furry loved one gets older). A pet health insurance policy can cover your dog and/or cat in the event of accidental injuries, emergencies, and illnesses. Many plans also cover office visits, prescriptions, diagnostic tests, x-rays, lab fees, vaccinations, and more. Go to www.PetInsurance.com for a free quote and more info.

**Homeowner's insurance** You have valuable goods (from engagement and wedding rings to all those expensive presents), and it's time to protect them. Merging households is a great opportunity to do a home inventory—which you'll be grateful to have if disaster strikes. And because you're insuring your home for replacement value, your stuff is probably worth more than you think. (You'll also need this inventory when you're figuring out the details of your will.) Start by going through each room and describing your possessions.

1. For each product, note as much as you can of the following: make, model, serial number, and other identifying information.

2. Attach receipts, purchase contracts, or appraisals to the list.

3. Count clothing items by category (pants, shoes, etc.), and note particularly valuable items.

Want help inventorying your home? Use our worksheet on page 271.

flip

4. Back up your inventory. Go room to room taking photos of valuable items (be sure to write the relevant info on the back of each picture) or make a video (you can say all the important stuff into the camera).

5. Once you're done, make several copies of your inventory and be sure to store some outside your house—with a relative or in a safe-deposit box.

If you're getting a mortgage, your lender will most likely require homeowner's insurance. And even if it's not required, do you really want to risk losing the investment you've made in your home?

A standard homeowner's policy generally covers four categories: one, the structure of your home (if it's damaged or destroyed by fire or most other natural disasters); two, your belongings (if they're stolen, or destroyed by fire or other insured disasters); three, liability (if you, your family members, or pets cause damage to anyone else or anyone else's property, or if someone is injured on your property); and four, additional living expenses (if you have to live away from home due to fire or other insured damage).

**Life insurance** It's not a topic any of us loves to contemplate, but you don't want your new family to have economic burdens if something happens to you. If you die, life insurance could help cover several things: your lost income, which would cover mortgage and other fixed costs plus future expenses for your spouse and kids; your outstanding debts and estate taxes; and funeral, burial, and health-care costs, depending on how you structure your policy.

There are two main types of life insurance, term and permanent. Term policies pay a set amount of money throughout the term of the policy. You pay a premium monthly, quarterly, or annually and receive a set of (much greater) benefits should the need arise. The pros? It's generally cheaper than permanent insurance. The cons? It doesn't have the additional economic benefits that permanent insurance does. Permanent policies, on the other hand, provide long-term financial protection to you and to your beneficiaries. Plus, you could potentially borrow against

## Legal Ease

What kind of lawyer do you need? Start with a general practice attorney who can usually do a little bit of everything from preparing a will to closing on your house to handling a criminal case if you get into trouble. As a young couple, a general practice attorney is your best bet to keep down fees and build a relationship. This person can often give you referrals to more specialized lawyers (see list below).

BANKRUPTCY ATTORNEY: This is if you need to file Chapter 11.

PERSONAL INJURY ATTORNEY: A trial lawyer who will help either defend you from or go after someone in the event of a car accident or other injury-inducing event.

REAL ESTATE ATTORNEY: For both buying and selling.

CRIMINAL LAWYER: If you really get yourself into criminal trouble, you'll need one of these for your defense.

TRUST AND ESTATES ATTORNEY: For complicated wills and inheritances, this type of lawyer can help with both planning and the aftermath of inheriting money.

MATRIMONIAL ATTORNEY: No, they're not just divorce lawyers. These attorneys also do prenups.

TAX ATTORNEY: An accountant can normally handle your run-of-the-mill tax questions and audits, but if you've really snuck some coin from Uncle Sam, you might need to hire a big gun.

what you've paid. Think of it as insurance for your "whole life." The pros? It's good for long-term financial planning—kind of like buying rather than renting your home. The cons? It's more expensive than term insurance.

Once you decide what policy you're interested in, you need to find a provider. Many companies provide their employees with life insurance free of charge. This is term insurance, with all its drawbacks. The advantage, of course, is that there's no cost to you. Some states require that your employer let you "carry" your insurance with you if you leave the company (kind of like COBRA, which lets you continue on your company's health plan for a fixed amount of time after you leave). As with COBRA, you have to pay for it.

Traditionally, insurance is sold through an agent or broker, who generally charges a commission—sometimes called a load. Some providers allow you to buy insurance directly, by phone, mail, or the Internet. These policies often do not involve commissions (they're called no-load). The downside is that they're harder to find and require more legwork than if you were to use an agent. Your final option: In some states, savings banks sell life-insurance policies.

Start buying insurance when you're relatively young and healthy so you can get a lower rate. Look into getting a convertible policy, which means term insurance could be changed to permanent insurance at a later date. You'll have to pay more at that time, but you'll have the long-term financial benefits.

## WHY A LIVING WILL AND HEALTH-CARE POWER OF ATTORNEY?

Nobody wants to think about it, but now that you're part of a new family unit, it's important to consider what you want to happen if you become incapacitated. If your wishes are on paper, your loved ones will have one less thing to worry about in the event of a crisis.

A living will spells out the treatment you would or wouldn't want if you were to be unable to speak for yourself or were terminally ill or permanently unconscious. A health-care power of attorney, an equally important document, spells out whom (your new spouse or your parents) you would want to make health-care decisions under a broader array of circumstances (for instance, if you're only temporarily incapacitated). While some states let you create a living will and a health-care power of attorney on the same form, it's a good idea to create two documents. You don't have to secure either, but doing so doesn't cost anything and could be tremendously helpful to your loved ones.

Once you've made the decision to create a living will and/or health-care power of attorney, here's how to follow through.

1. Get a copy of your state's form at a local hospital or online. Some states don't have official forms, but you can find a form that will be legal in your state at the U.S. Living Will Registry (USLivingWillRegistry.com). Every state has a statute or judicial decision governing these matters; to make our lives complicated, they're all slightly different.

2. After you've discussed the issues together, use the form as a springboard to discuss your general philosophy with your loved ones. Sure, it's a bit creepy, but it's important to make sure everyone's on the same page.

3. After filling out the form, give copies of it to your family and doctors and, if you want, a national registry such as the U.S. Living Will Registry, which will be able to make it available to hospitals and/or lawyers should the need arise.

4. Revisit and update your form every year or so, or if you have a big life event (move to a different state, have a child, etc.), if only to sign and date it. The more up-to-date it is, the more likely it is to hold up in court should a problem occur.

## CREATING A LAST WILL AND TESTAMENT

It sounds morbid, but a will is an important tool to have, even if you're young. A will allows you to control who gets your stuff (DH or parents or your favorite animal charity) in the event that something happens to you or your spouse. If your wishes aren't explicitly spelled out, the state has the authority to parcel out your possessions.

Putting together a will is simple and there are tons of websites that can help you, as well as software programs you can buy. After you write it up according to our guidelines, run it by a laywer, get it signed in front of two witnesses and notarized, and store it in a safe place—somewhere secure but not hidden, so people can still find it if the need arises. We suggest a safe deposit box (give someone else a spare key) or jewelry box.

**tip**
Each spouse should make a separate will, and you'll need to check with your state government on what's considered joint versus individual property.

**What will you include?** Make a list of your significant assets, which you should have already done for your insurance (see page 40).

**Who gets your stuff?** You'll need to decide who gets your engagement ring and other objects, especially if you want to make sure family heirlooms don't fall into the wrong hands.

**What if something happens to both of you?** Scary as it sounds, make a provision in the event that neither one of you outlives the other.

**Who is your executor?** Pick someone to manage your estate; if it's your spouse, have a backup (see above). Make sure you tell the executor and the backup where the will is.

**Who'll take care of your kids?** This is very important because you want to make sure that your children have a loving home if something happens to both you and your spouse.

Are you depressed yet? Yes, it's a downer, but just get it over with.

# >> Chapter 1: the takeaway

Here, the least you need to know.

**DECIDE ON YOUR MONEY STYLE.** Do you want to save a lot, spend freely and save a little, or wing it? While you each had your own way of dealing with money when you were single, you now need a unified strategy for where your money will go. Learn how to talk about it on page 3.

**SET A BUDGET.** What works for other couples will not necessarily work for you. Start with the basics: your monthly income and your monthly expenses. Then see what's left over and decide what you want to do with it. Follow our guidelines on page 25.

**MAKE A FIVE-YEAR PLAN.** Knowing what you want from life in the immediate future will make getting there easier. Examine your current financials and estimate your status in the next five years. Will you be able to afford a house? Will you start a family? Investing 102 starts on page 33.

# [ home ]

**Don't really feel grown up but know you at least** need to trick people into thinking you are? There's no better place to start than the privacy of your home. From finally sitting on a real couch to divvying up duties so your parties run like clockwork, it's time to take stock of your place.

## the nest test:
# your domestic style

Ask each other these quick questions before settling into the rest of the chapter. You may be surprised by some of the answers.

## 1. What belonging of mine would you throw out first?

**2. What's your least favorite household chore?**

3. Which is more your party style: "champagne brunch" or "keg party"?

**4. What's the next big thing we need to buy for our home?**

5. Which do you like better: making dinner or doing the dishes?

**6. Would you describe me as a slob? A neatnik? Or fairly tidy?**

7. How soon do you want to move?

8. What colors do you hate?

# living . . . together

Even if you've been sharing the same space for months, or years, that little piece of paper legally pronouncing your status changes things. The major ground rule? You need to treat your mate like you would a roommate. Don't let that unspoken code of respect for the other's space *and* style go out the window.

## MOVING IN MENTALLY

Moving in together is not just about packing boxes and hiring movers. It's also about welcoming the idea that you are going to be living with each other for the rest of your lives. And in order to ready yourselves, you each need to get in touch with

Moving in literally? We've assembled a moving to-do list like no other. See page 274.

what's essential to you for making a home a home. Write them down; share your lists. And be open to making them happen. For most, the little things (i.e., fresh-brewed coffee in the morning, a real couch, a cute mailbox, organization) give the most relief after a long day.

Also, you need to be prepared for the best *and* worst of cohabitation. The best: always having someone to come home to (or at least sleep next to); everyday habits like getting ready for work or a party being more fun with a partner; and starting to know your beloved inside and out, even better than you already do.

Now, the challenges: sharing space and TV/reading/leisure time; discovering quirks like leaving on lights or always soaking the bathroom floor. Your eating habits may change, too—especially if you're mixing preferred dinner times (six vs. nine), or if one

---

**Time Out**

## Go Dream House Hunting

It's so frustrating to get stuck in a daily rut of anxiety about money, where you're eventually going to live, the new chairs you want. Pick a Sunday, find out about all the open (dream) houses, and go fantasy house hunting. Put on some designer threads, maybe even flash some bling so the Realtors take you seriously, and have a daydream home day.

of you is a vegetarian or has dietary restrictions. Relax, these are all minor blips on the marriage radar. But knowing what to expect will help smooth out the adjustment period.

Another tip? In order to make your mental move-in easier, you need to establish house rules. They can be as simple as *kiss me when you get home,* or *let me have five minutes to unwind after I walk through the door.* Here are some general ones to subscribe to.

**Change your pronouns.** My place, your couch, my stuff—don't fall into this grammar trap (note: *your* dirty laundry on the floor is an exception). It's essential for both of you to start thinking of everything as ours, especially when one person moves into the other's space. Otherwise, one person could start feeling like a permanent guest.

**Agree to disagree.** There is nothing wrong with fighting when you first move in. Let's be honest with ourselves: It's not easy to share space—especially when it's yours that someone else moved into. Know that fights will happen, but the important thing is to agree to find a solution.

**Carve out your own area.** Even if you live in a small space, find a nook that's all yours. Privacy issues top the angst charts for newlyweds, and it's essential to create a place in your home where you can retain some independence. At the very least, be aware and considerate of your mate's desire for some me-time.

"He hates laundry and I hate dishes, **so we do the one we hate less.**"
—momokohime

**Appreciate quirks.** You can't expect another person to know all your little secrets (you need all leftovers transferred to Gladware, for instance). Even if you've been dating forever, weird stuff will come out of the deepest recesses of your personality once you're living together. *Nicely* point them out to each other. Decide together if it's worth indulging it.

**Cut each other some slack.** Remember, not every "bad" habit needs to be broken (hint: it probably can't be anyway). The trick is to find a solution that fits the habit: Invest in a water cooler to avoid the recycle pile-up or buy a basket to hold all those newspapers. And as with all habits, you can always blame your in-laws, as long as it's not in front of each other!

## RELISHING YOUR ROUTINE

Once you've begun to settle into your space as a married duo, it's surprisingly simple to fall into a routine (dinner in front of the TV, bagels on Sundays). It's only natural for your life to slip into a habit. The trick is to not take it for granted, and enjoy the everyday; there's something so romantic about knowing that without fail your spouse will pick up the wine (or milk, or cheese) on his or her way home. Another way to keep the routine alive? Establish a weekly—not daily—schedule for cooking, shopping, cleaning, hanging out at home, and morning routines. These rituals will keep you content and connected.

### Cooking for Two

Now that becoming a wife no longer means tossing in the towel on a career, couples' schedules are complicated, and the simple act of getting food on the table every night can become a source of frustration. Given that dinner is probably the most consistent time the two of you have together during the week, you need to make it something you both enjoy!

Break it up a little bit. Over the next five years, you'll need to decide what to have for dinner approximately 1,200 times (and that's just weekdays!). To keep your sanity and avoid low-blood-sugar-induced "what's for dinner?" drama, try creating a schedule. Here's our suggestion:

- three nights a week: you cook
- one night a week: you go out to dinner
- two nights a week: takeout
- one night a week: wild card (cereal anyone?)

   Your budget doesn't allow for ordering in? Substitute leftovers, frozen dinners, or pasta and jarred sauce for the "takeout" days. The point is to reduce the pressure of heavy prep and cleanup so you have time to indulge in another activity together (backgammon/reading a book/watching a movie) during the week.

**tip**
Promise yourselves not to eat pizza more than once a week. It's easy. It's delicious. It's also insanely fattening.

# Is Your Kitchen Complete?

Cooking supplies rank high on most newlyweds' registry lists, so you probably own many of these basics already. Use this checklist to take stock of what you have, and what you need. Keep a couple of items in mind for when your MIL asks what you want for Christmas. Feel free to buy yourself quality pieces as you hone your cooking skills.

## Gadgets & Utensils

[ ] Paper towels

[ ] Kitchen shears

[ ] Manual can opener

[ ] Bottle opener

[ ] Corkscrew

[ ] Large stirring spoons (2)

[ ] Slotted spoon

[ ] Wooden spoons with long handles (3)

[ ] Large fork

[ ] Soup ladle

[ ] Rubber spatulas, large and small

[ ] Pancake turner

[ ] Vegetable peeler

[ ] Wire whisk

[ ] Potato masher

[ ] Mortar and pestle

[ ] Grater

[ ] Juicer

[ ] Pepper mill

[ ] Funnel

[ ] Tongs

[ ] Rolling pin

[ ] Large flour sifter

[ ] Ice cream scoop

[ ] Skewers

[ ] Plastic chopping boards (2 to 3)

[ ] Vegetable steamer

[ ] Large strainer

[ ] Small strainer

[ ] Colander

[ ] Salad spinner

## Measuring

[ ] Measuring spoons

[ ] Quart-size glass measuring cup

[ ] Cup-size glass measuring cup

[ ] Set of dry measuring cups

[ ] Meat thermometer

[ ] Timer

**tip** Make sure to double check that you have everything you need for your recipe *before* you start cooking.

## Storage

[ ] 4 to 6 storage jars, light-proof and airtight

[ ] 6 or more tight-lidded plastic refrigerator/freezer storage tubs

## Small appliances

[ ] Portable electric hand mixer

[ ] Stand mixer

[ ] Toaster or toaster oven

[ ] Blender

[ ] Food processor

[ ] Coffeemaker

[ ] Coffee grinder

## Pots & Pans

[ ] Small skillet (4- to 5-inch)

[ ] Large skillet (8- to 10-inch)

[ ] Large stockpot (10- to 12-quart)

[ ] 2-quart saucepan

[ ] 3-quart saucepan

[ ] 4-quart saucepan

[ ] Large casserole, with lid

[ ] Roasting pan, with rack

[ ] Tea kettle

## Specialty Cookware

[ ] Wok

[ ] Asparagus steamer

[ ] Double boiler

[ ] Fish poacher

[ ] Egg poacher

[ ] Stovetop smoker

[ ] Fondue pot

[ ] Stovetop grill

## tip

Start with a good-quality chef's knife and paring knife that fit your budget, and add others from the list according to the kinds of food you like to prepare.

## Bakeware

[ ] Round 8-inch cake pans (2)

[ ] Pie plates (1 to 2)

[ ] Loaf pan (9" x 5" or 10" x 4")

[ ] 2 square cake pans (8" x 8" or 9" x 9")

[ ] Rectangular cake pan (13" x 9")

[ ] Mixing bowls, set of 3, glass or steel

[ ] Muffin pans (1 to 2)

[ ] Cookie sheets (2)

## Knives

[ ] Chef's knife (9-inch)

[ ] Paring knife (3-inch)

[ ] All-purpose utility knife (5-inch)

[ ] Long slicing knife and/or boning knife

[ ] Long serrated knife

[ ] Sharpening steel or electric honer

# Cooking à deux

As long as everyone knows his or her roles, making dinner together can be delicious.

ASSIGN CLEARLY. Even though you're working side by side, someone still needs to be the boss. Figure out who does what before you begin. You don't want to end up with a fantastic piping-hot stir-fry—but confusion over who was supposed to cook the rice.

STARVED? Never try to have fun in the kitchen when you are famished. Too many people lose their cool when they haven't eaten for a while. Snack first, or pull out the takeout menu instead.

HOLD YOUR TONGUE. "Dice" might mean ¼-inch cubes to one person and ⅛-cubes to another. If the task is not on your to-do list, then don't butt in on how your co-chef is handling it. Making things perfect (in your mind) isn't worth ruining the mood.

ALWAYS ADD WINE . . . or beer or an ice-cold martini. A great mix of music also helps turn dinner prep into your own private house party.

Swap sides. Unless someone has a much lighter workload and regularly gets home earlier, it's unfair for one of you to always do the cooking. Also, in many ways, food = nurturing = love, and making your mate a meal is an unspoken expression of affection no one should miss out on. On Sundays, decide who will be chef when for the coming week. If it's your night and you're suddenly running late, call home and ask your spouse to *do you a favor* and start dinner—this roommate-quality courtesy keeps anyone from feeling taken for granted.

Have specialties of the house. There's nothing wrong with declaring, "Wednesday is meatloaf night." In fact, we think that every cook in the house should perfect two to three dishes they are certain their partner loves. Knowing that Mike's Famous Fajitas are on the menu for Friday night will help you get through the afternoon at work without a trip to the vending machine. These simple traditions are both fun and comforting.

Be kind. Everyone wants to be a good cook—it lies at the heart of every classic ideal of domesticity. Don't be mean about each other's failures in the kitchen, particularly if you want your partner to keep cooking for you. As we said above, preparing food takes love, so even if a meal makes you want to gag, find a way to choke it down.

Respect food issues. If she's on a diet, don't make a big batch of pasta carbonara or prepare two huge bowls of ice cream with chocolate sauce for dessert. You not only show your lack of support for your spouse's health concerns, you also pit his or her desire to make you feel good (by eating your meal) against his or her desire to take care of themselves (by eating healthy). Same goes for vegetarians and spouses concerned with cholesterol and sodium intake—it may be annoying, but their health is far more important than you loving every meal.

Time to lose that newlywed nine? See our tips on dieting together on page 189.

### Stocking Up Strategies

Shopping for groceries and staples can suck up your weekends. These strategies can help you save time—or at least get the most out of the hours you do spend strolling the aisles.

**Make a ritual out of it.** If everyone knows that Saturday afternoon is time to hit the supermarket, it won't cause conflict. In fact, it might become something to look forward to. When you are done, have a standing date to indulge in a mocha cappuccino at the coffee shop next door.

**Buy in bulk.** Don't even try to shop for two. Smaller sizes are always more expensive, they contribute to the world's waste problems, and you have to go to the store more often (we're certain you could find something more valuable to do with your time!). Buy "family packs" and freeze twosome-size portions of meat—you'll save money and always have something on hand for dinner. Also, now's the time to join a warehouse club, particularly if you have the room to stock up on basics like toilet paper, paper towels, detergent, pasta, and other nonperishables.

**Add some adventure.** While far from scintillating, grocery shopping can pack in some simple fun. Divide the list, say "go!," and see who makes it to the checkout aisle first. Break open a box of your favorite kid cereal and munch as you make your way from the fruit to the frozen foods. Try one new item from the international aisle every time you visit.

**Find a greengrocer or a gourmet shop.** A great loaf of bread can make even the most basic meal taste better. Fresh herbs and vegetables from a farmers' market always pack in more flavors. And if you ask questions, you can get a full education on cheese, fruit, or coffee from a specialty grocer. Supporting smaller stores also keeps your neighborhood richer and makes your shopping more exciting.

**tip**
Meat will keep in the freezer for six months if you store it well: Wrap each piece individually in foil, put the items in a zip-closing freezer bag, squeeze out all extra air, and write the date on the bag with a permanent marker.

# Pantry 102

What does every couple need in their pantry? Take it a gourmet step beyond the basics and you will always have something to offer impromptu guests. Food retains flavor best if stored properly and used before the expiration date on the package.

### Food Stores

[ ] Assortment of beans

[ ] Long and short pasta

[ ] Fast-cooking rice

[ ] Basmati rice

[ ] Canned soup

[ ] Canned tuna

[ ] Whole peeled tomatoes

### Dry Goods

[ ] Vegetable stock or bouillon cubes

[ ] Cereal

[ ] Bread crumbs

### Baking

[ ] Vanilla extract

[ ] Sugar

[ ] Brown sugar

[ ] Confectioners' sugar

[ ] Flour

[ ] Baking soda

[ ] Baking powder

[ ] Cornstarch

[ ] Nuts

### Entertaining

[ ] Fancy crackers

[ ] Cooking wine

[ ] Soy sauce

[ ] Olive oil

[ ] Balsamic vinegar

### Spices

[ ] Sea salt

[ ] Peppercorns (and mill)

[ ] Cayenne pepper

[ ] Oregano

[ ] Cinnamon

[ ] Thyme

[ ] Nutmeg

[ ] Paprika

[ ] Rosemary

[ ] Basil

[ ] Bay leaves

[ ] Sage

**Shop online.** Order toiletries, prescriptions, batteries, lightbulbs, and other expensive basics online. There are many specialty sites that offer competitive prices, saved lists, and free shipping—and who needs to wait in line behind the woman consulting the pharmacist on her each and every ailment?

### Hanging Out at Home

Some couples plop on the couch and watch TV together every single weeknight. Now while we're all for nesting, switch it up a little to make nights at home just as fun as nights on the town. Our suggestion:

> Happy hour in your home one night.

> TV two nights (record all your shows for the week and watch them commercial-free).

> Technology-free activity one night (reading, cards).

> Wild card one night.

> Plan to go out on weekends.

### Grooving on the Daily Grind

During the week, the average couple probably sees each other a total of four waking hours a day. Most of that time is spent coming and going and getting organized. Depending on how you handle such daily interactions, these few hours together can be some of the sweetest—or the most stressful.

**Make your mornings count.** Every domestic duo has an A.M. routine. One hits the

## Shelf-Life 101

You'll want to confirm this tidbit by looking at the packaging, but most of your pantry supplies will last over a year when stored properly. An exception seems to be in the baking arena. After a certain amount of time, these opened ingredients lose their flavor, start to taste weird, or in the case of baking soda, go flat—all of which will yield less than stellar results.

- **Baking soda**         6 months
- **Baking powder**     3 months
- **Flour**                  6 months

shower first, the other picks up the paper—you get the point. Recognize it, revel in it, and dare to break it up every once in a while: Rise early and take a walk together; ignore your morning breath and have a roll in the hay before work; scrub each other's back in the shower. Breakfast (read: coffee) is also a key part of making the morning more blissful. Surprise your spouse with café con leche in bed, always have doughnuts to celebrate hump day, read the *Times* together over buttered toast with jam—and save ten minutes to discuss what's going on in the world before you head into it. If you kick off your day in a connected way, chances are you'll be a better doctor or teacher or shopkeeper.

**tip**
Never leave without saying good-bye— even if your other is in the shower. If they are still sound asleep, leave a note. It takes ten seconds, but it is worth hours of warm and fuzzy feelings.

**Learn each other's decompressing styles.** The standard pressures of work have a way of affecting one's mood—and people deal with stress differently. If post-work one of you likes to vegetate on the couch while the other kicks into organizing mode, there is going to be a culture clash. Likewise, if one party comes home all bubbly from a day of great deals and the other's day has been an emotional drain, there's the chance the upbeat person will feel the other is raining on their parade if they don't jump up and get all excited. When you are sharing a place, it is critical to give each other the space to deal with the day's ups and downs in a natural way. You can't expect to always stay on the same emotional page when you lead two independent lives.

**Celebrate the small stuff.** Finals are finally over. The annual budget planning at work is complete. The last box is unpacked. The tulips you planted last spring are blooming for the first time. It is expected to celebrate life's big holidays—but the little achievements often go unacknowledged. Now that you've got a 24/7 party partner, you can live a life of little special occasions. You don't need to make plans or spend money, simply take a moment to kick back at the dining room table or on the deck—preferably with a glass of something bubbly—and toast how lucky you are to have such a great life/smart wife/etc.

## DIVVYING UP CHORES

As soon as you move in together, or even start thinking about it, you need to have an honest conversation about how you plan to manage the day-to-day maintenance of your household. You might not realize it, but you have implanted, preconceived ideas in your head about how a man and a woman should share the domestic duties. If your mother was an old-fashioned housewife type, some part of you could assume that the female half of your duo will take on more of the cooking and cleaning than the man (with his role largely restricted to fixing electronics, mowing the lawn, and manning the barbecue). But if your mom worked outside of the home every bit as hard as your dad did, you'll probably expect an all-for-one attitude. And if your parents divorced when you were young, you might not have a clue as to how these things are "supposed" to work.

Once you've confessed your ideas about who should do what in the home, lose them and create a new, gender-neutral division of labor.

**Make a list.** What are the tasks that need to be tackled? Review it together one week after you make the list so you can actually see if you've covered everything, and then dole out tasks according to interest and ability (think team-captain style). As you choose your chores, agree on what counts as having done the job—or you could be eating microwave popcorn every time it's your spouse's turn to cook. Weekly errands are best tackled when you divide and conquer. Think about logistics here: If the dry cleaner is right near your office, then you should be the one to take on this task.

**Stay on track.** Check in every couple months to make sure each one of you is on top of your tasks, or consider swapping some chores to suit your schedules. Trading chores for a week once a month is also a great way to appreciate the other's "roles" and understand the work your partner is putting in (i.e., making the bed is harder than you think).

**Enforce rules.** If one of you still won't comply, create a fun system that penalizes the other person for skipping chores. Hand out "tickets" to the offender for not taking out the trash, for leaving mail on the counter, etc. The penalty: Whatever the fine is on the ticket ($1, $5, $10, etc.) must be deposited in a special savings account or stored in a money jar. Of course, it depends on how lenient a chore cop you both are.

**tip**
Everything doesn't have to be totally 50/50. If one of you is a much better cook, maybe you commit to doing the grocery shopping and making dinner most of the nights you're home; if the other is highly particular about smelly garbage (not a bad quirk), he or she can be in charge of that.

Want a painstakingly complete checklist of chores? Download it at TheNest.com/chores.

click

# Topic:
# are you lazy?

"

**I wouldn't say I'm lazy—my husband is just very high energy. Hey, more power to him!** —eland

"

**I feel like I'm lazy,** like DH does a ton of stuff around the house. I usually get home really late, so he does most of the laundry, all the cooking. I feel like a lazy bum.

—MollyAllison

**HA! I WISH. I NEVER SIT DOWN,** except to eat dinner, pay bills, and fold laundry. He parks it all night. —fig610

**Yes**—and I'm not ashamed to admit it. But I think it's fine because he works from home and I'm out of the house more than 12 hours a day. He hates me for it though! I just remind him that I'll be the one carrying our children for 9 months . . . that usually does the trick! —jellybean75

### nest note:

No matter how you look at it, it's not fair for one person to be in charge of all the household chores. If you work later than your spouse does during the week, make sure you pick up the slack on the weekends by taking over the items still on your sweetie's to-do list. The last thing you want is for him or her to feel taken for granted.

**Avoid being a nag!** If the other person *has* completed the chore, yet it's just not up to your OCD standards—or if he or she plans to do it, just not at the second that you're preoccupied by it—refrain from bursting a blood vessel. It's okay to let him or her know how you feel and what looks messy to you, but as long as mold isn't taking over your shower, or flies haven't infested your kitchen, is it really that big of a deal?

"My husband put all of the baby blankets in the dryer for me while I was out, and **half of them came out with rough patches** from the high heat melting the material. The poor guy was trying to help and I don't want to tell him what he did wrong."
—redhead

## THE CLASSIC CLASH:
## SLOB VS. NEATNICK

After money, the subject cohabitating couples butt heads about most is neatness. It's important that you realize that your idea of "normal" isn't superior to anyone else's—and that's especially important if your significant other has a different set of standards than you do. Here's how the neatnick can make it work.

**Make being tidy as easy as possible.** When dirty clothes wind up on the floor, not in the hamper, you must make the hamper easily accessible so the sloppier partner has no excuse for dropping socks and underwear wherever he or she pleases. But if that, coupled with begging and pleading, doesn't work, the neatnick just might have to accept that the slob is genetically hardwired to want to leave dirty laundry lying around.

**Hire a housekeeper.** You have no idea how many relationships have been saved by splurging on someone to clean up your home. That way, regardless of either of your behaviors, someone will come and do the work for you. The real silver lining: Once you get used to a clean house, you'll both become neater by default.

**Choose your battles.** And neatnicks have to ask themselves if it is actually so much work to pick your partner's socks off the floor and put them in the hamper. Or is it more the principle of having your preferences and requests ignored? It's probably better to save your anger for the big issues (read on).

# Spring Cleaning

Beyond the general above-and-beyond scrub-down that all homes need each season (pull out the fridge and sweep, send rugs out to be cleaned), take care of the things below in the spring. Book a date on the calendar so you both know what's coming and aren't surprised when "Spic and Span" Saturday rolls around.

**PAPERWORK.** There's no right time to tackle the filing cabinet, but "never" is the wrong time, so you might as well do it now. Dig down to the bottom of the pile of "to be filed" bills, receipts, and other fun stuff and get everything categorized. Don't just jam them into the filing cabinet when you're done. See page 21 for a list of what to store and for how long, and get ready to purge.

**WINDOWS.** Wipe them down inside and out. If you can't reach your second-story windows and they don't pop in for easy cleaning, call a pro. He might be the same guy who can deal with your gutters while he's up there, too. The pros tell us that the best cleaning solution to use is one teaspoon of any basic grease-cutting dishwashing liquid per gallon of water. There's debate on the whole paper towels versus newspaper thing, but all agree that a good squeegee is key.

**RUGS.** When was the last time you sent the throw rugs out to be cleaned? (If you're like us, it was a while ago.) Send them out to be steamed, and while those are out of the way, give your hardwood floors a serious mopping. The wall-to-wall should be steam-cleaned annually.

**FILTERS** Change the filters on things like the furnace, the central air, and air purifiers, and while you're thinking about it, swap out the old water filter, too.

**THE GARAGE.** The cars that dragged you through the slushy streets all winter tracked a fair amount of grit into your garage. And chances are, it was cold enough that you didn't spend as much time as you could have putting every last thing exactly where it goes. Haul everything out, hose down the floor, clean off and reorganize everything before you put it all back (this time in the right spot). If you've got anything in the house or in the basement that you've been meaning to store in a crawl space or an attic, this is a good time to deal with that, too.

**BASEMENT.** You'd be less afraid of things that go bump in the night if you were sure what all you had stored in the basement. Use a rainy spring afternoon to organize, categorize, and throw things away. Are there boxes down there you haven't opened in a couple years? Think about whether you can pare down the contents. Look in corners of ceilings and floors for any signs of water or structural damage, and once all is clear, you can run back upstairs to the safety of the rest of the house.

**CARS.** A lot of car maintenance is supposed to be done on a schedule that relates to mileage, but if your car is due (or, ahem, past due) for a tune-up, take it in. If you're all set for oil changes, tire rotations, and the like, check out smaller things, like replacing the windshield wiper blades that worked themselves to death over the colder months. Fill all the fluids (radiator, antifreeze, washer, etc.). Take out the stuff you had to tote around in the trunk for the winter—scrapers, sandbags, shovels, blankets, whatever—but leave a spare tire, a jack, and jumper cables. Then, finally, take the car to the really good car wash and say yes to all of the additional options on the menu, especially the one that gets down and dirty with the grime on the underside of your vehicle.

**CLOTHES.** Clean out the cold-weather clothes you didn't wear last winter and those warm-weather things you don't intend to wear in the coming season and make a Salvation Army run. Chances are, if the style is out this season, it will be next spring, too, so why wait?

**COMPUTER.** Edit down your electronic photos. Delete cookies, delete items you don't use off the desktop (or move them to a file), get rid of out-of-date "paperwork" that's clogging the hard drive, and update your software.

**tip**

Spring's not the only season to deep clean. In the fall, before winter rolls in, change the furnace filters, seal your deck, and clean the last of the leaves out of the gutters.

# The Perfect Wash: Get Loaded with These Tips

You're going to be taking care of this particular chore for the rest of your life and now is the time to master it! Follow this three-step guide and you'll be ahead of the pack.

1. Sort clothes by color and crudiness. Zip zippers and hook hooks to prevent snags and also empty the pockets (the problems a hidden tissue can do to a load of laundry!).

2. Fill the washing machine with water (for a general wash, warm is best) and then add the detergent so it can disperse properly. The recommended amount of detergent on the bottle is based on an average load of five to seven pounds of clothes (about the size of a laundry basket) that are somewhat soiled (not your nasty workout or gardening gear) and washed in hard water. When the conditions change, you need to change your detergent accordingly—more soap for really dirty clothes or large loads; less for a small load or those done in soft water.

**tip**

Some things (your delicates, his sentimental or sartorial faves) each of you should always wash for yourself. A rule of thumb: If the thought of rending the garment in the spin cycle rips you up for more than a few hours, do it yourself. No need to compound loss with resentment.

3. Once the soap has had a chance to dissolve, load the clothes in—don't pack them in—and make sure they are covered by water with room for the clothes to move around and get clean. For a top-loading machine, fill only to the top holes of the basket. For front-loaders, leave 1 inch of space in front of the door. An overloaded machine will result in wrinkled, less-clean clothes (and if you use powdered detergent, you might notice undissolved clumps have settled in the creases of your clothes).

# decorating as a duo

The look of your home (what's on display, your wall colors, the furniture) is one expression of who you are. Both of you came into this relationship with accumulated stuff from your previous lives, and it's likely that you both want much of that stuff to stay with you, too. With a little compromise, you can create a new look without losing your individual styles. The goal is to blend your personalities and tastes to ensure that you both feel comfortable in and excited by your space.

## DEFINING YOUR COUPLE STYLE

First, assess what you've each brought to the table. If you and your mate have remarkably similar taste in décor styles, color schemes, and art, decorating your space should be simple. But if you often disagree on aesthetics, you can find a common ground no matter how disparate your tastes are. The following exercise is a great way to discover where your styles converge.

Round up two or more months' worth of home magazines and tear out *all* the pages showing decorated rooms. Look for photos of homes in nondecorating magazines, too. Once you have a big stack of torn-out pages (aim for at least fifty, but ideally more), look through them and put a Post-it on the back of each photo you like. Don't overthink it—just go on your gut reaction to each room.

When you're done, pass the entire pile to your partner, face up so he or she can't see which pages you've put Post-its on. Your honey should then go through the pile and set aside the pages that appeal to him or her. When done, look through your partner's "yes" pile and pull out the pages that *also* have Post-its on the back indicating your approval.

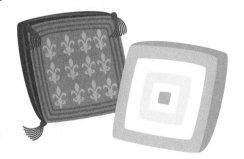

Then, the two of you can flip through the set of pictures that appealed to you both and see what the common elements are. Sure, there will probably be some looks you love that your partner won't go for, but agreeing on a style actually makes the whole decorating thing much easier.

# Buying Your First Home

Ready to ditch the rental for a love shack of your own?

DECIDE IF YOU'RE READY TO DEAL. Frozen pipes. Overgrown lawns. Leaky roofs. Property taxes. These will all be your responsibility once you become homeowners. The costs can be quite substantial when you first buy a home. They will be worth it if you stay there for several years, but if you doubt you'll be living in the same city in a year, buying a home may not be for you.

FIGURE OUT WHAT YOU CAN AFFORD. You know what you pay now for rent and other home expenses. How much more per month can you take on while maintaining some quality of life and contingency funds? In addition to the cost of the house, don't forget to think about taxes, maintenance fees, repairs, PMI (private mortgage insurance), and closing fees. The closing fees can range from 2 to 5 percent of the price of the house and are typically paid by the buyer, not the seller. That's a nice chunk of change for random fees like checking your credit (yes, you have to pay for them to check your credit), and many first-time homebuyers forget to consider this necessary evil when budgeting for a home. Ease the burden by calculating this additional cost into your mortgage. If it's structured into your monthly mortgage payment, you won't have to pay it immediately out of pocket.

You might also want to set up an emergency fund for unforeseen repairs, because you'll get the bill when the boiler breaks. The bottom line: Don't max yourselves out on your mortgage payments and forget about budgeting for all the extras.

FIGURING OUT YOUR DOWN PAYMENT. Many homebuyers opt to put 20 percent down, but this is not the only option. Some lenders, such as Fannie Mae, offer programs for first-time homebuyers that let you make a smaller down payment—but keep in mind that you may need to purchase mortgage insurance if you put down less than 20 percent. And remember that the down payment doesn't include closing fees, which can cost anywhere from $5,000 to $15,000.

**CHOOSE YOUR MORTGAGE WISELY.** There are two basic types of mortgages: fixed-rate and adjustable rate. Fixed-rate mortgages have interest rates that stay the same throughout the loan's life (usually fifteen to thirty years), while adjustable rate mortgages (ARMs) have interest rates that vary over the course of the loan. Usually, your ARM's interest rate will be tied to an economic index, such as the going mortgage rate. When rates are high, your rate will be high. When they're low, yours will be low.

If you're buying a home when interest rates are "historically low," it may be wise to choose a fixed-rate mortgage. If interest rates are high and you think they will decline, you may want an adjustable rate mortgage.

**CHECK YOUR CREDIT REPORT.** This is the time to revisit your credit history (see page 5). Your credit report is an objective way for lenders to quickly analyze how risky it is to lend you money, in this case for a mortgage. A credit score or FICO score of 650 to 700 is considered average, according to MyFico.com. The best score range (760 to 850) will allow you to get the best interest rates because you'll be less of a credit risk to lenders. In dollars, that extra 20 points can change your payment difference by about $200 a month. A bad credit score won't necessarily ruin your chances of getting approved for a loan; upgrading your credit score by establishing a good line of credit (paying your loans on time, carrying a balance of 30 percent less than your maximum balance on credit cards) will show you to be less of a risk for lenders.

**GET PREAPPROVED FOR A MORTGAGE.**

This means you apply for a mortgage on a hypothetical house in your price range and the application is preapproved. Before you apply for a mortgage, address any lingering blots on your credit record (see above). The lender commits in writing to fund your loan for a

**tip**

Wondering how much those monthly mortgage payments will really be? Trying to decide whether it's worth it to haggle over a lousy fraction of a percentage point? Take a look at the figures below.

Monthly Payments (per $100,000)

| Interest Rate | 15 yrs. | 30 yrs. |
|---|---|---|
| 5% | $791 | $537 |
| 6% | $844 | $600 |
| 7% | $899 | $665 |
| 8% | $956 | $734 |
| 9% | $1014 | $805 |
| 10% | $1075 | $878 |

To find out which type of mortgage is best for you, visit LendingTree.com.

click

# Buying Your First Home (continued)

specified period of time, provided the home you choose appraises out in value. (Translation: The lender hires an appraiser to examine the dollar value of the house to confirm you're paying what it's worth. It's their way of making sure you're not getting ripped off with their dough.) Getting preapproved enables you and your spouse to know what you can spend and to use that as a negotiating tool. Because most lenders are hooked up to bank databases, applications for preapproval can be processed in twenty-four hours.

DEFINE THE DREAM. Once you've got a rough idea of your financial picture, it's time to determine the parameters of your dream home. Think about the kind of neighborhood you want to live in: Is it urban, suburban, exurban? Is it filled with DINKS (dual-income, no kids)? Do most of the houses have swing sets in the back-yards? Is it brand-new with saplings, or do you need tree-lined streets? Are recreational facilities (pools, tennis courts, etc.) nearby? What about the schools? Next drill down to the house itself. How much square footage do you want? What about the size of the yard and number of rooms? What kind of layout works for your life? After dreaming, get a little practical and rank these elements in order of priority. Consider location, structure, price, and size, and don't discount factors like the way you felt as you drove up to and then toured the house.

START YOUR SEARCH. Once you've thought about potential neighborhoods, price ranges, and amenities, it's time to start your search. Start with the Internet to find listings and price ranges in areas you like. Drive around communities that best suit your lifestyle. Chat with friends, coworkers, and family to get references for real estate agents and Realtors, and information on open houses. (You can also jot down agents' names from the "For Sale" and "Sold" signs you see.) Don't forget to communicate your time line (when you want to purchase; when you'll have to vacate your current home) with your Realtor or broker.

**tip**

Home inspectors are not repairmen, and they do not inspect septic systems. It's best to get a septic inspector to evaluate the system before you make an offer.

**KNOW WHAT TO LOOK FOR.** Here's what to consider as you hunt for homes:

- Original details: molding, floors, etc.
- Layout
- Square footage
- Lighting
- Room for expansion
- Location
- Neighborhood feel
- Investment potential

**INSPECT YOUR INVESTMENT.** Once you've found your happy home, it's time to bring in the professionals. Home inspectors are trained to look at the overall condition of the home prior to purchase. If they see a problem, they'll recommend having a professional (plumber, electrician, carpenter) estimate the cost of repair, which can often be used as a bargaining point or deducted directly from the purchase price. (It can also save you from making costly discoveries, such as a leaky roof or a boggy foundation, after the home is yours.) Find an inspector in your area using the American Society of Home Inspectors (ASHI.org).

**REVIEW THE FINE PRINT.** Lawyers review the paperwork involved in the purchase of a house and deal with the title company to ensure that your contracts show you are the legal owners of all the negotiated property. They also know the ins and outs of town regulations when filing a deed or making exterior or interior changes to a house, and can translate your new homeowner documents for you. In some states you can use a title company instead of a lawyer, but it's advisable to rely on a trained real estate attorney. Find referrals from friends and family members, or the bar association in your state (www.ABAnet.org). For more on hiring lawyers, see page 41.

**SEAL THE DEAL.** When you're ready to put in a bid, that offer must be presented in a contract, written by your Realtor or real estate agent, laying out the details to the seller. (This letter will include closing dates, appliances wanted or not wanted by the purchaser, mortgage contingencies, and inspection documents or citations for any necessary repairs to the property.) It can take six to eight weeks from the date you and the seller agree on a purchase price to "close" on the house, so keep that in mind when you're working out a time line.

**tip**
Closing the deal on a new home could be your biggest newlywed challenge yet, but before you realize your dreams of bay windows and balconies, you'll need to land a mortgage. Don't panic, go to thenest.com/mortgage for a cheat sheet of pertinent facts, terms, and tips.

No matter which style says you two, you need to put your aesthetics into action. Most likely, you're not going to have the funds to entirely refurnish your space. Instead, find a way to work with what you have, identify what you eventually want, and shop for what you can't live without.

**Shop together.** If someone's stuff dominates the décor of your new space, it's not going to feel like a married home. Joint purchases can help create a home that represents both of your personalities. Shop together for small things such as frames, place mats, and lamps.

**Find a middle ground.** His life-size cutout of Marilyn Monroe or her fuchsia throw rug might mysteriously "disappear" in the move, but don't completely delete your partner's style from your apartment. Nurture each other's interests and comfort colors with splashes of personality to make the place still feel like home to each of you. For example, buy a coffee-table book of Marilyn photography or get pink picture frames to place on your bookshelves.

**Get organized.** A lot of times things can stay if you just have an (out-of-sight) place to put them. If his baseball collection rivals Cooperstown's and her magazine rack hasn't been picked through since she read *Seventeen*, forget the spring—it's time to clean now. Once you file the must-haves in binders, boxes, and trunks, you can have fun with decorating around them. And if you want to do your partner proud, honor the booty with a unique display that makes it look more like art than junk (i.e., you don't need every single Kewpie Doll in the collection but place two strategically as bookends). However, the rule for clothes and gadgets is if you haven't used it in two years, it's a goner. Just think of all the money you can make auctioning it off online.

**Maintain "me" space.** You don't need a top designer to designate a quiet area where one of you can zone out. Set up a comfy chair and ottoman that don't face the TV and place a side table next to them with books, journals, and possibly candles to set a Zen mood. Then, when one of you is taking over the main living space with a gender-specific interest, head to your chair for some me-time. It's like time-outs just got fun.

**Relax.** You don't have to decorate your entire home in a weekend, and the décor doesn't have to be worthy of a design magazine. Take the pressure off yourselves by focusing on the big picture—mixing and matching your styles to create a home that expresses you as a couple.

# Need Inspiration?

Here, a few basic terms to get you inspired and educated for when the sofa salesperson asks you about your vision.

MID-CENTURY MODERN Best defined by sleek, minimal pieces with punches of color and pattern, mid-century modern evokes the clean, streamlined furniture designs of the '40s, '50s, and '60s. Stylish simplicity is key here: Think Eames chairs and George Nelson bubble lamps. This style is ideal for any space where minimalism can reign without need for clutter. If you'd rather not go basic white, you could choose a bright rusty orange or bold blue or other splash of color for the walls.

CLASSIC CONTEMPORARY Gorgeous texture, rich woods, and a comfortable feel define this style. Contemporary, clean lines are seen in traditional pieces. Choose wallpaper patterns of deep reds, heavy creams, or amber yellows and chunky urn-shaped lamps for desks and side tables. Folding screens add immediate interest, and zebra throws and mirrored end tables contribute an unexpected dazzle.

VINTAGE CHARM For a lived-in look, choose a celadon green, canary yellow, or basic white paint for the walls. Hit consignment shops and tag sales for old-school canisters, Victorian upholstered sidechairs, and wood benches. To fill vacant walls, frame vintage postcards or hang old family photos—even if they're not yours.

ETHNIC/GLOBAL This look is rich with deep colors (reds, purples) and hits of metallics (golds and coppers work best). Think Bedouin tent with gorgeous Persian rugs, colored pillar candles, and lots of comfy velvet pillows to sit on. With this look as popular and simple to put together as it is, you can shop everywhere from the local mall to an exotic destination to get pieces for your palace.

COTTAGE CHIC Mismatched patterns and light pastels give this style an antique country feel. To start, give everything a whitewash of paint: Walls, wood floors, side tables, upright chairs, and picture frames are all easily transformed for a bright clean background. Fill the walls with conglomerations of mirrors and collections of varied tag-sale plates. Cover white-based lamps with whimsical shades decorated with lace, ribbon, tassels, or pastel-printed patterns. Pile on a mix of light-colored floral throw pillows.

ECLECTIC The challenge here is to keep your look cohesive. This is a great solution for combining stuff. Unify your palette by going for a neutral with two accent colors. Since a person is usually attracted to items that complement each other, see what happens when you put up that chandelier you found downtown, your collection of framed fern prints, those jars of shells, and the adorable hanging cabinet you haven't yet figured out how to use. Odd paintings or prints can work well together too if placed in similar frames.

## ROOM-BY-ROOM RULES

Try to tackle decorating projects one room at a time. Of course, it's never that cut and dry—if you're looking for a great bed, you may stumble on the perfect mirror for your living room. Your best move is to arm yourself with the following room rules.

### The Living Room

Your living room is the space you'll likely obsess about most, decorating-wise, since it's probably where you'll spend the bulk of your down time and where you'll entertain guests.

THE GOAL: Show off your couple style (and impress your guests) while still being very comfortable.

THE FOCAL POINT: Your couch. It's where everyone gathers 'round and is probably the largest piece in the room.

THE RULES: Think about ways you can make what you have work together better. Stain or paint wood pieces the same shade; or, if you have a single wood piece that clashes with the others (say, one mahogany item in a sea of maple) think about painting it white so that it fades elegantly into the background. Poorly coordinated upholstered pieces can always be slip-covered, which means you never have to throw away a perfectly comfortable sofa just because it doesn't match your significant other's slipper chairs.

Tie the room together with accessories. Throw a coral striped throw on the sofa, place coordinating pillows on each of the chairs, and set a coral vase on the mantel. The repetition of color will trick the eye into thinking all the underlying furniture is as well coordinated as the accent pieces are.

Arrange furniture to fit how you use the room. Do you frequently move from the sofa to the stereo to switch CDs? Then make sure there's a clear footpath between the two, so you don't bruise yourself on an end table while playing deejay. If there's a certain chair you love to hunker down in with a book, make sure it's situated next to a side table with a good reading lamp. If you frequently have small groups of friends over for drinks, create a cozy seating arrangement around the coffee table. And if you two have couch-potato tendencies, make sure the TV is situated right in front of the sofa, and that you have a cushy ottoman to rest your feet on.

Put some personality into your living room. It won't come alive unless you put your personal stamp on it—through wall hangings, photographs, and mementos that reveal who you are as a couple. Choose pieces that have personal meaning: Think photos of your favorite vacation spot or a print or framed museum poster picked up on your honeymoon. Fill the room with photographs of family and friends (your wedding photos are probably the most professional you have), stack coffee-table books that show off your passions, and decorate surfaces with pretty souvenirs from your travels together.

### The Bedroom

It can be tempting to focus most of your nest-feathering efforts and budget on the public areas of your home and give your bedroom short shrift, but don't ignore this special space. Sure, it's only the two of you hanging out in there, but if you make it look fantastic and feel soothing, you'll get a dose of instant happiness when you enter it at the end of the day.

THE GOAL: Create a sexy sanctuary.

THE FOCAL POINT: The bed.

THE RULES: Make your bed your haven. If there's one thing you should definitely invest in, it's the bed. You don't need to spend thousands on 1,000-thread-count Italian linens, but the stuff you sleep in should look inviting and feel delicious against your skin. After all, you spend a third of your life in bed and it's where you get it on (most of the time, anyway). So talk to each other about what your fantasy bed would look

## Quick Clean

There's nothing like cleaning your house from top to bottom, but who has time? Why not take some clean-up short cuts? (Don't worry, we won't tell Mom.) To get it all done, each pick a task, as opposed to a room, to maximize efficiency.

BATHROOM: Keep a box of disinfectant wipes and glass-cleaning cloths under the sink for a two-minute touch up. Use the glass cloth to do any other mirrors in the house.

ALL FLOORS: Skip the vacuum and use a disposable dust sheet on one of those handy mops to pick up pet hair, dust, and more. FYI, you can use both sides.

FURNITURE: Use one of those dust sheets to run across all your furniture.

CLUTTER: In the closet keep a large tote designated for stuff you haven't registered as junk yet and vow to go through it once every two weeks.

# Quiz
## finding your couple style

**You can learn a lot about how to decorate** your home from the things you like to do and the items you wear. Instead of boring you with a dissertation on style, take this quiz to identify your couple likes, find your style, and get tips on decorating.

### 1. Your bookcase has mostly:

**a.** John Irving's collection.

**b.** Dan Brown's latest.

**c.** Kafka.

**d.** Autobiographies of B-list celebs.

### 2. The shoes you both tend to wear on weekends are:

**a.** Flip-flops. ✓

**b.** Customized sneakers.

**c.** Cowboy boots.

**d.** Wellies.

### 3. The movie rental you guys would agree on most is:

**a.** Anything starring Will Ferrell.

**b.** Something from Sundance.

**c.** A Bollywood film with no subtitles.

**d.** Anything by Woody Allen.

### 4. At home, what CDs are most overplayed?

**a.** Dave Matthews Band.

**b.** Maroon 5.

**c.** Seventies glam rock.

**d.** Show tunes.

### 5. Where's your next ideal summer vacation?

**a.** Nantucket, for the sailing.

**b.** Bali, for the exotic nightclubs and beach life.

**c.** Tibet, for the culture.

**d.** Anything one of our folks pay for.

### 6. Describe the sheets on your bed.

**a.** Muted solids.

**b.** Designer anything.

**c.** Mismatched stripes and plaids.

**d.** Mickey Mouse.

## 7. Where do you get your Saturday morning coffee fix?

**a.** At Starbucks.

**b.** From our new home espresso machine.

**c.** At my health-food store.

**d.** Any place that sells it.

## 8. What's hanging above your couch?

**a.** A black-and-white Ansel Adams poster.

**b.** A Warhol-esque portrait of our dog.

**c.** A great flea-market find.

**d.** My struggling artist friend's creation.

## 9. Your weekend ritual includes:

**a.** Brunch with friends.

**b.** Gallery hopping.

**c.** Browsing used bookstores and flea markets.

**d.** A road trip—without a map.

## 10. If you two could buy any vehicle, what would it be?

**a.** A Land Rover.

**b.** A Mini Cooper.

**c.** Anything hybrid.

**d.** A vintage VW bus.

# results

## mostly as
**You're "Classic."**

You're the couple who shops at stores like Crate & Barrel for contemporary, clean lines. Your dream home has gorgeous texture and rich woods, yet a comfortable feel.
**The quick fix:** Invest in one high-quality piece of furniture—whether it's a table, a bar cart, or a chandelier.

## mostly bs
**You're "Trendy."**

Trendy when it comes to home design is best defined as mid-century modern. You should start designing your home around modern, minimal pieces with punches of color and pattern. Don't be afraid to raid your granny's attic.
**The quick fix:** Slipcover your couch in a neutral color and top it with tons of graphic print pillows.

## mostly Cs
**You're "Boho."**

Your style is boho (short for bohemian). You're the couple who can take a scrappy old chair and make it into a showpiece. And a scarf can work wonders on a side table.
**The quick fix:** Hit a flea market for rich, perhaps Indian, fabric and make drapes to start working your boho style from the outer periphery into the room.

## mostly ds
**You're "Eclectic."**

Your style is a little trickier to distill because your range of likes (and dislikes, we bet) is so varied. When it comes to your home, your challenge is keeping your look cohesive.
**The quick fix:** Unify your palette by going for a neutral with two accent colors. And remember: You don't need to display an entire collection of anything, like we told you on page 70.

like, whether that means crisp white cotton, romantic lace, or Zen shades of gray, then make that fantasy a reality.

Invest in your sleep. Make sure what's on the inside is just as spectacular (we're talking mattresses, of course). A quality mattress is an investment that should last until your diamond anniversary. Even if you two shared a bed long before marriage, upgrading to a quality queen or king mattress will do wonders for your relationship (and your sex life).

Keep ugly stuff out of sight. This may be hard if space is a big issue, but avoid amassing a lot of work-related stuff or paperwork in your bedroom. If your bedroom is the only place in your home where you can fit a desk, at least keep it tidy, and not overflowing with bills, file folders, and office supplies. And don't let your bedroom turn into a storage space—try a screen to shield your desk area or find another place for extra furniture and other homeless items. If necessary, rent a storage space. Your bedroom can't feel like a sanctuary if there's clutter and reminders of the outside world in view.

### The Kitchen

It goes without saying, the kitchen (if it's big enough) is where people congregate—especially when you entertain—so it's important to make an impact. You can color-coordinate your appliances, but a few beautiful-but-functional items (a great teapot, a sculptural fruit bowl) will also dress up the countertop, and save you money.

THE GOAL: Maximize your countertop, and add color to make the décor fun.

---

## Mr. & Mrs. Manners

# Color Clash

Q. I love red. He has bad memories of a red rec room as a child. How do we compromise?

A. It's not unreasonable for your husband to balk at red if it hits a sore spot. Instead of painting an entire room red, look for items that use red as an accent color or mix red with hues like brown, charcoal gray, or bright orange in stripes or a graphic print. But if he simply can't stomach the slightest hint of red in your shared possessions, you'll have to accept that and express your passion for it with things like red toenail polish.

# Topic: your DH and decorating

How invested is your husband in decorating? **Does he have tons of opinions,** or does he just let you do what you want? —Lesalita

**I can't put a new picture up without his input.** —doril

Sometimes, **I think my DH cares a little too much** how things are decorated. Just this past weekend, we were going to get some flowers to plant. He said that he wanted input on what I picked out. I told him, 'Honey, that would be like me telling you that I wanted to pick out all the wood you were going to use to make your next project.' —sfrazier

**I CONSULTED WITH HIM ON EVERYTHING,** but he would just nod and say okay. —manther225

**Only if it has to do with his black leather armchair.** —DansWife

We used to battle about every decision—from what color to paint the bathroom to how to organize things in the kitchen—we finally just decided to divide up the rooms and each have our own areas to decorate. Fortunately, I got the living room! —TX505

**nest note:**
Don't forget that your first home is your home together. You may have very specific ideas about what you'd like to do with the space, but shutting your spouse out will make your home look more like a boring catalog photograph. Try to incorporate both of your belongings and styles into your rooms—you may be surprised how well they merge to reflect your partnership.

# How to Hire . . . a Decorator

If you feel totally clueless when it comes to decorating, or have tried to style your place yourself with only so-so results, you might want to hire an interior decorator.

- **WHAT THEY DO:** Because having expert third-party advice will prevent bickering over issues such as whether turquoise throw pillows work on a pale green sofa, bringing in a professional can be an especially smart move for couples. Also, professional decorators have access to many fabulous furniture brands, fabrics, and other items that are only available "to the trade," so you'll have infinitely more options than what's available at your local mall.

- **HOW THEY WORK:** Some charge by the hour (usually between $50 and $250), and others charge a one-time, nonrefundable fee. In addition, you will pay a markup on any furniture, upholstery, and other items and services you purchase through the decorator. If you're on a tight budget, consider contacting local design schools to see if there are any recent grads, or even current students, who might be willing and able to decorate your home. They'll likely be willing to do it for a very small fee, or even for free, simply to get to put your home in their portfolio.

- **HOW DO YOU KNOW THEY'RE RIGHT FOR YOU?** We always say go with your gut and think about whether or not you and your collaborator can make decisions with this person. If everything a decorator has shown you is French country and you want mod and sleek, this might not be a good match. After the pro passes the gut check and the aesthetics tests, always call references and ask, Was the project completed on time? Was the decorator able to stay within budget and, most important, did he or she both listen to your ideas and provide new inspiration and guidance that fit the vision?

THE FOCAL POINT: Countertops. Don't clutter them with kitchen gadgets, extra pans, mismatched tea towels, and dirty sponges.

THE RULES: Keep it organized. Arrange your kitchen so that the things you use frequently—the sauté pan, the chef's knife—are always within easy reach. Store these everyday items in the cupboards and drawers closest to the stove, but keep waffle irons, juicers, and any other items you don't use all that often in the cupboards that are less accessible. Ample counter space is essential around the sink and stove.

Food storage is very important. Sure, it's great to have a new set of copper pans, but what if you can't find the chicken broth to simmer in them? Create an organization system that works for you (for example, soups on one shelf, cereal and pasta in labeled Tupperware) to prevent double buying at the grocery store.

## The Bathroom

You don't need to do much to decorate this room—basically in the bathroom you should just make sure the shower curtain, bath mat, and towels coordinate.

THE GOAL: Organize it well and keep it clean.

THE FOCAL POINT: The sink area. A great mirror and similar containers to store soap and other sundries is key.

**26%** of newlyweds say they're equally messy, while 38 percent blame the household Y chromosome

THE RULES: Show off the pretty items, hide the ugly stuff. If you have more bathroom items to store than you have storage space, you'll have to keep a few things in plain view. You might as well put out the aesthetically pleasing things and keep the less pretty stuff hidden away. Stack fluffy towels on a wall rack, or keep them in a basket next to the shower; display your perfume bottles or prettiest toiletries on the vanity, but keep the razors and pill bottles in the medicine cabinet.

Experiment with color. Because of its smaller size, the bathroom is the perfect place to inject bolder colors or try new painting techniques. Just be careful of going too dark—darker hues will make a room look smaller, and most bathrooms can't afford that. If your spouse is dying for a color like navy, suggest painting stripes, or buying navy towels as a contrast to light blue walls.

Clean this room first! If your living room hasn't been dusted in a while and the bedroom carpet could use a visit from the vacuum, it's not *that* big a deal, but if you let things slide in the bathroom, your whole home could suddenly just feel, well, gross. To make sure this room stays spic and span, keep a separate set of cleaning products and tools under the sink. If you always have an all-purpose cleaning spray and a sponge at arm's length, you'll be much more likely to give the rooms the frequent touch-ups they require.

### The Home Office

If you're lucky enough to have a home office, your best bet is to keep the décor neutral. That space may be the first to flip into a nursery or a guest room as life takes it course.

THE GOAL: Create a cohesive space for both co-owners where productivity and creativity trump clutter.

THE FOCAL POINT: The desk. Keep it free from mounds of paper—don't let it become a mail graveyard.

THE RULES: Take into account your work styles. If one of you gravitates toward the couch with your laptop, don't force that person to work at a big corporate-style desk. Set up a space that works, such as a reclining chair with a side table.

Choose function over form. We're sure that your Mies van der Rohe drawerless puzzle table looks awesome, but will

## Manage Your Mail

If mail tends to accumulate and clutter your counter space, it's probably because there's nowhere else to put it. Create a system for organizing your mail.

### Establish an in-box

Make sure all incoming mail has a place to go—whether it's an in-box on your desk, a tray in your entryway, or a basket in the living room.

### Set a sorting schedule

Whether it's every day, or every three days, choose a time to tackle the in-box. Toss junk mail and flip through catalogs. If there's anything of interest, tear out the page (make sure the phone number or website is listed on the page), and file it in a designated folder.

### Divvy it up

Anything other than personal letters or magazines (like bills and intriguing credit card offers) should be placed in a designated spot on the bill payer's desk.

# How to Buy a Mattress

If your current mattress is more than nine years old, if its surface is covered with bumps and lumps, if you wake up feeling like you haven't even slept (and it's been nine hours!), or if you need to be pried from the sinking sag in the middle, you're ready for a new mattress. Here's how to get the right one.

### SIZE UP YOUR SPACE

Obviously, your bedroom layout will determine how big a bed your bed should be. Be on the lookout for manufacturer-specific sizes—some companies now offer a slightly larger queen size marketed as a "European Queen." Arm yourself with a tape measure and jot down the exact size of the mattress, and then compare it with these standard bed dimensions.

**California King:** 72 x 84 inches

**King:** 76 x 80 inches

**Queen:** 60 x 80 inches

**Full ("double"):** 53 x 75 inches

**Twin:** You should not be buying one . . . or two!

(All dimensions may vary by +/– ½ inch)

### SET A BUDGET

Comparison shopping can be tricky when it comes to mattresses, as models vary tremendously between retail stores. Instead, find a sleep set that feels just right, then measure it against similar comfort and support levels of mattresses in another store. Prices differ greatly, but you can expect to drop about $1,000 for a reputable queen mattress with box spring—essential to prolonging the life of your bed. Top-of-the line brands can reach a whopping $20,000.

### DO A BED TEST

In order to find the perfect fit, grab your mate and head to a trustworthy mattress store. You should both lie down in your favorite sleeping positions and test out mattress comfort levels, from plush to firm. Pay special attention to how the mattress supports your shoulders, hips, and lower back—too little support can lead to back pain and too much can add unnecessary pressure.

### LOOK INSIDE THE BOX

It's the quality of the materials used and how they're put together that determine how long a mattress and foundation will provide comfort and support. The best mattresses have more springs, which have been intricately arranged and hand-tied with loving precision. Look for details like a complex coil shape (it will provide better weight distribution) and a thicker wire diameter (for greater resiliency). Each spring system suggests a different feel, so let your body be the judge.

your pens and paper clips fall into the cracks? Where will you store your paperwork? If you just have to have that long table, look for attractive containers, like wicker baskets or fabric-covered boxes, for utility.

Steal space. When you can't devote an entire room to the home office, look for double-duty furniture like antique secretaries that can house your laptop and accordion files. Consider the age-old office/guest room combo with a day bed or sleeper sofa. Or, screen off a portion of the room to make it seem like a separate space.

# entertaining essentials

Why do you need a party primer? Well, entertaining as a couple is a bit different from entertaining as a single. Expectations are much higher for the quality of the gathering. The guest list changes; the menu seems a bit more sophisticated; and others expect you to play host much more often. Especially if you've moved into an amazing new (and bigger) space.

First, you need agree on your entertaining style. If you have differing views on opening up your home, compromise. For instance, selective entertaining (see below) is a good solution for the überentertainer/carefree-entertainer couple combo.

## WHAT'S YOUR ENTERTAINING STYLE?

**Natural-born entertainers:** You feel happiest in your home when it's filled with friends. You're as at ease having friends over for takeout pizza and a salad as you are hosting a formal dinner for eight.

**Selective entertainers:** You like to invite others into your sanctuary on special occasions. You might consider entertaining a chore or a bore, so opening up your home requires a good reason. If occasions become few and far between, though, friends and relatives might think you both a bit antisocial.

**Carefree entertainers:** You feel comfortable having people over at the last minute, even if things aren't totally tidy. You don't need to dot all your hosting i's when having people in. A carefree style can be welcoming, but make sure your guests have enough to eat and drink.

# Topic:
# do you like having houseguests?

Just wondering. DH is like, 'We should get a daybed or futon for our office for when people stay over' and I'm like 'Um . . . **I don't really want to encourage people to sleep over . . .'** Does this make me a bad person? —ChrisnFrankie

"

**There's an old saying: Fish and houseguests begin to smell after three days.**

—WillowStreetCA

We have a spare bed but don't really want to encourage people to stay over. Honestly, IT JUST MESSES UP MY SCHEDULE. And I don't like sleeping over at other people's houses either.          —finally:)

I LOVE HAVING HOUSEGUESTS! DH and I both like to entertain & our family lives OOT. However, it is nice to have your space back when it's over.

—AmandaRae1980

"

## nest note:

If you're worried about houseguests overstaying their welcome, make sure you tell them ahead of time about an engagement you have on the day they're set to leave. This will let them know exactly what time they should be packed and ready to go.

# Hosting a Houseguest

Here, some dos and don'ts for making friends and family feel comfortable in your married home.

**DO:** Test out your guest room (or pull-out couch). That way, you'll know if the bed is comfy enough, if there are enough blankets, pillows, etc.

**DON'T:** Test out the guest room with your mate and forget to wash the sheets. It goes without saying, but you should always make the bed for guests with clean sheets—even if they were the last people to sleep there.

**DO:** Give a house tour. Be sure to explain how to use the coffeemaker, TV, shower, and alarm clock so your guest won't worry about interrupting the happy couple.

**DON'T:** Go for midnight snacks. If you don't know your guest too well, an accidental rendezvous at the fridge in your sleepytime skivvies will create an awkward atmosphere for everyone.

**DO:** Make sure the bathroom is clean, especially the tub and shower curtain, which are often neglected in a spare room. Leave a can of air freshener (or matches) in close reach, since guests might feel self-conscious asking for them after the fact. And put extra toilet paper in a visible spot (try a basket on the floor) so guests don't need to rummage around looking for a roll.

**DON'T:** Take a shower together (you and your spouse, that is). Especially if you only have one bathroom.

**tip**
Fresh flowers, fluffy pillows, current magazines, and books tailored to your guests' tastes will make them feel extra welcome.

**Überentertainers:** You like to entertain only when you have ample time to organize and plan everything perfectly. Hosting is something you consider sacred and you want Emily Post–style perfection when you have people over. Don't get so caught up in perfection that you never let anyone visit.

## THE GUEST LIST

Before you start planning the details of the food and drink, think through the most important ingredients of any get-together:

**Keep it close.** For small or casual gatherings, you may want to simply invite a group of friends who know one another well, but for bigger events you should aim to create an interesting mix. If everybody in the crowd is already well acquainted, your gathering could have a bit of a "same old, same old" feel. Invite some new faces—cool coworkers, friends of friends, somebody you hit it off with in spinning class—to give the party more energy.

**Mix it up.** You could try to bring together different types of people whenever possible. Balance out the married couples with some singletons, and combine the business types with the more laid-back and creative people in your life. Mixing up diverse people is what makes a gathering dynamic and memorable.

## CREATE A FESTIVE VIBE

As the hosts, how you interact with your guests is largely what determines whether or not your party will be a success. If you're ultrahospitable and seem to be having a fabulous time yourself, everyone will leave the bash with great memories, even if some of the food didn't turn out as delicious as the recipes promised. But the most lavish Champagne and caviar–fueled affair won't be fun if you two aren't on top of your game. Keep in mind these three principles of being a standout host:

**Don't disappear to the kitchen.** It's easy to get caught up in obsessing over the food, but remember that the primary reason your guests came was to spend time with you; if eating was their first priority, they would have gone to a restaurant. So get out of the kitchen and mingle! If you're throwing a dinner party, linger at the table between the courses, rather than quickly jumping up after every course to clear plates or pour water or prepare the next thing. Your friends aren't in any sort of rush to get home, so don't rush them nervously through the meal. It's essential that you make time to connect with them.

**Nix your host anxiety.** Nothing extinguishes a party's spark like a stressed-out host. If you're overwhelmed by mixing drinks, visibly disappointed that your entrée doesn't taste as great as you hoped, or anxiously running around cleaning up used napkins and empty glasses, you'll look like you're having a terrible time (or like hired help)—and your guests will feel guilty for putting you through such an ordeal. Stay cool and collected at all costs. If you feel tension creeping up, take a deep breath and watch your guests talking happily among themselves. Remind yourself that you've created an opportunity for other people to have fun and that's the only thing that matters.

**Play (platonic) matchmaker.** If people are feeling shy, think of things two strangers have in common and then introduce them to each other with a lead-in that will get them talking (e.g., "Jason, you should meet Eric—he used to live in Beijing. Eric, Jason is planning a trip to China" or "Lisa and Jack, you should meet Christine and Rob. You guys are neighbors."). Then move on to work your hosting magic on another set of guests.

**Stay on top of your guests' needs.** Even though you should relax and have fun at your own gathering, that doesn't mean you can have four glasses of wine the first hour and

## Mr. & Mrs. Manners

# Rules of Regifting

Q. As wedding gifts, some friends bought us great decorative vases and picture frames to match our living room. Thing is, we've redecorated and now they clash with the style of our new room. Is it wrong to regift? (We've never used this stuff.)

**A.** If it is a truly great gift, but something you already have or don't need, it's not wrong to regift, but you have to be careful, because it is tacky if you get caught. If you can, it's better to return the item to a store and use the credit to get your friends something that's actually from *you.* But if you do decide to regift, make sure to follow a few simple rules. Never regift a present from Person A to an individual who Person A might know, no matter how distant. You don't want to wind up at a friend-of-a-friend's barbecue only to have your giftee tell Person A that the lovely figurine in their living room is from you. Secondly, make sure you scan your present thoroughly for any indicators that it was bought by someone other than you—store tags from another state or a gift receipt and a copy of your registry in the box are giveaways that you got this gift before you gave it. Tip: Keep a log of gifts given and gifts received with our worksheet in the back.

figure the party will just take care of itself. Periodically check in to make sure there's fresh ice in the drinks, ample appetizers on the table, and enough toilet paper in the bathroom. Luckily, being part of a team makes this easier. Before the party begins, decide who will do what during the event. For example, one of you can be in charge of the drinks and the music and the other can take on food and tidying-up duties. And we love the idea of hiring an intern from your office, or a local college student, or even a friend's kid sister or brother to help with serving food, dealing with the "we forgot" list, and cleaning up.

## PERFECT PARTY FORMULAS

Even if you're terrified of hosting a party in your home, there will come a time when you won't be able to escape it—the boss is coming for dinner, a cousin's having her first baby, no one is stepping up for the Super Bowl. Here, we've broken down some basic parties and given you the tools you need to pull it off with aplomb. If you're already a party pro, create a signature soiree that you're known for: a New Year's cocktail party, a Halloween ball, or even an Oscar party. By going all out with one party every year, expectations for spontaneous entertaining from you will diminish.

### Housewarming 102

A housewarming party is a fun way to get all kinds of friends and family together and put an end to the "When do we get to see the new place?" question. Because the party's usually an open house, you can really expand the guest list—coworkers, friends you haven't seen in ages—basically anyone who's heard you discussing the travails of house hunting and moving. And don't forget your new neighbors!

WHEN: Though there's no "official" time when you should host this party, it's tough to get away with calling something a housewarming when you've been at your place for more than about four months. After that, people will assume that the house is plenty warm and that instead of sharing the excitement of a new start, you're just plugging them for prezzies. (It's not mandatory to bring a gift to this party, but many people will want to.)

WHAT YOU NEED TO DO: The key to success with a housewarming party is an informal vibe (which will be convenient if you still haven't found all your serving pieces, or gotten to know your oven well enough to tell when you've got to shave a few minutes off the recipe times). Go buffet—you can order in vegetable trays, wings, sandwiches, and sides like macaroni and chicken salad, and make one warm entrée and a dessert. Plan to offer a couple tours, and revel in the first of many great times in your new space.

WHAT TO WATCH FOR: People will be poking around your place (legitimately), so you've got to find a really good hiding spot for anything you want to keep a secret. Open houses can sometimes result in guests who over-stay their welcomes. Let the lingerers know it's time to go by asking if they need a ride, seeing if they know how to get home, or, if you're desperate, mentioning that you've recently moved and just can't wait to get some rest!

**37** % of couples would rather host a party than attend.

**Casual Cocktails**

BEST FOR: 4 to 10 guests*

TIME: 8 to 10 P.M. (so everyone knows dinner won't be involved)

WHAT YOU NEED TO DO: Having just a few people over for drinks is the easiest way to entertain—and since everyone would so much rather be in your cozy home than sitting around a bar, you'll still earn lots of points for hosting. All you need to do is offer a few basic beverages—say, beer, wine, vodka with mixers, or whatever liquor you've got on hand—and put out some simple snacks like olives, nuts, and a cheese plate with a sliced baguette.

WHAT TO WATCH FOR: Running out of supplies. Stock up on mixers that go well with most types of liquor, such as tonic water, sour mix, and ginger ale so you won't be stuck serving whiskey and grapefruit juice. Follow this formula: For a three-hour party, guests consume two drinks per hour.

BRILLIANT IDEA: If you want to set up two of your single friends without making a big drama out of it, invite them both over to a laid-back gathering like this without spilling your intentions. It's totally low pressure for all: If they're a good match, they'll be able to quickly discover it in such an intimate setting, but if they don't hit it off, it won't be awkward since neither of them knew it was a setup in the first place.

*All numbers exclude you and your mate.

### Spontaneous Dinner Party

BEST FOR: 2 to 6 guests

TIME: 7 P.M. (gives you time after work to pull it together)

WHAT YOU NEED TO DO: Invite friends over for a low-key meal (great on a weeknight or when you've made plans at the last minute) and make it clear to them that you won't be pulling out all the stops, host-wise. You can even order takeout for the main dish, or buy prepared sides such as salads and roasted veggies. This takes the pressure off, and can be just as fun as a more formal affair.

WHAT TO WATCH FOR: Flaky friends. If you're going potluck style, most people jump at the wine or bread option. But if you've given certain pals cheese or dessert duty, make sure you have a backup plan in case something comes up and they forget to bring it or have to cancel. Stock the fridge with ice cream and chocolate syrup, have a stash of nuts—they may not make up your dream menu but at least you'll have something to serve.

BRILLIANT IDEA: Make a one-dish meal (like chili, paella, or just pasta with chicken and veggies) so you don't have to fuss with side dishes. Ask one of your guests to bring a salad, and another to bring dessert.

### We-Are-Adults Dinner Party

BEST FOR: 4 guests

TIME: 7:30/8 P.M.

WHAT YOU NEED TO DO: Choose a menu that's elegant but still easy to pull off. Start meal planning early in the week by selecting a mix of recipes you've mastered and new ones you've been dying to try (hint: look for at least one recipe, maybe a dip or a dessert, that can be made the night before). Create a master grocery list and tackle the shopping together. Then, create a schedule (either mental or actually written out) of what steps you need to take in what order to have everything ready by go time. You don't want to be freaking out that you forgot to preheat the oven as guests start to arrive.

WHAT TO WATCH FOR: Early birds. As much as we hate those who are fashionably late for an intimate dinner party, sometimes super-early guests can put you over the edge. To keep yourself calm, cool, and collected, make sure the hors d'oeuvres are ready first, so early arrivals will have something to nibble on, and don't select laborious entrées that have to be served piping hot. Otherwise, you'll be stuck in the kitchen while your guests are filling up on cheese.

BRILLIANT IDEA: Set the table for dinner before you even get started cooking (see our instructive illustration below). That way, if you start running behind schedule in the kitchen, you'll have one less thing to stress about and you will *look* more organized. Place a row of flower-filled bud vases down the middle of the table (or, if the table is round, group them together in the center). They'll look beautiful without blocking your line of vision.

### I-Wanna-Dress-Up-for-Drinks Party

BEST FOR: 12 to 24 guests

TIME: 8:30 P.M. to midnight

WHAT YOU NEED TO DO: Every once in a while you should treat your friends to a sophisticated soiree. Stock up on libations and *lots* of ice, put out platters of elegant, bite-size appetizers, light votive candles in every corner of the room, and cue up some softly sexy music on the stereo.

WHAT TO WATCH FOR: Competing deejays. It's no secret that music sets the mood for any party. But be aware of who's looking through your CD collection: If your ballad-loving friend takes control, your party could be over quicker than a one-hit wonder. Your best bet? Create a few party mixes ahead of time that everyone's bound to love.

BRILLIANT IDEA: Create a house drink! Establish your very own couple cocktail that your guests can (excitedly) expect every

For music to motivate any party, go to TheNest.com/partymusic.

click

# Stocking Your Bar for a Party of 10

A well-stocked bar is a valuable tool for entertaining guests, decorating the house, or dealing with visiting in-laws. Here's everything you need.

**LIQUOR:** You can't go wrong with 1-liter or 750-ml bottles of moderately priced brands (no more than about $20, sometimes much cheaper) that have name recognition—Jose Cuervo, Jack Daniel's, Absolut, etc. For a party of 10, have on hand:

[ ] Gin (1 liter)

[ ] Vodka (1 liter)

[ ] Rum (1 liter)

[ ] Bourbon (750 ml)

[ ] Tequila (750 ml)

[ ] Sweet vermouth (750 ml)

[ ] Dry vermouth (750 ml)

[ ] Cointreau (750 ml)

[ ] Single-malt Scotch (e.g., The Glenlivet 12-Year-Old)

[ ] Irish whiskey (e.g., Black Bush)

**WINE:** Sample several different kinds under $20—not all in one night—then pick your two favorites and serve them as your house wines. Keep five bottles on hand.

[ ] White wine (2 bottles)

[ ] Red wine (2 bottles)

**MIXERS:** Buy in smaller packaging that can be stored if it isn't consumed.

[ ] Cranberry (64 oz)

[ ] Orange (64 oz)

[ ] Tomato (1 liter)

[ ] Cola and diet cola (4 liters)

[ ] Lemon-lime seltzer (1 liter)

[ ] Ginger ale (2 liters)

[ ] Tonic (2 liters)

[ ] Seltzer (2 liters)

**GARNISHES:**

[ ] Maraschino cherries (1 jar)

[ ] Green pitted olives (1 pound)

[ ] Lemons (6)

[ ] Limes (6)

**EXTRAS:**

[ ] Ice (1 pound per person)

[ ] Cocktail napkins (4 per person)

## tip

On average, expect your guests to have two drinks per hour and plan on one pound of hors d'ouevres per person.

time they come to your house. It not only gives your soirees a signature, but you'll save a bundle stocking a huge bar. Think mojitos, mango martinis, or a Champagne punch—and make gallons of it in advance to serve with beer, wine, and nonalcoholic drinks.

### Everyone's in Party

BEST FOR: Inviting as many people as your place can hold!

TIME: Any time.

WHAT YOU NEED TO DO: An easy, inexpensive way to entertain a ton of people all at once, a beer bash is perfect for a summer Friday or when there's a big game to be watched. Just load up the fridge with brews or buy a keg. You can keep the food light and casual (think pretzels, potato chips, veggies and dip) or serve up appetizer-sized versions of unpretentious classics, like mini grilled cheese sandwiches and pigs in blankets with mustard and ketchup for dipping.

WHAT TO WATCH FOR: Guests who won't leave. The beauty of a bar? There's a closing time. If your friends are having such a great time (and, of course they are—you're the hosts, after all) and don't seem to be making moves to leave, drop subtle hints. Start collecting empty glasses and bottles, load the dishwasher, and even yawn once or twice. If all else fails, pile their coats on the couch and tell them that you're pooped but they should feel free to stay as long as they want. (Guess what, they won't.)

BRILLIANT IDEA: If all that beer makes your guests crave greasy food, order up pizzas toward the end of the party.

For more great party ideas, tricks, and lists, go to TheNest.com/living.

click

### Weekend Brunch

BEST FOR: 4 to 10 guests

TIME: 11:30 A.M. to 2 P.M.

WHAT YOU NEED TO DO: It's an easy, low-pressure option when you feel the need to entertain but are too lazy to deal with a dinner party. Wake up a little on the early side and pick up all the brunch basics: orange juice, bagels with a selection of cream cheeses, and coffee cake or muffins. Either make eggs to order for your guests (one of you can play short-order cook while the other chats everyone up over coffee) or, for an easier option, make a quiche or two in advance, so your guests can get a protein fix without any last-minute cooking. Serve coffee and Bloody Marys or mimosas if you're in the mood.

# Party Crises Solved

**CRISIS: You run out of an essential.**

SOLUTION: Make light of it. You could always send a friend out, but if it's late in the night acknowledge and joke about the situation ("Better get more tonic next time. How about club soda?"). To keep this from happening in the first place, err on the side of buying too much—more napkins, ice, liquor, and lemons than you think you'll need. And when you postmort the party together afterward (the other great thing about being a hosting couple!), take note of how much liquor was consumed and how many supplies you went through, and record it on your computer. That way you can consult it the next time you're planning a party and aren't quite sure how much to buy.

**CRISIS: Uncomfortable silence.**

SOLUTION: As host, it's always a good idea to have a few talking topics in the back of your mind in case the party conversation stalls—a new restaurant in town that you just tried, some interesting (and controversial) article from the paper, or even a work dilemma that you need advice on. Go so far as directly asking someone what they would do in your shoes.

**CRISIS: You ruin the entrée.**

SOLUTION: Accidents happen . . . especially in the kitchen. Don't hesitate to find your favorite takeout menu and order in ASAP. Have a sense of humor about it and your guests will, too. There's no need to apologize incessantly, or to hide the fact. Your ability to be honest and unselfconscious about it will make your guests feel less stressed about entertaining at their houses.

**CRISIS: A guest has spilled red wine on your carpet.**

SOLUTION: Don't freak out—that will only make your guest feel even worse. First, assure him or her that accidents happen (you might even want to crack a little joke, like "That's it! The bar is closed for you!"). Then use this technique (which utilizes items you probably already have around the house) to get the stain out: First, blot the area lightly with a clean white or light-colored towel to absorb any excess vino. Once most of the liquid is cleaned up, dab at the stain from the outside in with a solution of one part white vinegar and two parts water (seltzer will work if you don't have vinegar). Keep dabbing until the stain's pretty much gone. Next, to neutralize the acid in the vinegar, use a solution that's one part ammonia and two parts water on the stain and finish it off by splashing some clean water on the area. If your carpet is a light color, you might want to go the extra mile by hitting the area with household-strength peroxide and then rinsing with more water.

**WHAT TO WATCH FOR:** Famished guests. Since brunch is somewhere between breakfast and lunch, early risers may be very hungry by the time they get to your house. Anticipate this with brunch hors d'oeuvres. Why not? Create pigs in a blanket with breakfast sausage; make mini quiches and mini muffins; and assemble a tray of cheese and baguettes (any time is the right time for cheese).

**BRILLIANT IDEA:** To make this basic brunch menu special-occasion worthy, serve smoked salmon with the bagels, add Champagne to the orange juice, and a dollop of caviar to the eggs.

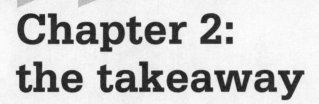

# Chapter 2: the takeaway

**Prepare yourself for living together.** Instead of battling each other's habits, find a way to compromise on the quirks. Read our foolproof plan on page 49.

**Pick two spots to focus on.** Trying to redo your entire house to fit the latest décor scheme you've hatched is a recipe for frustration, burnout, or at least massive credit card debt. Instead, start small by identifying two areas for focus: the one room that you spend the most time in and the one room that drives you the most crazy with its haphazard look. Follow our room-by-room advice on page 72.

**Host a real party.** Once you've worked with your permanent roommate to create a place you both love coming home to, show it off! Whether you have an intimate dinner or an invite-all-your-friends cocktail party, entertaining is a wonderful opportunity to make your newly decorated house a home. Hosting essentials start on page 82.

# [ friends and fun ]

**You promised to love and honor—
the vows** didn't say anything about becoming total bores. Being a couple doesn't mean cocooning with Moo Shoo for the rest of your lives. Corny as it sounds, you also need to get out there and keep your lives connected. The perfect couples' social life takes a balance of time together and time with friends (both sets). Pull out your calendars now.

## the nest test:
# squaring away
## your social circle

Mull over these questions alone, and then together with your partner, to help get on the same page in the fun with friends department.

1. **What social obligation would you love to permanently get out of?**

2. **Who are the five friends you most hope to still have in ten years?**

3. **Are you okay with me having friends of the opposite sex?**

4. **What's your idea of a great date?**

5. **How often do you want a girls'/guys' night?**

6. Do you think we hang out enough with your friends?

7. **Do we spend too much time together?**

# your social calendar

FRIDAY

Jeff out w/ the guys

meet Michelle dinner at 8

SATURDAY

8pm @ Bistro: Jane + Sam Rosie + Rob Kathleen + Casey

You may be thinking, "What's the big deal? We've been going out for a while and we already spend every moment together." And even if you don't think anything needs to change on the social front, the fact is that people perceive you differently when you're married or living together. Other couples may be more eager to invite you places now that you're officially a duo, and some of your single friends might be uncertain where they stand in your new universe.

You'll suddenly feel obligated to get to know your spouse's work colleagues and any of each other's friends you haven't bonded with yet. You may also find that some of the Saturday-night activities that seemed so exciting even a few months earlier may start to lose their appeal. Here's how to master the fine art of social planning.

## STICKING TO A SCHEDULE . . . FOR FUN

When you're first falling in love, your relationship is all about good times—you plan cool, unique dates; hit the road for romantic getaways; and generally blow off responsibility whenever you can in order to spend more time savoring each other's company.

Then, when you're certain the other person is there for the long haul, having fun tends to fall much lower on your list—well below things like advancing your careers, establishing your home together, starting a family, or whatever your personal couple priorities are. That's not a bad thing, because one of the reasons we seek out our soul mate in the first place is to have a partner for tackling life's serious projects. It's essential, however, that you continue to make fun and playfulness a key part of your relationship, even when—*especially* when—you feel like there's no time for it.

If you cease to be each other's partners in crime, you'll soon just be each other's partners in the practical details of life (the mortgage, the household chores, the family responsibilities), and that can suck the electricity right out of your relationship. Even when you're busy with these other priorities, you can't have a hands-off approach to recreation, assuming it will take care of itself; you have to plan the social stuff—as a couple.

The big reason to establish a strategy for your new social life is that it's important for you two to be on the same page about it. Agreeing, or at least compromising, on how often you want to go out, who you want to go out with, and how you're going to make your joint plans is essential for avoiding conflicts—say, when the weekend rolls around and one of you has lined up back-to-back parties while the other is hoping to stay in and catch up on the week's TV shows.

**Mr. & Mrs. Manners**

# Double-Booking Dilemma

Q. What if we each have good friends getting married on the same weekend?

A. This one is tricky—neither of you wants to miss your good friend's vows, but if you split up and go to separate weddings, they won't be nearly as fun as they would be if you were there as a pair. Bite the bullet and choose one event, and send a really extravagant gift and apologies to the other. Since this is a scenario that's likely to repeat, make a mental note of who made the friendship sacrifice and make up for it with the next conflicting engagement.

First, discuss your free-time expectations—use the questions at the start of the chapter to get the conversation flowing. It's easy for one person to feel hurt or offended if the other makes independent plans on a night they thought you'd be spending together. The secret to sublime couple time? Plot your play schedule (loosely, of course) with a little help from our suggestions on how best to spend your free hours.

## Scheduling Time for Two

Though you made plenty of plans together when you were dating and engaged, you now need your individual calendars to be more tightly coordinated. If you each schedule outings without checking with the other, you'll throw your calendar into chaos, but if you wait to talk over every little potential detail, you might find your social lives fizzling from indecision.

Use this system to avoid confusion: When one of you receives an invitation or talks to a friend about plans for a particular night, tell your friend the plan is tentative until you check with your spouse. Quickly shoot your partner an e-mail or text message to make sure that you guys are free and up for the plan in question. To keep these e-mails from getting lost in your in-boxes, flag them as "high priority" or put something unsubtle in the subject line like READ THIS NOW. Once the plan is confirmed, you both put it in your individual calendars so you won't double book.

If one of you is more of a planner but the other hates to feel like the weekend is all booked up before it's even begun, agree to block out some "no plans" time on your weekend calendars, then wait and see what you feel like doing when those hours roll around. You can spend them just unwinding together, or make last-minute plans with whichever friends are around and able to be spontaneous with you.

### Our Free-Time Formula

What does a killer social life for couples consist of? Here are our guidelines for balancing the one-on-one time with more social gatherings:

**Weekly**

- One just-the-two-of-you date
- One double date or night out with a few mutual friends or relatives
- Alone time where you each do something you love, such as having a session with a celeb gossip rag or fantasy football for an hour after watching your favorite TV show together

**Twice a month**

- A party or night out with a big group of friends
- Dinner or drinks with just the girls/guys

**Monthly**

- Gathering at your place—whether it's just dinner for one other couple or a wild cocktail party

**Every three months**

- A weekend getaway

**Yearly**

- Proper vacation (that means at least a week long), ideally to someplace neither of you has visited before
- Blowout bash at your place, whether for a birthday, the holidays, or no reason at all

**Time Out**

# Hot Nights at Home

Sick of drumming up the small talk when you're out with your mate's mates? Take a break from socializing and have a date night at home. Have a picnic on the floor, dance to a sexy song (think salsa), or read to one another . . . in bed.

They say that when you marry an individual, you're really marrying an entire family; these days, it seems that you're *also* marrying into a whole new group of friends. The average age of individuals marrying for the first time is higher than ever, and most people who stay single into their postgraduation years acquire a bunch of buddies almost as tightly knit as a group of blood relatives. So now that you've acquired this new clan, what to do with them? And how do you ensure that your spouse learns to adore your friends as much as you do? Follow these rules for getting to know and (hopefully) love each other's amigos.

**Make time to connect with them.** At your wedding, it's likely that there were friends on your partner's side of the aisle who you still don't know all that well ("Where is he from again?" "What does she do?"), or vice versa, so make sure to get some quality time on the calendar with them within three months of your honeymoon. (If they live far away, six months is more reasonable.) If these are people you two hope to have in your lives for the long haul, it's important that you all get to know one another, because if you don't make the effort now, your first anniversary will roll around to find you realizing you haven't seen the friend in question since the wedding.

**65%** of couples say they wish their mate would take the initiative more when it comes to making plans.

**Try to merge groups.** Unless you're unusually lucky, your respective friends aren't going to morph effortlessly into one big happy clique, but that doesn't mean you shouldn't try to help things along! Forging some bonds between the two groups will make your social life as a couple infinitely easier to manage, because you'll no longer need to divvy up your weekend nights between the separate sets of friends. Get the two groups together as much as possible—by hosting dinner parties chez you, or simply by organizing everyone to head out to a concert together—and see what happens. It's inevitable that at least a few of your favorite people will hit it off with your spouse's—your freshman roommate and his or her former colleague could discover they both have a passion for collecting vintage vinyl LPs, and your ex-turned-friend could hook up with your spouse's co-worker (and ask you two to be in the wedding!).

# Topic: your friends

"

**MY DH HAS A TON OF FRIENDS FROM HIGH SCHOOL**—the wives, girlfriends, fiancées are very cliquey and even though I've been with DH for almost two years, I am still 'the new one.' There are times when everyone is together and I'm just sitting there alone. One won't even return my phone calls.

—Mrs. Chach

My husband's friends don't seem to get the fact that he's married now and **isn't available to go out to bars** whenever they call.

—Jax0812

**Most of DH's friends are bachelors.** Up until recently, we've really just hung out with the guys. But for the past two Saturdays, we've hung out with my girlfriends and their husbands . . . and we've had the best time! I'm seeing how much fun it is to hang out with married people instead of being the only girl among a crowd of men.

—mrswilliamsin05

**We're the only ones in our group with a house,** so whenever anyone needs a place to stay they assume they'll just stay at our place. One friend just postponed an overseas move and wants to stay with us for the extra week. Have people never heard of hotels?

—Jenimac

DH's two female friends came over, and **one of them spilled her margarita on my new furniture.** Every time these girls come over they spill or break something—and my husband defends them.

—spiffyone

## nest note:

Sure, his or her pals have probably been around longer than you, but that's no excuse for being disrespectful. The moment you said "I do" you became the most important person in your spouse's life—and if any of the amigos has a problem with that, it's your mate's job to set them straight.

**Accept that you won't agree about everyone.** Your counterpart is guaranteed to have at least one friend you simply don't click with, and he or she will be equally unenthusiastic about somebody in *your* circle. In other cases, you'll like your partner's friend just fine, but find that friend's partner totally repugnant. Here's how to mediate this situation: You should accept that you're obligated to spend at least some time with the friends in question (and remind yourself that at least they have great taste if they like your spouse so much!), and your spouse should try to minimize the one-on-one time you have to clock with the people you don't like. Arrange to see these people in group outings, where you can limit your direct contact and be buffered by other people you do like.

## tip

If you don't feel the need to meet new people because you can barely find time to keep up with the friends you already have, take a class or form your own club with a group of friends. It ensures that you all get to see one another regularly without the hassle of making plans and coordinating schedules. And if your spouse tends to pout when you go out solo, he or she will probably be much more accepting of it if you're heading to a class or a "poker night" rather than just out to a bar to throw back drinks with your pals.

## MARRYING FAMILY

Of course, if one or both of you have large families who live nearby, a lot of your social time might be spent with them. If you have siblings who are close to you in age, or just progressive parents who *seem* your age, they can double as some of the best friends of all. But it's important that you and your mate understand how the other feels about logging lots of social time with the relatives. Even if your spouse gets along famously with your family, he or she probably won't be able to forget the in-law factor and totally let loose around them the way he or she can with regular friends (or vice versa). Talk it over and discuss how you're going to draw boundaries. Some guidelines:

**Family events take priority** (unless your family has "events" five days a week). As a general rule, when family gatherings conflict with those of your friends, the family event wins—one of you shares blood with these people, after all. But if one of you has a huge family or just a supertight one that expects you to hang with them 24/7, there need to be some exceptions or else you'll never have time to see nonfamily friends.

**You don't have to include your family in every invitation.** Of course you're going to want your kin at any big parties you throw, but you don't need to extend an invite to them every time you have other couples over for dinner or an intimate drinks gathering. If you're having another couple over for dinner and think your brother and sister-in-law will feel excluded, try to avoid telling them that you're hosting, and if they find out, deflect attention from it with an invite to come over in the future ("The beef satay we made for Eric and Karen was delicious, I can't wait to make it for you guys").

Keep far-flung family up on all your news with a website: TheNest.com/webpages.

**Create a balance.** Feeling smothered by your significant other's kin? Gingerly explain to him or her that you need some time for other friendships—not because you don't love the in-laws to death (yes, it's okay to exaggerate a little) but because there are only so many hours in a week and you need to devote some of them to the rest of your social circle. You can always point out, "The wonderful thing about family is that I know they'll always be there for us no matter what, but if I keep blowing off my friends because of family commitments, I'm scared I'll lose those friendships."

## SURVIVING OFFICE PARTIES & OTHER OBLIGATIONS

One of the duties of marriage that your officiant never mentioned is the obligation to accompany your spouse to boring social events. There are many occasions where people simply expect you to show up as a twosome, so even if you'd rather lose a toenail than attend your other half's office party or family reunion, it's your job to go and try to have a good attitude about it. Here are some of the most common social obligations you'll be faced with, and how to make them more bearable.

**The office party:** There's no question that you need to put in a command appearance at any of your partner's work affairs if they are for families or spouses—after all, this is the organization that helps you pay the bills every month. Befriend the other spouses (especially those of higher-ups) and try to charm the assistants and interns (you never know when you'll need a favor). If it's an especially stuffy or tedious gathering, make a secret game out of it with your mate by taking a sip of your drink every time you hear somebody utter an industry-speak phrase like "deal structure" or "drill down." Just make sure that no more than one of those drinks is alcoholic—getting tipsy and risking the slightest embarrassment or inappropriate behavior simply isn't worth it.

**The extended-family gathering:** By now you've hopefully learned to love, or have at least negotiated an unspoken peace accord with, your sweetheart's immediate family—but some of those uncles and cousins and great-aunts might be harder to stomach. They're a little too distantly related to feel like kin, and if you have less in common with them than you would with, oh, the average stranger on a city bus, it can be awkward. Plus, they may talk about people and things that make you feel excluded. To make large family affairs less painful, find ways to look like a team player that don't require you to chat up Aunt Iris for an hour. Throw yourself into helping out in the kitchen (a little work always makes time pass quickly), or play ball or a board game with the young cousins.

**Couple clubs:** Maybe one of you plays in a baseball league that has regular family BBQs, and the other is in a book club with people who think regular "include the spouse" nights are a great idea—either way, you'll have to do some fraternizing with the people your sweetie spends extracurricular time with. Think positively. Hard though it may be, look at these obligatory outings as opportunities to absorb new information and broaden your network of acquaintances. There's likely to be someone at the event who shares some of your interests or can hook up a great work connection, or tell you about the best bargain Italian restaurant in town. Who knows, you might even find yourself having fun!

# get busy

We know you love your newlywed nest. But just because you've been homebodies for the last few months (or even years) doesn't mean you have to stay homebodies. Whether it's once a week, every two weeks, or even once a month, if you've really drifted apart and have tough schedules, you need to get out of the house, together.

## DO DATE NIGHTS

Yes, it might feel strange at first to schedule a "date" with someone with whom you've become locked in a couples' routine, but just about any busy twosome will tell you that regularly scheduled outings are essential to keep their union strong. For one thing, it reminds you of your early dating days, taking you back to that time when

# New Date Night Ideas

There's nothing wrong with the classic dinner/movie combo, but when you want to mix it up, try one of these unique outings.

- Go on a mini bar crawl. Hit three different watering holes and sample a different drink and appetizer at each.

- On warm spring and summer nights, go on a hike or a bike ride and bring along a picnic.

- Be spontaneous. Pick a day, and then don't solidify plans until you have the current weekend arts calendar, weekly happenings magazine, or daily paper's events listing in your hand.

- Take a one-night class on something new and fun like Malaysian cooking or the wines of South Australia.

- Broaden your cultural horizons. See a foreign film, hit an art gallery with evening hours, or sip your drinks at a jazz bar.

- Make like teenagers and go parking. Stock the car with snacks and sodas and drive to a lookout spot with a killer view. It's simple, dirt cheap, and sexy.

- Play pool. Most cities have some form of billiard hall. No clue about pool cues? Try bowling. Head to the driving range. Play some one-on-one at the local playground.

- Be charitable. Spend an afternoon volunteering together—visiting an elderly person, preparing dinner at a shelter, delivering food to the housebound. It's a less traditional—but far more enriching—form of fun.

you were so dazzled by each other that you could barely manage to eat the food in front of you. Plus, sitting down to a proper dinner or drinks in a public place forces you to have longer and more in-depth conversations than you typically do at home—where it's so easy to be distracted by the television or the Internet or the many household tasks.

The most fun date-night strategy is to take turns being cruise director—one week you make all the arrangements, reservations, or ticket purchases, and the next week your significant other does. When it's your turn, you'll enjoy the challenge of planning something that your partner will enjoy, and when it's his or her turn, you'll get to savor the indulgence of having somebody else arrange a fun evening without your having to lift a finger.

Scared you'll be forced to sit through a horror movie marathon or a quilting bee? Set up a two-veto system—each choose two events that you *refuse* to go to no matter how much your darling thinks it sounds like fun. Beyond that, let your tastes and convenience be your guide and pick one thing to attend. If you can't decide (or nothing is really jumping out at you), cut your list into tiny strips and draw one, or choose the date based on distance from home, alphabetical order, or some other random way you invent. This is great for partners who don't know their schedules until the last minute or who are terrible at sticking to plans. Even if you wind up not really loving the outing, you'll wind up with a hilarious shared memory of something that *nobody* else did.

Suffering from a dearth of date ideas? Go to Nest.com/dates. click

## DOUBLE DATING

Shortly after you become a committed couple, you'll need to begin the search for other couples you both enjoy spending time with, equally, and who feel the same about you. The goal is to have dinners where the girls can get totally engrossed in one conversation while the guys get caught up in another, but you can all have a great time chatting as a foursome, too. Have a few sets of great couple friends. Once you get in a pattern of seeing them regularly, they provide a no-fuss social outlet, and they can be your go-to partners for those activities—think concerts, wine tastings, and outdoor adventures—that are often more fun when it's not just the two of you.

Unfortunately, such couples can be frustratingly hard to find. Often your spouse just won't click with your best friends' partners, and vice versa. Or you might find one of your friend's mates totally unbearable yourself. The point is you need to put a little energy into finding and cultivating friendships with great double-date partners. Here are a few pointers on finding and nurturing quality friendships with other couples.

**Turn friendly acquaintances into friends.** Think about it, you probably know a few seemingly cool couples—whether they're friends of friends, work associates, or whatever—with whom you just haven't crossed the friendship threshold. Go ahead and put yourself out there by e-mailing to see if they'd like to have dinner sometime. Your first official night out together should be something low-key or interactive so that it's low-pressure and there's something to do and talk about—think bowling, a Japanese dinner like shabu shabu or hibachi, a haunted historical site tour, or any other activity that automatically provides natural conversation fodder.

**Make sure the communication isn't dominated by one gender or the other.** When you first start hanging with another couple, it will be either the girls or the guys who take hold of the planning, depending on who knew each other first. But after you've started seeing this couple somewhat regularly, the other gender should try to stay in touch, too. Let's say the women are old college friends who recently reconnected and

## Wanted: Couple Friends

Finding new friends—who are also couples—to hang out with is not as easy as it might seem. You actually need to put some effort in and view it like dating. Try looking for them in these places:

- **Work.** Maybe there's someone in accounting who is always mentioning how you and his wife have a lot in common. Why not suggest brunch or an after-work drink with the four of you?

- **Couple-friendly vacation spots.** Not necessarily a too-hot-for-teacher Caribbean resort, but maybe an organized wine trip in Napa or a bike tour in Holland.

- **School.** Take a cooking class or wine-tasting class offered specifically for couples. If none are available, sign up for one on Valentine's Day.

- **Yoga studios.** Many places offer classes for couples, and chuckling over downward dog will always break the ice.

the four of you have had fun dinners a few times. Ideally, the men should start to form their own friendship by shooting each other e-mails once in a while, or even going out for beers occasionally without the wives. If there are solid bonds on both the male and female sides of the equation, your friendship as a foursome will be more satisfying.

**Turn foursomes into six-somes.** Once you've found one compatible couple, see if they have any other couple friends you can add to your new crew, since the easiest way to make new friends is through other friends. Remember those parties when you were single and had to bring a single friend? Change up the rules, and make it so couples each have to bring a couple that no one else knows. What a fun, easy way to extend your newlywed network! The perfect setting: a casual get-together like a barbecue or game-watching party, or even a buffet-style dinner party.

---

## Mr. & Mrs. Manners

# Restaurant Checks and Balances

**Q. How do we handle paying when out with a group?**

**A.** By far the simplest way to handle a restaurant check when you've dined with a big group is to divide it evenly among the number of diners and have the waiter divvy it up between your credit cards. If you're out with other couples, one member of each couple can throw down plastic, though if it's a mix of singles and couples, it's more complicated for the waiter, since he'll have to put twice as much on some cards as on others. If there's an extra single woman in your party—say if it's you two and another couple, plus a single girlfriend—it's a chivalrous move for the men to split the check evenly and not ask the single woman to pay. Try to resist the urge to tally your individual share (I don't drink and only had a salad!); think of it instead as the price of admission to this dinner event and everyone pays the same, just like a movie or concert.

It's a fun topic, but one that you and your significant other may not have talked about too seriously: your travel dreams and goals. You need to have an honest chat about it early in your relationship, because people have very different tastes when it comes to travel. Some feel they won't die fulfilled unless they've visited every corner of the earth; others don't see much reason to leave the comforts of their home states. Some think *vacation* simply means heading to a place where you can order alcoholic beverages without leaving the swimming pool; others like to pack multiple cities and cultural sights into a week.

Here are four basic vacation categories. Think it over and talk to your spouse about how often you'd ideally like to experience each (e.g., twice a year, yearly, every two years, every five years, never).

Adventure travel, during which you check out a beautiful corner of the earth and do some invigorating outdoor exercise in the process.

Cultural travel, in which you visit a foreign land (or an intriguing American city) and soak up the site's history and atmosphere by visiting museums and cultural institutions, dining heartily on local cuisine, and shopping.

Pure relaxation travel, which usually involves a beach, secluded cabin, or golf course and requires you to do nothing but lie around with a good book and a fruity drink, get spa treatments, and maybe participate in some low-key water sports.

Family-oriented travel, which isn't so much about the destination as it is about spending quality time with your kin.

If you find you're not entirely on the same page when it comes to your vacation days, work out a compromise. Maybe one year you journey to a far-flung locale to fulfill your wanderlust, the next you rent a house at a local lake or visit a nearby country inn to make your homebody partner happy. You could also settle on a vacation spot that offers something for both of your personalities—a spot where you could spend three days lounging on the beach and three days sightseeing and doing other activities, for example.

One thing is certain: If you don't plan trips in advance, there's a good chance they'll never happen. Although many newlyweds think they don't have enough money or time for a vacation, it's essential that you treat yourselves to occasional getaways. Realistically, demands on your time and bank accounts will probably only increase in the next few years (especially if you have children), and if you wait for the perfect time to travel, you may wind up putting it off until your Centrum Silver years. One way to ensure you can afford vacations: Set aside a small amount of every paycheck for your travel fund. If you each save just $50 per two-week pay period, you'll have more than $2,000 to spend on an end-of-the-year trip in about ten months.

When it comes time to spend your well-saved money on a trip, assign a point person (you can swap the responsibility every trip) to do the research, create a general itinerary, and make final travel arrangements. With one person in charge, not only will the planning get done, it will be easier to stick to a budget (it's often cheaper to book plane fares and hotels together). And don't forget to view visiting friends as a mini vacation. Sure, you aren't dying to go to Detroit, but a fun weekend away with friends is a great, inexpensive way to add to your travelogue.

# socializing solo

Now that you've got couple-time covered, it's essential to maintain your individuality. At the very least it will give you something new to talk to your mate about.

## STAYING TIGHT WITH SINGLETONS

The more committed your romantic relationship, the more challenging it can be to maintain close connections with your single friends. They might invite you out less on the assumption that you're too busy to do swinging-single stuff. They might get sensitive if you don't call and constantly invite them out, because they're paranoid that you'll lose interest in them now that you've entered the coupled-up world. Here are a few rules for keeping these bonds strong:

**Don't do too much "we" talk around them.** To keep your single friends from thinking you walk on a whole different planet now that you're hitched, don't dominate the conversation with topics like your baby plans, your house shopping, or your in-law drama. Obviously you need to be honest about what's going on in your life, and you can't dish about dating and hooking up since you're no longer doing those things, but focusing too heavily on the couple-y side of your existence can alienate others in a less blissful romantic situation. Be sensitive. Talk about work and family and hobbies and all the other things you

# Split Personality Paradises

### Tripping for Two

There's nothing wrong with the classic eight-day, seven-night beach vacation, but why not try something a little more memorable? Trust us, you'll have bragging rights for ages. A good rule of thumb: Make every third vacation one of these.

**LONDON, ROME, PARIS:** Think of this as the Grand Tour à Deux. The trifecta of classic European cities is a great place to visit with your mate–as opposed to your college roommate–when you can actually afford to stay in a nice hotel and eat at fine dining establishments.

**CHINA AND JAPAN:** Hitting every continent is key, so don't miss out on Asia. While you could of course add more spots, like Thailand and Vietnam, the Japanese and Chinese cultures give you a great taste of what this part of the world has to offer. Start saving your frequent-flyer points now.

**SOUTH AFRICA:** Lions, tigers, and elephants? Check. Fine wine? Check. Indigenous African culture? Check. Need we say more? From luxury safaris to in-depth tours of the burgeoning wine country and Johannesburg's melting pot, the tip of this exotic continent is a must-visit.

**BELIZE:** Two words: rain forest. Don't you want to tell your grandkids you zip-toured the jungle back in the day? In addition to the ecological experience, you will enjoy some dramatic diving and snorkeling on one of the world's most dramatic reefs.

**SCANDINAVIA:** Meander through fjords and marvel at the colorful glow of aurora borealis, aka the northern lights, in the northern countries of Norway and Sweden, if for no other reason than to take the best pictures of your life. There's also the fact that the sun barely sets in summer.

**RIO DE JANEIRO:** There are few spots better for the kidless couple than Rio—where the nightlife goes on into daylight, the food is amazing, and the beaches are beautiful (especially the remote ones off the coast you can day-trip to). Think of it as your last hurrah.

## Don't Miss Birthdays

Keeping in touch with faraway friends can be tough for anyone, not just the married kind. The simplest way to show them that you care (and remember): Send a birthday card. Head to our birthday calendar on page 277 in the resource section and fill out *all* the birthdays of anyone and everyone important to you. You'll never be belated again. And another easy way to stay in touch with far-flung friends? Send holiday e-cards.

focused on before you met your mate.

**Take a lighthearted approach to setups.** Setting up your single friends, whether with friends of your mate's, eligible people from your office, or whomever, is one of the most generous things you can do. Sure, it's risky—they could hate each other, or, worse, one might be smitten and the other disgusted, or, *worst of all,* they could tumble into bed and then never talk to each other again, creating an awkwardness that will still be rearing its head years later at your annual holiday party.

Nonetheless, there's always that slim chance they'll actually fall for each other, and the rewards of that—you'll gain both tons of good karma and another cool couple to double date with—make it all worth the risk. Two tips: Don't do it unless both parties are game and don't overanalyze setups. If you know two willing, eligible, and nice people, take a chance. They're adults and can handle whatever happens, and you can feel virtuous no matter what for making the effort.

**Set boundaries without guilt.** If your single buds frequently invite you out without including your spouse, don't feel guilty about saying no some of the time. If Thursday night is your regular date night, or you and your partner have declared Saturday night off-limits for girls'/guys' nights out, don't be shy about telling your single friends exactly that. They'll probably understand, and if they don't, just remind yourself that they eventually will down the road when they're in serious relationships of their own.

### FRIENDS OF THE OPPOSITE SEX

It's not a secret that guys and girls often build close friendships with one another. It's our differences as much as our similarities that make us want to spend time with someone. Chances are that by the time you got married, your spouse had a chance to meet your important opposite-sex pals and it's not even an issue. There may be periods in

# He Said/She Said

*If he doesn't seem too thrilled about a double date, don't worry—it's not you. He'd rather talk guy than girl (and women do tend to dominate couple conversations). Here's what you both need to know.*

**HOW MEN SEE THEIR FRIENDS:** When guys converge, the conversation is usually light (sports, movies), the television is on (again, sports or movies), and the beverages are alcoholic. When guys hang out with their friends, they're looking to put their professional and personal lives in the very back of their minds. No, their communication *isn't* limited to grunts. Hanging out with his pals is just a guy's time to forget about his problems and talk about the things that mattered when life was less complicated—like whether a shark could beat a bear in a fight.

**HOW WOMEN SEE THEIR FRIENDS:** When a woman meets up with her friends, laughs are sure to be shared, and a drink or two might be tipped back. But where men look to escape life's stresses, women *talk* about their problems with one another. A guy might gripe about a bothersome boss, but women probably know most of their friends' coworkers by name (even the ones they've never met). A woman's time with her friends is a chance to let it all out, knowing full well that her girls will offer a receptive ear and helpful advice.

**HOW TO MEET IN THE MIDDLE:** One way to close the gender gap when men and women are together is to have a few topics in mind that everyone will be interested in. If you're all Packers fans—great! Talk about what they need to do to win the division. But if the men and women are segregated, subtly start chatting up a couple men and women about things like current movies, books, or travel. The groups will merge for a bit, and lots of mingling and varied conversations always make for a good time.

# Quiz
## are you a smug married?

Is your wedded bliss driving your unattached friends to distraction? Answer these questions and find out.

1. **When your single friends tell you about their dating life, you think:**

   **a.** Good for them—it's fun meeting new people.

   **b.** I really hope they all get married soon—it must be so lonely being single.

   **c.** Thank God I never have to go on another date again!

2. **While wishing your single girlfriend a happy thirtieth birthday, you slip in:**

   **a.** You look better than ever!

   **b.** You look better than ever—you're sure to meet someone soon.

   **c.** You'd better hurry up and get married if you want to have kids.

3. **You have plans with a few married couples, and a single friend wants to join the fun. Your initial response is:**

   **a.** The more the merrier!

   **b.** I would never hang out with couples solo, but if it doesn't bother him/her, then it's fine with me.

   **c.** *Now* what are we going to talk about? It's so much easier going out only with couples.

4. You meet your friend's new boyfriend, and when you and your pal have a moment alone, you tell her:

   **a.** You guys are great together!

   **b.** Where do you think this relationship is headed?

   **c.** You'd better not mess this one up—single men are hard to find!

5. During a night out on the town, a single pal gets a little tipsy. You think:

   **a.** Hey, we've all been there.

   **b.** She's never going to meet a guy behaving like that.

   **c.** Poor thing—she's probably depressed over being single.

6. You set up a friend with your spouse's coworker, but at the end of the date it's clear that there's no spark between them. You turn to your sweetie and say:

   **a.** Oh, well, I guess I'm not meant to be a matchmaker.

   **b.** Are there any other singles in your office? I really want her to meet someone.

   **c.** No spark! Doesn't she know beggars can't be choosers?

(continued on next page)

7. **When it comes to seating at dinner parties, you like to:**

   **a.** Mix it up. I like to seat different people together so they can mingle.

   **b.** Seat single people together—maybe somebody will make a love connection.

   **c.** Seat single people at one end of the table and couples on the other end. It's just too hard numbers-wise to do it another way without splitting up some of the couples.

8. **A friend is feeling a little down, so to cheer her up you offer to:**

   **a.** Treat her to a mani/pedi—you know that always makes you feel better.

   **b.** Take her to happy hour. You'll buy her a few drinks and scope out single guys for her.

   **c.** Pay for her first month on a singles website. She wouldn't be so depressed if she had a husband!

9. **You haven't caught up with a single girlfriend in a while, so you decide to send her an e-mail. As you update her, you:**

   **a.** Fill her in on the stuff she can relate to, gloss over the more couple-y topics, and ask about getting together soon.

   **b.** Notice all the sentences start with "we," so you go back and throw in some "I"s and a few things that have nothing at all to do with your DH.

   **c.** Always include how much fun going to concerts/traveling/cleaning your ears is now that you're part of a couple.

## 10. A single friend asks you to grab dinner at your fave Mexican restaurant on Wednesday night. You say:

**a.** Sounds good. Let me double-check with DH and I'll let you know for sure. (Then you double-check quickly and, unless you've forgotten about plans you've made, you go for an evening of guac and girl talk.)

**b.** Yes, but I can't stay long because DH and I like to watch *Lost* together.

**c.** Sure! What time should we be there? (Everyone knows you and your DH spend all of your spare time together, so the invite was obviously for both of you.)

- - - - - - - - - - - - - - - - - - - - - - - - - - -

# results

## mostly **a**s

**You're not a Smug Married!**

While you're happily hitched, you don't think everyone else needs to be in order to feel content. You treat all your friends with respect no matter what their marital status may be, and while you'd love for your single pals to find true love, you're not putting any pressure on them. They'll get married when the time is right.

## mostly **b**s

**You're a borderline Smug Married.**

You see your comments simply as helpful advice. But unless a single pal specifically asks for it, it's best to keep your thoughts and feelings on the subject to yourself. If you have trouble holding your tongue, remember that once upon a time you were single, too. Did you enjoy having family and friends constantly prodding into your love life? Didn't think so . . .

## mostly **C**s

**You're a full-blown Smug Married!**

For you, there's nothing better than being married—and nothing worse than being single. Although your unattached pals say that they're perfectly happy, you just don't believe them, and you can't help but feel sorry for them. Keep in mind that different lifestyles make the world go round, and some people are (gasp!) happier single than married. Besides, even if they were unhappy, is it nice of you to constantly remind them of the reason? Remember, friends are supposed to be supportive!

your marriage, though, when one partner becomes jealous of the time the other is investing in an opposite-sex friend—particularly if it's a relatively new addition to your stable of friends or, let's be frank, if the friend's super-good-looking. Here are a few guidelines for keeping these friendships happy and healthy for everyone involved.

**Introduce your two main men (or women).** Before you even consider hanging out one-on-one with an opposite-sex buddy, it's good form to introduce him or her to your spouse if they haven't already met. You don't have to make it a big three-way date, but you can invite the new person to swing by for coffee with the two of you, or make plans to attend the same party. Introducing the two sends a message to everyone right away that you've got nothing to hide, and your spouse has nothing to worry about. It may sound paranoid, but it's really not about pre-empting accusations of impropriety—it's just polite. Your new pal and your spouse may have nothing in common, so we're not going to tell you you have to include one any time the other is around, but the more time you spend with your friend in groups—of other people, not necessarily your spouse—the less anyone will wonder.

**Draw the line if things get weird.** When you're hanging out with someone of the opposite sex, flirtation happens. And as a newlywed, when it does, you may feel ashamed or horrible. But flirtation isn't a bad thing—it usually just makes you feel saucy and happy, which *improves* your marriage. The red flag should go up when you start looking forward to times with your new pal so you *can* flirt and feel good. It's a long way from having an affair, but starting the habit of going to someone else to get what's missing from your marriage is a bad, bad habit. If there is *any* discussion of or overture toward hooking up, start downgrading your friendship and avoiding one-on-one hangouts. Seriously, those are the early behaviors of someone who wants to make a move, and letting them continue will likely lead to an affair years later that "just happens." Also, try not to vent about marriage problems to an opposite-sex friend who you think could have even the slightest feelings for you. You're unlikely to get good advice or perspective from this person and he or she may even feel drawn into a psychodrama of wanting to "rescue" you from your "horrible" spouse. And listen: Any

"I trust my husband and he can definitely have female friends (regardless of their marital status). After all, I have single male friends that I hang out with sometimes."
—amanjay

# Topic: going out

## My husband is going to a bachelor party in Vegas.

I feel a twinge in my stomach because I don't want him to go, but I know he deserves to have fun with his friends. I try to look at it this way: He gets his guy fix, and I get the house to myself for a few days. —LALASEPT05

My girlfriends love to go to lounges and drink martinis, while DH's pals are strictly sports bars and beer kind of guys. **Needless to say, our groups don't socialize much.** —crsd99

**I'M AN EXTROVERT WHO WANTS TO BE AROUND PEOPLE ALL THE TIME**; my DH is just the opposite. I'm slowly learning, though, that it's okay for him not to come out with me all the time, while he's learning that he does need to be out a bit more if he wants to be an integral part of the group.

—EastCoastBride

Years ago a friend told her boyfriend that she could only see him on either Friday or Saturday night—not both because the **other night was for her girlfriends.** I have never forgotten this. There is no way that my DH, who is just wonderful, could substitute for my friends! —LucyMax

**MY DH LOVES TO PARTY AND CAN STAY OUT UNTIL 4 A.M.** He gets annoyed when I'm yawning and falling asleep. I finally realized I can go home without him so he can have his idea of fun and I can get my idea of a good night's sleep.

—newlywed26

## nest note:

Spending time together is healthy for your relationship—and the same goes for getting together with your pals. And don't worry if your different groups of friends don't click or you simply need some alone time with your BFF every now and then. Hanging out with your friends solo is fine—as long as you don't spend more time with them than you do with your sweetie.

friend who encourages you to walk out on your marriage without even being asked for an opinion has a hidden agenda. We strongly advise walking out on *that* friendship ASAP and surrounding yourself with positive people.

**Be honest and fair.** If you're secretly jealous of your spouse's friendship with another person, do both of you a favor and bring it up. (Note that we didn't say: Tell your honey to stop hanging out with the person under penalty of couch-sleep.) Just talking about it will likely result in your partner reassuring you about what's going on—and will teach you about what he or she is looking for in a friend. You'll probably find out it's something totally non-threatening like "someone who can talk for hours about '40s sci-fi TV." It's also good practice to state your insecurities so when something truly threatening does come up, you know how to navigate the conversation. You should talk about what you're really scared of: It's probably not the friend specifically, but the idea that you one day might be cheated on, or you've always worried that you'll never be entertaining enough to make your spouse happy. You may even find out your spouse feels a little bit confused when *you* spend an evening with *your* opposite-sex friends, too. That brings us to our second point—turnabout is fair play. Whatever rules you set for your spouse—it has to be a group, you have to know about it, etc.—you have to be willing to follow them yourself!

**tip**

One great way to make sure your individual social circle stays wide and varied is to join a club or take up a hobby where you'll get to interact with lots of other people. Look at them as cliques in a post-high-school kind of way: no immaturity, no gossiping (well, maybe a little), a group of people with a common bond. Think book clubs, card nights, sports teams, volunteer organizations, or classes (cooking, wine tasting, painting) where you'll have the chance to bond with a bunch of people at once.

## WHY YOU NEED ALONE TIME

Just because you're head over heels and feel positively *incomplete* without your sweetheart's company, don't make the mistake of thinking you no longer need time away from his or her side. Taking time to be alone with your thoughts is important to your psychological well-being, and getting centered will make you a better partner to your spouse. Here are a few ways to work a little alone time into every day:

# The Ex Files

**It's likely that at least one of you has an ex who's still in the picture. If a solid friendship has risen out of the ashes of your burned-out romance, it's totally reasonable for you to want to keep up that relationship even though you're committed to someone new. There's bound to be a tiny bit of jealousy—it's only natural and not a bad thing. Think about the ego boost when an ex sends you an e-mail. Think of your other half having a tinge of jealousy. It's okay to maintain a friendship with ground rules. Some tips:**

- Talk to your partner about how you can be friends with your former flame in a way that won't make him or her feel uncomfortable. Maybe you agree to get together only for weekday lunches, or only when your current partner is present.

- Be straightforward about all your ex interactions. If you don't mention a meeting or conversation with your ex and your significant other finds out about it anyway, you'll look beyond shady. Why risk getting in hot water when you don't have anything to hide?

- Be honest with yourself. Do you really want to maintain a friendship with your ex, or are you simply looking to maintain the feeling of having someone secretly pine after you?

- The more your spouse gets to know your old infatuation, the less threatened he or she will feel; so make sure to include the ex in dinner party plans.

- Give it up graciously. If your spouse simply can't get comfortable with the presence of someone with whom you were so intimate, let it go. No single friend is worth driving a wedge in your relationship.

**Get some exercise:** Working up a good sweat, whether at the gym, on a jog, or in a yoga class, provides a great chance for your brain to work through any issues that have been nagging at you. If you've been struggling to find inspiration for a work project, or need to think through a personal problem, you'll probably find that answers come more easily during or after a workout.

**Keep reading:** Nothing beats a good book as a means of escaping from everyday life. If you love to read, designate a half hour every day for uninterrupted reading time.

**Stay creative:** Artistic endeavors like painting, playing music, or scrapbooking can be some of the most relaxing and restorative solo activities of all because you tend to get so wrapped up in them that concerns and stresses fall way. Plus, creating something beautiful will give you a sense of accomplishment.

**Keep journaling:** Put your pen to work and write down what's going on in your life—even if you feel like you have nothing to say, the seemingly mundane details of your newly married life will be a treat to revisit months, or even years, later.

# Chapter 3: the takeaway

Those things you can do right now to get the party started.

**Make a plan for plans.** Sounds silly, but you and your sig need to decide together how much free time, couple time, and alone time you need. Follow our guide on page 99.

**Schedule a date night.** Don't just assume nights out will happen—plan them. Date nights work—see why on page 106.

**"We"–ed out your vocabulary.** Remember your single friends? There's a direct correlation between how much you talk in the plural and how much your friends still like you. Find out how to keep them on your side on page 112.

# [ in-laws ]

**Along with fine china and crystal, you also** registered for a whole new set of parents. Unfortunately, this family business doesn't come with a liberal return policy. The only true law of in-laws: All you can do is learn how to love them as best you can—and quietly vent about them to your friends.

## the nest test:
# your in-law issues

These open-ended questions can help you and your honey start to talk about what makes your in-laws tick—and what just ticks you off.

1. **Do you wish we saw your parents more? Less? What about mine?**

2. **Would you accept a loan from your parents?**

3. What topics are off-limits at your family's dinner table?

4. **Are you going to tell your parents all our plans about kids, etc.? Or do you believe in privacy?**

5. **What do you love most about my parents?**

6. **What do you hate most about my parents? (Be honest, I can take it.)**

7. **What will happen when your parents get old?**

8. **Which holidays do you hope to spend with your family?**

# anatomy of an in-law

What's an in-law? An extremely close family member you didn't get to choose. What used to be a comfort zone (the amicable nature of your family) can become a world of confusion the second you bring another person into the mix. But there are some basic reasons why your respective parents are acting strangely. Here are the inherently complicated bonds formed by marriage.

## MOTHERS-IN-LAW

### His Mom Explained

Any time two powerful women come in contact with each other, there are going to be some issues. And no one has more power in a man's life than his mother or his wife—no wonder there are sometimes tugs-of-war. Oftentimes, though, the conflicts that arise between MILs and DILs are due to simple miscommunication. The wedding-planning process usu-

> "My mother-in-law still gives me the evil eye over the time I told my husband to stop acting like a toddler and get his own drink for dinner."
> —SuzeeQ

ally, shall we say, brings out the defenses. It's an emotional time for her (she feels like she's losing a son); it's a stressful time for you (you are probably annoyed by her constant interference). And since she's not *your* mom, your comfort level for confronting her and talking it out is probably pretty low. But you have to understand that, to her, the wedding is a changing of the guard as to who's the number one woman in his life. Now, most moms realize that a wife can never replace a mother, but nevertheless, she's bound to feel threatened and stake her claim to some degree. And that means staying involved and keeping close.

HOW TO DEFUSE THE BOMB: Woo her. If she's tech-savvy, drop an e-mail every now and again (once a week will probably suffice) about something new in your life. It really doesn't have to be that important: Maybe you finished a big project at work, or you and your guy have decided to have a tag sale. Giving an inch will ease a mile of involvement issues. If the phone's the only way to go, use the same tactics but just establish from the start that you have only a second to talk and wanted to check in.

Hopefully, over time, you will join forces and start to understand each other more (like how similar father and son can be!). But if you just can't seem to break the barrier with his mom, know that mothers can, like anyone, be coddled, cajoled, and confronted into respecting your life. Just listen to what she is saying. Remember, your husband's parents have been the loving influence upon him for his entire life and, as such, deserve credit for how your beloved has turned out.

### Her Mom Explained

A son-in-law is a big deal to most moms—he's a reflection on how well she raised her daughter and can also be a way for her to relive the courtship-dating-planning-relating of her youth. Usually, as long as a guy is "good enough" for a MIL's baby girl—and dresses nice for family events—things between a husband and his mother-in-law can be smooth (okay, so no guy will ever be good enough in her mother's eyes, but you know what we mean).

Now, that doesn't mean your wife's mom is out of the picture—lots of times, the psychodrama in a marriage takes place between an advice-giving mother and an independence-seeking daughter, and the husband will clearly be caught up in that. And the natural reactions, like taking sides, forming opinions, and feeling frustrated, can cause tension.

HOW TO DEFUSE THE BOMB: Do not, under any circumstances, talk badly about your wife to her mom. Even if it's only to "take the mom's side" for once and win brownie points, you'll only be convincing her that you're not a perfect match. Your best bet? Mind your manners, maintain good spirits around her family, and keep out of the mother/daughter spats. If you get dragged into it, drag yourself out. If there's no way out, play the role of unbiased mediator. If all else fails, punt it to her dad.

## FATHERS-IN-LAW

### Her Dad Explained

Because they're men themselves, fathers-in-law are naturally suspicious when a guy comes sniffing around his precious daughter. Of course there will always be a few peeing contests between men and their sons-in-law, and most of them boil down to "Are you taking good care of my baby?"

HOW TO DEFUSE THE BOMB: Show him that you *are* taking care of his baby by being affectionate, thoughtful, and caring (btw, you should be doing those things anyway). But at all costs, avoid any flattery of his daughter that makes a reference to her body parts—dads do not like to think of their daughters in that way, and it will just make him suspicious of you. Another tactic: Ask for financial advice. It's probably not a good idea to mention dramatic career-change thoughts, though—strong and steady, and above all deferential, wins the race.

**His Dad Explained**

If you think about it, most adult men are more than aware of the fact that they don't understand women. Fathers-in-law have had a lifetime of marriage to realize that it's a pain in the butt to argue with their wives, so the last thing they're going to do is bother trying to pick a fight with someone *else's* wife. Plus, most women know how to charm their husbands, and so it's a natural jump to easily winning over their husband's father.

Of course, there are plenty of exceptions—the blue-blood dad who looks down at his son's middle-class wife; or the emotionally distant dad who incurred the rage of his daughter-in-law for how he treated his son growing up. But even these tensions are rarely direct—the dad's disappointed in his son, the son's not as concerned about his emotional abandonment as his wife is, etc. We're not saying it can't go wrong; we're just saying that, usually, it's relatively quiet on this front.

HOW TO DEFUSE THE BOMB: If there is a reason to call in the dogs, follow your hubby's lead. He probably knows the best way to deal with Dad (like asking him about the latest biography he's reading).

## STEP IN-LAWS

The dynamics between you and a remarried in-law's spouse often take a similar form to the ones between you and a biological in-law, especially if your sig other grew up with him or her. But there can be more to it than that. Some steps may try to buddy up with you, or create strange triangles. And if there's lingering bitterness, you may find yourself an unwitting ally.

HOW TO DEFUSE THE BOMB: Say your mate's dad's new wife *hates* his first wife—she may try to exploit the fact that you don't like the first wife's candied yams. Yes, it can be tempting to know that someone on your spouse's side *gets* what's wrong, but all you're asking for is trouble if you start cleaving with steps on family

**tip**
Feeling frustrated by your new family? We know it's essential to communicate when problems arise, but sometimes what you really want to say needs to be seriously censored. So have an old-fashioned vent session. Write down everything you'd like to say but can't. Show the list to your spouse (if he or she can take it), then rip that document to shreds.

# Calling All In-laws

**For many couples, knowing how to address the people who parented the love of your life can cause stress. Is calling them by their first name disrespectful—either too casual or too formal? Is calling your MIL "Mom" telling your own mother you don't need her anymore?**

**The solution:** Just copy what the rest of their family does, get your spouse to suss it out, or ask the question yourself. Here, four casual but totally inoffensive ways you can find out what your in-laws like to be called.

- "I know [name of another child-in-law] uses 'Mom'—is that what you'd like me to call you also?" If you have issues with calling your in-law "Mom" or "Dad," just add, "I'm having a hard time thinking of you that way because I automatically think of my own parents—what do you suggest instead?" They might prefer a first name, or a tweak like "Mother" or "Mom Z".

- "Come on in! Oh, I forgot to mention that a friend might be stopping by. I feel weirdly formal referring to you as 'Mrs. Johnson,' but however you're most comfortable. Just let me know what I should call you!"

- Picking up the phone when an in-law calls . . . "Hello? Who is this? Sorry, I've got a really bad connection. Who is this again?!" Whatever they say, there's your answer.

rivalries. You seem like you're siding with a step over your spouse's actual parent, you're promoting discord in the marriage between her and the father-in-law, and the more you dwell on how much an in-law annoys you, the more you'll *notice* how much she annoys you. Try to treat your step in-law like family—the kind with whom you don't stir up trouble.

## DIAGNOSING YOUR IN-LAW ISSUES

Now you can kind of understand where the in-laws are coming from. But those generalizations don't help you deal specifically with your new family. Sometimes a family member who interferes is insecure about his or her role in your lives. Playing on these insecurities will only make matters worse. Your best plan? Figure out what type of in-law you have . . . and learn to act accordingly.

### Booster Shot In-laws

It doesn't matter if it hurts, because they're around so rarely. Some people call them distant, others call it dreamy—you've got an Easter-and-Christmas–type family that helped you pay for a wedding and then stepped back out of the spotlight. You know they love you, you know they're there, but geography or personalities keep you from having day-to-day overlap beyond the occasional phone call or birthday check.

YOUR BIGGEST CHALLENGE: Growing comfortable enough with their communication style to let them know when you really do *need* them. (It's okay to want more mom-in-law time—really!) There's no rule that says you can't start a new family holiday, like an end-of-summer get-together.

### Excedrin In-laws

You take 'em when you need 'em. Most people have some form of in-and-out in-laws, and this is one of them. Yes, they'll

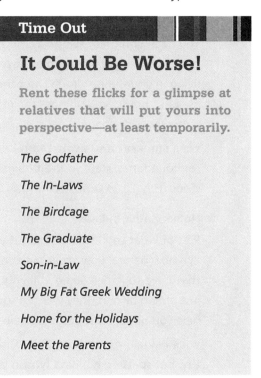

**Time Out**

# It Could Be Worse!

Rent these flicks for a glimpse at relatives that will put yours into perspective—at least temporarily.

*The Godfather*

*The In-Laws*

*The Birdcage*

*The Graduate*

*Son-in-Law*

*My Big Fat Greek Wedding*

*Home for the Holidays*

*Meet the Parents*

descend for a week here and there, get a little over-bearing just when you need the quiet time the most, but all in all you've got a good relationship with them. You know you can go to them if you need help, and they're also not so in-your-face that you have to pray they'll go away. Excedrin in-laws are perfect because while they can sometimes be a pain, you also know you can reach for them to help you relieve headaches you can't handle on your own.

> "This is the question of the century: how to deal with a MIL who won't let go? I made my feelings crystal clear to my DH—I am his wife, and as such, I should come first!"
> —MrsBDA

YOUR BIGGEST CHALLENGE: Learning to speak up when an issue does come up. You've really got it made. But, if one of those so-called headaches that made you call them in for support turns into a full-blown migraine, the involvement level may shift. And when things are running smoothly, it's tempting to quash any minor complaints—why fix what's pretty much working, right? Unfortunately, stifling your concerns often results in the issue getting (unnecessarily) bigger.

## Birth Control In-laws

You deal with them every day . . . and they make you long for family-free living. Seriously, why would you need to have kids when you've already got two needy humans living in your house? You've got the punch-line family structure. They see your house as "our" house, your life as "their" little fixer-upper project, and your spouse as their wittle pwecious baby.

YOUR BIGGEST CHALLENGE: Learn to exploit them (in a good way) for their helpfulness, set boundaries, steel yourself mentally when they get too overbearing, and take it in stride. Hey, Little Orphan Annie and Oliver Twist would have killed for your problems.

## Homeopathic In-laws

Part of what you love most about your spouse is the relationship with his or her family—how natural they act around one another, how welcoming they are, how much fun they have together. Some in-laws just get it: They relish the fact that their family has just grown by one. They want to spend time with you, on *your* schedule. They want to help you out because *they* had help starting out. You've got it good with these in-laws.

YOUR BIGGEST CHALLENGE: Guilt. It should be about the quality of the time, not quantity, but splitting holidays (which we tackle later in the chapter) and limited visiting time can make you feel badly about not reciprocating the same wonderful care and attention your respective parents dole out. Just show them that you care through the little things: frequent phone calls, handwritten notes, even forwarding links to interesting articles.

# keeping the peace

You're not going to change your in-laws . . . and you should be wary of asking your partner to. Honestly, no one needs to hear again and again how kooky his or her parents are. What will it do besides make your spouse feel defensive?
Instead, follow these rules to promote family harmony.

## FAMILY-FRIENDLY MOVES

Every family has a different way of doing things, even if on the surface they seem eerily alike. Once you start to understand both families' cultures (and quirks), you'll be able to navigate your way through the landmines.

**52%** of Nesties feel happy about the amount of time they spend with in-laws. **16%** want to spend even more time with their in-laws.

**Help settle any misunderstandings or skirmishes.** Instead of rolling your eyes and saying, "Oh, it's just my mom—ignore her," take responsibility for helping to manage your own mother and father since you likely know how best to deal with them. If you shrug it off, your spouse will think you don't care that your parents are being hurtful—even though to you they're just being their usual annoying selves. Remember: You're not an innocent bystander caught between two warring factions—you're the person they have in common and the whole reason they're talking to each other in the first place. No, you don't *have* to appoint yourself the peacemaker, but you can do it a lot faster and more successfully than anyone else in the picture, so for the sake of everyone, don't shy away from your job as the in-law moderator.

**Address the issues.** It's not going to be easy to tell your family members that you don't want them doing something they consider second nature. They're not going to react with a resounding "I understand!" every time. But you have to acknowledge that if

# Spilling the Family Beans

**Maybe your mate doesn't realize that eating in the living room is a cardinal sin. To make sure you're both on the same page, compare notes on your families' secret rules for these common situations:**

**EATING:** This seems to be the biggest area of conflict for many families since it's the primary occasion for time spent together. Some parents think it's weird to have dinner before eight; some think it's offensive to eat past seven. Some families put all their eggs in the dinner basket (be prepared for a five-course meal), while some eat like the French (big lunch, don't-be-hungry dinner).

**DRINKING:** Hand and hand with eating, "to drink or not to drink," is the real question. Maybe red wine is like water at your dinner table, but your mate's family thinks more than one glass is a sure sign of alcoholism.

**BEDTIME:** What's the cutoff time for someone to phone? Nine, midnight? Is it a little-known fact that Mummy gets tired (read: cranky) after seven, so if you want to ask a favor, do it in the morning? Is sleeping late seen as the supreme sign of laziness?

**TACKY SUBJECTS:** Obviously tread lightly around dirty jokes, but what about the telling of other stories? Should you never discuss work or health problems at the table? What about money?

**GIFTING:** When they set a price limit, do they really stick to it? Or is lots and lots of generosity the name of the game? Are birthday gifts a big deal, while holiday presents are seldom exchanged or reserved for youngsters only?

you *don't* say anything, it's almost guaranteed that the thing that's bothering you or your mate *won't* change.

Suffer in silence or communicate in awkwardness—we know which we'd recommend. Even though your comments may temporarily bruise their egos, most in-laws really do want to foster a good relationship with you both, so consider this an investment in your long-term happiness.

**Think before you speak.** It should be common sense, but we'll repeat it: When it comes to topics like sex, politics, and religion, all the good arguments in the world aren't likely to change someone's mind, so err on the side of genteel and avoid these topics whenever possible.

**Prep your partner for what *not* to say.** You may have learned on the second date that your husband's Uncle Jim-Bob spent time in jail during the '60s, but if the rest of his family considers it a black mark on their family history, you don't want to make a joke about it over Thanksgiving dinner. Think about all the things your family is squeamish about discussing, too, and let your spouse know it's best not to unearth those issues.

A glimpse of the skeletons in your family's closet will also prepare your spouse for what might otherwise appear to be weird behavior. Sure, it may be uncomfortable to explain that Aunt Thelma was raised in an orphanage (or by lemurs in the jungle), but armed with this knowledge, your spouse will be better able to understand why she gets all emotional when she sees newborns clinging to their moms (or eats leaves with her hands at the dinner table). And when your spouse can empathize with even the nuttiest member of your family, he or she's less likely to pick a fight.

**Compare backgrounds (just this once).** Maybe you never start eating dinner until you've each said a short prayer. Maybe touching someone with the left hand is considered abhorrent. Maybe certain terms (like *ass*) are considered disrespectful. Whether it's a religious, cultural, or etiquette tradition that your family sticks to, it's always worth explaining ahead of time. Sure, your spouse might have already caught on or known not to do something, but reinforcing behaviors that your parents are sensitive to can prevent countless hurt feelings and awkward misunderstandings. We all want our parents to

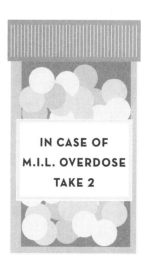

IN CASE OF
M.I.L. OVERDOSE
TAKE 2

# Topic:
# would you be mad if MIL called you "what's her face"?

**My MIL did this in front of my husband's family while we were out to dinner.** It is not like she forgot my name—she just did it to be a snarky ***.
I told him she was rude, and he seemed to just go with the flow, like that is how she is. —gyspy2482

**Holy crap that is rude!**
—Kimberlina05

I HATE WHEN GUYS MAKE EXCUSES FOR THEIR MOTHERS' RUDE BEHAVIOR.
Why is it that we have to just 'let it go' while MILs can make whatever rude, ugly, nasty comments they want? —newlywed26

The fact that your husband wasn't bothered would be more upsetting to me than anything.
—EastCoastBride

**Even 'what's her name' is better than 'what's her face'!**
—njbride

" If it wasn't taken as funny by the group then it reflected poorly on her, not you. **BEING GRACIOUS AND LETTING IT PASS** made you look even better. —livinitup

like our significant other, so discuss anything that might make you feel embarrassed, like bad table manners or potty jokes. No one's a mind reader, so let your partner know your mom will take it as an insult every time he or she refuses seconds at dinner. The secret to success? Promise to respect each other's family traditions, within limits, of course. If you've been asked to dress up as Turkey Tom for their annual Thanksgiving parade, figure out a way with your mate to politely decline.

## GROUND RULES YOU CAN AGREE ON

Sometimes the issue isn't really with your in-laws at all—it's about getting in sync with each other. Sometimes changing your spouse's mind is as simple as saying, "Well, I prefer they not," but other times your cutie might not really see why it's a problem and you'll have to, as ever, compromise. The most important lesson is learning to maintain a united front.

It's also important that you learn to stick up for yourself while at the same time respect your partner's ability to live his or her own life. So your mate's mom calls *every* day and you don't want to talk? Stop answering. Meanwhile, if your spouse takes the calls, no good can come from barking at him or her to cut the apron strings—your mate has the right to talk on the phone to anybody he or she feels like. So together, agree to follow these basic ground rules—our secret tricks for getting in good with the in-laws.

**Deal with your own.** If something about your partner's family is really getting under your skin, chances are it will sound better if your spouse is the one to sound off about it. Remember: You know how to handle your own 'rents, whether it's smooth-talking, a tiny present, or just the sight of their baby begging for help.

**Maintain your boundaries** (i.e., never spend more than three days under the same roof with your in-laws). If you cringe when a father-in-law touches your sheets, for example, or roots through your pantry and alphabetizes your spices, it's because he's invading your space. The big breaches that come up with in-laws: when to visit and how to behave when you or they do. Before you make any visit, first talk to your spouse and map out a plan. Accept an invitation to spend time with the in-laws, but tell them ahead of time that you know space is tight and don't want to inconvenience them. Instead, spring for a hotel and park yourselves there. You will get some needed space (and alone time), and even though they probably won't admit it, your in-laws will be grateful for the break, too.

**Try (really, really hard!) not to bash each other's parents.** If your MIL comments that your house is a mess and maybe one of you should stop spending so much time at the office, don't let harsh words fly to your mate. So what do you do? Do you boil inside instead of telling your spouse what's really ticking you off? Or do you cause a family rift by screaming at everyone at your sister-in-law's housewarming party about how dysfunctional they are? How about neither? You have to pick and choose your battles.

If it's something minor, like your MIL saying something stupid that annoyed you, keep your mouth shut. If, on the other hand, she steps way out of line, talk to your spouse about it tactfully. It's important not to psychoanalyze by saying: "Your mom really has a ____ problem. . . ." Instead, say something like, "I was really confused by something your mom did today."

**Prove that you're making an effort.** Call or e-mail your mother-in-law once in a while to say hi, even if it kills you. We've said it once and we'll say it again: Keep her close, but not too close. Make a biweekly or monthly call or drop an e-mail. You can even call when you know she's not going to be there and leave a "just thinking about you" message.

Keep her on the periphery of personal matters, too. If she asks how work is, you can say it's been a bit busy or stressful but you don't have to tell her you're thinking of quitting. You can tell her you saw a great movie, but you don't need to tell her who

## Mr. & Mrs. Manners

# Caller ID Please

Q. My MIL has gotten in the habit of calling me every time a new thought pops into her head. How can I make it stop?

A. Start dialing her digits. You need to take control of the chats and set the schedule for calls. As the conversation seems to teeter off, specifically state when you will call her again. Keeping in touch will help her feel secure about the relationship, and her involvement with both of you. If she keeps calling anyway, use that ever-powerful Caller ID. Call back a couple days later and say, "Oh no, of course I'm not avoiding you—work's been busy, and I've never been a phone person. Even my best friends from school don't hear from me more than twice a month. Now, how are you?"

# [L]

# Making the Rules

**Fill out this form to help you see the concrete issues when you're hashing out what you need to do—or not do—about an in-law situation (or any other kind of conflict!). Then keep it, to remind yourselves that you agreed on the same result.**

**1.** What's the specific issue? (i.e., MIL constantly buys me preppy clothes that she wishes I would wear.)

_____

**2.** What would you, the husband, like to see done about it? (i.e., Tell her to stop buying me clothes.)

_____

What would you, the wife, like to see done about it? (i.e., Nothing, she's just being generous.)

_____

**3.** Why is this topic important to you, the husband? (i.e., I feel like she wishes I was someone I'm not.)

_____

Why is this topic important to you, the wife? (i.e., I feel like he's being so ungrateful.)

_____

**4.** How can I, the wife, make the problem it causes for my husband go away? (i.e., Ask my mom to stop shopping for him.)

_____

How can I, the husband, make the problem it causes for my wife go away? (i.e., Wear some of the clothes with other items in my closet to make my own look.)

_____

**5.** List all the other options available: (i.e., Return the clothes; have them sit unused; give them away.)

_____

**6.** Write down the most doable solution, and give examples of how you're going to make it easier. (i.e., I'm going to suggest some other gift ideas to my mom, and he's going to wear some of the items when we're with my family.)

_____

you went with. If she starts grilling you, say politely, "That's such a long conversation and I actually have an appointment; maybe we can talk about it later?"

**Never criticize your spouse within earshot of his or her family.** Want to get on your new family's bad side fast? Chastise your spouse in front of his or her mom. This is her baby you're talking about, and whether you're right or you're just plain cranky, your mother-in-law is not going to take criticism of her brood well. Save the wisecracks until after they leave or for the car ride home. It will keep you looking like the darling child-in-law they know and love and you can still keep your spouse in line.

**Determine what's off topic between you two and the in-laws.** Even if you tell your parents everything, your spouse may have a very different relationship with his or her parents. So set up some privacy rules—decide what you're comfortable having your respective parents knowing about you, your spouse, or your marriage. And if one of you does dish (with your partner's permission, of course) to your parents that you're considering a new career, make sure they're aware that this is confidential information and you may or may not be sharing it with both sets of parents.

**Don't overanalyze every move.** Remember, your in-laws are the parents of someone very special—your spouse. And he or she has spent twenty-plus years with them, developing habits and routines. So if he sides with his mom once (and only once), or if she takes financial advice from Dad without consulting you once (and only once), let it go. Explain why the in-law infraction upset you, and then drop it. Some habits are hard to break.

*"Whenever my mom would schedule a last-minute get-together, I would chicken out and let my wife call and decline. Well, that plan backfired. My mom always took it out on my wife."*
—Daveyb

**Present a united front.** This rule should be tattooed on your bum. Once you and your spouse have come to an agreement about what behavior you expect from an in-law, it's crucial that you both commit to that stance. If you overlook a verboten behavior when your spouse isn't around, you may look like the good guy in the immediate moment, but you're sabotaging the trust you have with your spouse and also encouraging a potential divide between your parent and your partner. Whether letting them tell you the right way to arrange the pillows on the love seat or how many kids you should have, if you've agreed on a position, being inconsistent only makes things worse.

When couples can't stand up to their parents on the small things, it's even harder for them to draw (sometimes painful) boundaries about the larger issues down the road.

And the more tiny fights build up over the years, the more contentious the in-law relationship will be—both sides will be primed for a fight when there *is* a big disagreement.

All it takes to show your parents you're siding with your spouse is to say, "Well, I completely understand where you're coming from, but for now that's how we want things" instead of "*I* understand where you're coming from, but for now that's how *she* wants things." Not only does the latter pit your spouse against your parent, but it pits you against your spouse in the eyes of your parent—you're basically saying "I want *this* but she's making me do *that*." If a parent senses discord, they may be (rightfully) concerned about the marriage as a whole and start finding even more issues with you two as a couple. And *everyone* should want to avoid that.

## DEALING WITH YOUR OWN BAGGAGE

There comes a time in every newlywed's life when they lash out at their in-laws for doing something perfectly, well, benign. Shocking but true: Sometimes, you're annoyed because it's *them*, not because of what they've done. To keep you from wasting your energy getting mad over stuff that has no real emotional currency, ask yourself two questions:

**Is this really an attack on me?** Yeah, your FIL leaves a check when he comes, but it's not because he thinks you're a crappy provider if he does the same thing with *all* his grown kids. The truth is, sometimes when you get bent out of shape over what you perceive as criticism, it's actually just you being self-conscious of your own flaws.

> Need reassurance that your in-laws *aren't* the only ones who drive newlyweds mad? Read and post your biggest complaints: TheNest.com/inlawtalk

**click**

**Does this affect my life negatively?** Okay, it annoys you that your MIL wanders into your bedroom and makes the bed so it's hospital perfect. But you have to ask yourself, Is she taking your housekeeping skills to task or is it a habit from her nursing days? Worst-case scenario, you wind up with a neater bedroom or a little extra cash for the vacation fund. You can live with that, right?

If you answered "no" to both these questions, no matter what your in-laws are like, you're projecting your own emotions onto them. We recommend doing some perspective-gaining exercises (remember people who have wronged you, list reasons your

# [L] Out of the Mouths of Mothers-in-Law . . .

Sure, her comments can hit below the belt, but that doesn't mean you have to stoop to her level. Here's how to get the last word and still look sweet.

**Remark #1: "Oh, you're looking so . . . healthy [i.e., fat]!"**

THE REASON: She's probably self-conscious about her appearance and is projecting her low self-esteem on you. Of course, nasty remarks about someone's looks are childish and narcissistic, so it means she is emotionally immature (no big surprise here). Your best defense? Don't sink to her level.

THE RESPONSE: "Thank you! I feel great." Your confident approach of shaking off her comment should stop her in her tracks, letting her realize she's not getting to you. If she keeps saying it, you can take her aside and say something like, "I'm sure you don't mean to hurt my feelings, but you're making me feel very uncomfortable by talking about me like that." This should end the discussion.

**Remark #2: "Hmm . . . that's not the way we make stuffing."**

THE REASON: Cooking is probably her claim to fame, and she is afraid your recipes will overshadow hers. She may also be resistant to change, or fear that she's losing her status as matriarch (culinary or otherwise) of the family.

THE RESPONSE: "I'd love for you to try mine this time. You might like it." Remain confident, loving, and sincere, and she will realize that you're sweetly standing by your conviction—and your cooking.

**Remark #3: "That's his favorite. Trust me, I've known him a long time."**

THE REASON: She wants acknowledgment from you that she has prior claim on her son. To her, you are a newcomer, and she is probably still mourning the loss of her role as the most important woman in her son's life.

THE RESPONSE: "You're probably right. He has all kinds of secrets that I haven't learned yet." This will show her that you're not trying to take over, and that you're deferring primary importance. But for your sake, it should also end her bragging, since you've kindly reminded her that you are not competing.

**Remark #4: "Is that how you're wearing your hair now?"**

THE REASON: Your MIL doesn't like change. Or she has an idea of how she'd like to see you look, and wants to be your beauty confidante. If she has good style herself, this may be critically important to her self-esteem; she wants to get close to you by helping you choose a hairstyle.

THE RESPONSE: "Yes, [insert name of DH] loves it." If you say this nicely, your assertiveness might nip her rude comment in the bud, and you won't sound rude yourself.

**Remark #5: "Don't treat/talk to my son that way."**

THE REASON: She can't let go of protecting her son, and it's possible she never will. She doesn't trust him to handle his own affairs and sees him as a child who needs defending.

THE RESPONSE: If she sees you and DH in an argument, say, "I don't like fighting either. I don't like what just happened, and I'm especially sorry that you had to see it." This ends the discussion and holds DH just as accountable as you are.

If her comment comes without a clear catalyst, say in a genuine manner, "What do you mean? What am I doing that's upsetting you?" And listen to her answer. If you discover that a certain behavior pushes her buttons, then don't do it around her.

## tip

It's important to let your husband know about the communication you've had with his mom, but not in a way that makes you look like a tattletale. Say something like, "I had a discussion with your mom today. She doesn't like [such and such] . . . I told her [such and such] . . . I just thought you would want to know." You should especially give him this warning if there's a way MIL could spin the discussion in her favor. Hint: Say things neutrally so it doesn't sound like you're attacking his mom. Talk about your feelings, not about her. He can complain all he wants, but if you start, he may defend her.

in-laws might think they're being helpful, watch a half hour of news about people with *big* problems) so you can save your rage for when it's truly warranted! On the plus side, being a bit more self-aware might help you be a better offspring-in-law, which may sunny up your relationship to the point that they'll even stop bothering you with the *real* stuff!

# in-law landmines

When you're fully prepared for the slings and arrows of an extended family, you'll be able to handle these (and any other) issues that surface. We take you through them, from big to small, but the same tools that will help you address a loan from your hubby's grandpa will also help you with laying down no-touching-the-big-screen-TV rules for his nephew—we promise.

## HOLIDAYS

**Why it's an issue:** The holidays are, obviously, an important time for many families. For far-flung clans, it's often the one time a year when (almost) everyone can be together. The pressure to spend it "their" way is doubled when you've got both sets of extended families handing out invites—and more than that if you've got divorced parents involved.

The holidays are crucial times, but physics (not to mention your budget) makes it impossible for you to be at both houses at once. Then there's the shocking reality that you might not *want* to spend every one of your ten vacation days this year with a relative.

**Saving-grace solutions**

CALL DIBS ON BIG DAYS. The holiday considered most important may differ between your family and your spouse's. For example, Christmas may be *the* event for some groups, while others would never miss a Fourth of July ice cream social or a Chinese New Year. The simplest way to make sure everyone winds up happy is to each choose one holiday for which your family will get priority. If there's no conflict, you've got the problem already solved. But if it turns out you both want, say, Passover at Mom's, read on . . .

**TAKE TURNS.** Look at the whole year's calendar and set expectations early. ("We'll be in Seattle for Christmas, but with you for New Year's Day and Christmas next year.") Sounds simple, but how are you supposed to pick between two demanding families? Our suggestion: Instead of randomly deciding on one or another, choose one for an emotional reason (it's the last holiday before his brother moves to Germany, a cousin just had a baby, or a family member has been ailing). It makes your choice seem sensitive. Your family will be better about holding their tongues—provided you make good on your promise to be with them the next year.

**SPLIT UP.** If you've both got pressing reasons to be at home (deep-rooted traditions, sick family members on both sides, ludicrous amounts of guilt trips), remember that you are two separate people and if you're comfortable doing so, you can spend the holidays apart. Of course, this isn't the best solution on holidays that you'd like to make an important ritual for *your* new family, but minor celebrations can certainly be attended solo. Assure your family early that there's nothing wrong with your relationship, you just both want to attend to what's important. Make sure the missing spouse sends regards in a very special way, like a handwritten note or homemade cookies.

**JOIN FORCES.** Whether both sides are wild about having huge reunions or you have a big family and your spouse is an only child, many families invite their in-laws to one site. (You can even have a holiday celebration in a third-party location that's central to everyone.) Or invite people to your place—that way, instead of making *you* decide where to spend your time, *they'll* have to (it's why they gave you all that china anyway, right?).

**PARTY HOP.** If you've got the budget to do so, you can do a timeshare on families. You may not get to spend the exact day with the entire family, but just making an appearance is often enough to reassure your in-laws that you're a loving member of their family.

**tip**

If there's something your family did that was important to you as a child or even now, whether it was a holiday observance or just everyday behavior, find a way to incorporate it into your joint family times. Keep a bowl of fortune coins by your front door, head to midnight mass after your Hanukkah dinner, or give all of the kids in the family gift-wrapped bananas on their birthdays just because your parents used to. By bringing your favorite traditions to your new life together, you'll wind up creating your own family rituals.

## VISITS & FAMILY VACATIONS

**Why it's an issue:** Houseguests, by their very nature, infringe on one's comfort. There's a constant pressure to please, and often you feel like your house and your life are on display. When your houseguests are your in-laws, this pressure is intensified. They may feel that the general rules of houseguest etiquette (notifying you of arrival times, how long they plan on staying, restraint from clutter criticism) don't apply to them.

Family vacations, on the other hand, are the ultimate in time turmoil: Imagine your visiting issues combined with the turbulence of choosing whose house to go to for the holidays. We're assuming you have only a couple of weeks vacation for the whole year: Start divvying that up between some solo time with your spouse; weddings, college reunions, and other fun friend trips; and holidays, and what do you have left? Barely a day for your family's annual Colorado ski trip and his family's time-share on the Carolina coast.

### Saving-grace solutions

**MAKE A VISIT PLAN.** For out-of-towners, agree on the length of stay well ahead of time so there are no surprises. Create a general schedule of what they'll do during the visit. Don't feel like you have to entertain your in-laws every minute. Suggest fun things for them to do; otherwise, you'll end up resenting them. If you have other obligations during that time, let them know in advance so it doesn't seem like a white lie.

**START NEW VACATION TRADITIONS.** Maybe you can rent a house or houses—have your own Kennedy compound!—in Cape Cod for both families? It may be close quarters and high emotions, but at least you won't have to suffer through another guilt trip that starts with Colorado powder.

**31** %
of Nesties (the majority) see their in-laws once a month, but almost 10 percent only see them once a year!

## tip

If you're inviting a family member for the holidays and aren't sure how they'll react to your modified celebration, ask them to contribute their own favorite element to the celebration at your home. Whether it's a dessert you consider out of season or an advent calendar they hang each year, you'll make them feel welcome, which is the best gift you can give during any season.

**Why it's an issue:** Money isn't just a big deal with in-laws—it's a big deal with any relationship. On the other hand, few of us are independently loaded to the extent we'd like to be, and when it comes to big-ticket items like a house, it's common to turn to family for financial help. Your spouse's family may be lavish with gifts of money and it's no big deal, but if your family doesn't feel the same way, it may make you uncomfortable to ask for a loan. Again, you need to talk to your spouse.

That doesn't mean you should never look to the United Bank of In-laws when financing an important purchase, but be forewarned that there *will* be strings. Some in-laws express a sense of entitlement after helping out with a loan or "gift." Some give money even if you don't ask—and refuse to take no for an answer. Others' concern over financial matters and savings goals can seem invasive and judgmental if you're more private about money than your spouse.

Even when they're financially self-sufficient, some adult children become resentful when another sibling gets more money from their parents—a resentment that's easily passed along to their spouse. It can also create uncomfortable feelings in a marriage when one set of parents contributes more to one couple than the other. On the flip side, expenses relating to your parents can be equally diverse, as footing the bills for your parents' ailing health or housing needs can be an unforeseen, financially draining surprise that causes many couples to argue over just how deep their obligations run.

**Saving-grace solutions**

GET ON THE SAME PAGE. Fully discuss your feelings about your financial obligations to and expectations of your respective families *before* they become an issue. Don't tell your families you're starting to look at houses before you know the answer to the "do you need help with the down payment" question. In confidence, discuss your families' financial backgrounds with each other. If his dad has been paying down the debt of a failed business for fifteen years, it would explain why he can't chip in when your times get tough.

PUT IT ON PAPER. Though it sounds rather rigid, if you do borrow money from your in-laws, always draw up a contract that spells out a repayment plan. Once you both agree to it, the element of "When are we ever going to get our money back from those ungrateful kids?" is removed (assuming, of course, that you are scrupulously conscientious about making the payments).

## GRANDPARENTHOOD

**Why it's an issue:** When your ILs start asking nonstop about when you and your spouse are going to start a family, it's easy to read it as pressure to get reproducin'. The first thing to keep in mind is that they could just be curious—and a little bit competitive. The way you felt if *all* your friends got married before you is similar to how people in their age bracket sometimes feel about who's-got-the-first/best/biggest grandbaby. Grandkids are bragging rights the same way you used to be.

Of course, once you do have kids, a whole new set of struggles comes with them. Who gets to see the new addition more often—*his* mom or *her* mom? Who spoils the baby more? Who does the infant like better? Some in-laws are desperate to baby-sit—others struggle to get their children to *stop* treating them like a built-in nannies. And when it comes to childrearing, you've got two sets of parents giving input to another completely unique set of parents. If you think toes won't be stepped on and egos bruised, you're related to pod people.

### Saving-grace solutions

SET EXPECTATIONS EARLY. If you don't plan on procreating for a couple years, don't deflect the kid question, because it will just boomerang back on the next visit with your in-laws. If you have an idea of your schedule, make it clear. And if in-laws hit below the belt with topics like the female decline in fertility after the age of twenty-six, it's time to take them aside and tell them to back off.

FORGET THEM BACKING OFF. Don't ever tell parents that your kids are none of their business. Grandparenthood is a blood line and they have a right—barring, of course, abusive behavior—to be a part of it. You can, however, begin to set boundaries long before your babies are born.

TAKE INTEREST IN THEIR OPINION. When you're concerned about a cough or want to know when babies begin to crawl, you can take advantage of all those child-raising skills they've spent decades accumulating. They will be thrilled to be involved, and you'll be able to put their know-how to the test.

## KEEPING HOUSE

**Why it's an issue:** Just as with raising kiddos, maintaining a house is a skill that in-laws have had a lifetime to perfect. They may sound overbearing when they tell you to switch your wood polish or recommend an organizing system for your shoes, but chances are they're just trying to be helpful. After all, when's the last time you asked your accountant mother-in-law to tell you about changes to tax law or had your forester father-in-law explain the life cycle of a deciduous tree? It's human nature for us to want to share our expertise with people who are dabbling in the same field, and chances are, your ILs just see cleaning, cooking, and organizing as an area where, by age alone, they're the authorities.

### Saving-grace solutions

MAKE AN EFFORT. It can't hurt to try to make a good impression when you know the in-laws are coming over. Clean the common areas, pay special attention to the guest room, add some flowers, and pack away the clutter. If you're busy or have too-tidy relatives, you can hire a housekeeper to give your place a once-over to add polish just before they're due to arrive.

CLOSE SOME DOORS. Politely insist that disaster areas (your bedroom, the shed, the workshop downstairs) remain private, and practice shrugging off any comments that you interpret as veiled criticism.

WHEN COOKING, BE INCLUSIVE. Spring for nice food for dinner (you're less likely to be careless about burning an expensive cut of meat, after all, and quality will make up for any mistakes in preparation). Ask advice. Unless you are a graduate of the Culinary Institute of America, you can afford a little input from someone who has been cooking for twenty years. Have his dad taste the marinade. Ask her Italian mom to make sure the pasta is al dente. Better yet, ask them to bring a recipe and teach you how to make it.

## CARETAKING DUTIES

**Why it's an issue:** When a parent becomes too ill to live by himself or herself anymore, the barriers will fall down and your in-law issues may intensify. Having a parent move in with you will affect everything from your daily schedule to your sex life. Are you expected to be equally responsible for sharing the duties of your spouse's parents—driving them places, picking up prescriptions, checking in with their doctor? What happens when your spouse thinks it's perfectly reasonable to move to a new town to help their parent with daily chores—and you don't? Or, if you've decided to put a parent in a nursing home, who is going to foot the bill?

# The Tactful Turn Down

**Whether it's sayonara Santa Claus or you're just trying to avoid a visit, follow these relationship-saving rules.**

**DO: HAVE EACH OTHER'S BACK.** Calling your parents when your spouse isn't home to say, "Yeah, his mom's *insisting* that we spend Labor Day at their beach house—apparently it's some big tradition for them," may get you off the hook in the short term, but you're sending the message to your family that your spouse is in competition with them and trying to trump their wishes.

Instead, be very honest about the reasons for choosing, and make it clear it's something you worked out as a couple. "It was really hard for us to decide, but her family only gets together for Thanksgiving, so we'll come see you guys next month for Christmas" is fair, true, and placating. (Plus, showing your parents what a great team you are makes it easier for them to respect other twosome decisions you make in the future.)

**DON'T: BLAME FINANCES, EVEN IF THEY'RE A REASON.** You don't want to get any families yapping about your money status, because that's a precursor to, "Oh, so you've got enough money for an Audi but not for your family?" judgments. Plus, if they offer to pay your travel expenses, you'll have to come up with *another* reason to say no.

- - - - - - - - - - - - - - - - - - - - - - - - - - - - - - - - - - - -

**DO: RSVP "YES" FOR A FUTURE SPECIFIC EVENT.** "We'll definitely be there soon," sounds like a blow-off (probably because it usually is), but if you can promise them a definite visit, you'll win points. Whether it's pinky-swearing that you're going to do next New Year's at their place or vowing to attend Uncle Mikey's ninety-fifth birthday in the spring, letting them know when they'll see you lets the family keep bragging rights to hanging out with you.

**DON'T: LIE ABOUT WHEN YOU'RE GOING TO SEE THEM NEXT.** Just because you'd *like* to spend next Thanksgiving at your mom's, don't say you will unless you've cleared it with your spouse first. Being up front about missing events will help prevent bitterness about the resentment, but reneging on concrete plans just feeds that kind of issue. You have to cancel only once to unleash a torrent of, "Oh, so I suppose your in-laws made you a better offer—so sorry I'm not good enough anymore."

---

**DO: SEND SOMETHING USEFUL AND SWEET.** It doesn't have to be expensive—even a grocery gift basket you put together yourself—but anything out of the ordinary will let them know you wish you were there. Think s'mores kits for a household where the fireplace is always lit after October, a homemade batch of cookies, or some sort of serving piece that's perfect for one of the would-be-host's specialties.

**DON'T: LET GUILT (OR RELIEF) KEEP YOU SILENT.** You may feel so bad about choosing one set of parents over the other that you hesitate to make any special gestures toward the ones you skipped. But radio silence during the all-important family-togetherness-holidays just gives the abandoned relatives a *reason* to be upset that you're not with them. Instead, call the remote in-laws when you arrive at the house (and at least once on the big day) to make them feel like they're still a part of your holidays even if it's not in person, and be sure to throw in a little gratuitous "I sure wish we were there, too!"

---

**DO: INVITE THEM OVER.** The next time you can, ask them to join you. Doing so will make it clear that while you can't come to everything they invite you to, you do want to spend time together.

**DON'T: EXTEND AN INAPPROPRIATE INVITATION.** Asking them to a cocktail party when they eschew alcohol or having them over to watch the playoffs when they're not sports fans will look like the empty gesture it is.

# Topic: MIL wore white to the wedding

**I've been married nearly 4 months and this is still bothering me.** My MIL wore a white poofy dress to our wedding and claims it was champagne. She got a dress with a sweetheart neckline (just like mine). I feel that I should confront her about this. —JanuaryKim

**Sounds like a real monster-in-law!** —newlywed26

**You can't control her, so just let it go.** —kriscross

I can totally understand why you were irritated. However, **I think it's time to let it go.** —lilrunner

SHE OBVIOUSLY DID IT TO BOTHER YOU, so make like it didn't! Don't let her have the satisfaction of knowing that you've been steaming about this for 4 months! —bambam80

**Your MIL was being an a\*\*** and the guests at the wedding know it. —Jennifer5.04

Seriously, do you think for one moment anyone at the wedding got confused over who was the bride? Besides, **she was the one who looked like an idiot.** —Squishy'sGal

In your wedding photos, HAVE HER DRESS PHOTOSHOPPED TO NAVY OR PINK or black. When she asks why, tell her the truth. —SUwife

### nest note:

We agree with our fellow Nesties—why let someone's stupid behavior ruin memories from the best day of your life? And who knows, a few years from now you might be able to look back on this and laugh. Okay, maybe not. Still, don't let it affect your newlywed bliss for one more second. Simply keep in mind that your MIL was the one who looked bad that day—not you.

# Feuding Families

Q. Our parents act civilly when they're in the same room, but after they part ways, it's obvious they don't like one another. How can we help them make peace?

A. There are several different issues here: your parents' insincere behavior when they're together, the passive-aggressive hostility that comes out in the days that follow, and your own belief that you can or should smooth over their disagreements. Accept that they aren't going to like each other, but refuse to be dragged into the mudslinging. You're just increasing your own aggravation by taking part in conversations that have nothing to do with you. Next time one of your family members goes off, cut them short with a neutral statement like, "I know they're not like us, but I consider them my family now and am really working on accepting them for who they are." That'll take all the fun out of gossiping for your family member and you can change the subject. Your families may still grumble among themselves, but you and your husband will have plenty of peace and quiet.

## FAMILY DIFFERENCES

**Why it's an issue:** Okay, be honest—you've got a few things you could say about your in-laws' lifestyle, don't you? (They have a nice house, sure, but it's mortgaged to the hilt; or she's a total tightwad who wears ugly shoes.) It's human nature to have opinions about how people spend their time and money . . . and a lot of those opinions are rooted to some degree in jealousy. (Sure, they're fiscally irresponsible, but you'd kinda like a big house, too; you wish you were more financially conservative.)

It's only natural that when your parents and in-laws meet, judgments will be passed. The way you view your in-laws' lives is at least partially informed by the values you learned from your parents, so it's likely they'll feel kind of the same way. That means the post-game may entail you and your parents (or your spouse and in-laws) discussing the odds and ends of the other set's lifestyle. When it's your family being critiqued, it will definitely feel like you're being ganged up on or judged. Who can blame you for getting defensive about yourself and your family?

**Saving-grace solutions**

PUT YOUR PARTNER ON PATROL. Let your counterpart know in private that while you may even agree with what your in-laws have to say, you're sensitive about hearing your parents criticized, and ask him or her to be proactive about steering the conversation away from so-what's-their-deal talk. (In exchange, you've got to be vigilant about doing the same.) Your in-laws probably don't even realize they're doing it, so they'll be just as sated if they voice their opinions to their offspring at a later time when you're not there.

BUILD SMALL BRIDGES. Facilitate some interfamily bonding by bringing up things they have in common and arranging meetings on common ground.

DITCH THE "BEST FRIENDS" DREAM. As long as both sets of parents are civil to one another when they meet in person, who cares what they think about your mom's stock picks in private?! We know it smarts to hear, but there are bigger things to get upset about.

## MOVING AWAY

**Why it's an issue:** Close your eyes and you can almost imagine how it would go: You're eating with the in-laws one night when your spouse half-consciously mentions a job you're looking at in Dallas. Suddenly, your in-laws are launching a massive you-can't-move campaign: "Would you really want to live there—it averages three hundred degrees there in the summer!" The after-dinner football game cheers get particularly hateful when your FIL's team is playing the Cowboys. Your e-mail in-box fills with links to stories about crime rates, public school rankings, and pollution in Dallas. Even though your spouse encouraged you to apply for the job, your in-laws are blaming *you* for "dragging their baby away from home"—even though you haven't even had an interview. What's the freaking deal already!?!

> **tip**
>
> If you do move away, send strong signals that the distance is only milege, not emotional. Visit within two months of the move (even with all you have to do). Forward deals on flights you find and ask them to come help you unpack. The effort you put in early will pay off.

**Saving-grace solutions**

START BY UNDERSTANDING. Okay, their reaction may seem extreme when you're on the receiving end, but it's not really so nuts. Think about how you'd feel if a good friend— particularly one who's just gotten married—told you she was moving cross-country. "But all your friends are here!" you'd pout (at least inside). Now imagine if you'd spent twenty-plus years being responsible for that friend's well-being—you'd feel like you were losing control and facing a big separation from someone you invested a lot of time in. Then add in that for most of those twenty-plus years, that

# Buttering Up the In-laws

Hopefully by now you've realized that battling with your in-laws is an energy-drain that should be undertaken only as a last resort. To help reduce tension and actually help build a loving, productive relationship with your new parents, we recommend trying a few of these IL-impressing moves. They require little to no effort, but the payoffs can double (or triple) your success as not just a couple but a *family*.

- **ASK QUESTIONS.** Act curious about your in-laws' past—their marriage, their moves, their careers. We often forget that small talk is an option with older people, but novel conversations like this can make the days with the in-laws fly without even hinting at the "Where are my grandbabies?" topic. Plus, it will help you see them as a dynamic couple, just as you want them to see you and your spouse. You may even discover some surprising things you have in common.

- **GIVE COMPLIMENTS.** Letting your in-laws hear how magnificent you think they are (at hosting, at golf, at picking out the perfect hot pink lipstick to match their tracksuits) will only make your time together more pleasant (some studies have found that a compliment doesn't just create a buzz in the person being praised, but the person giving it, too!). It can also be a good move to rave about the areas where your in-laws are harping on you—say, your cleaning skills. "Wow, I never see a speck of dust in your house. I can't keep my place clean for anything!" Your in-laws will melt at the flattery and maybe even back off a bit when they realize you're aware of your shortcomings.

- **FORWARD IDEAS.** Clipping newspaper articles, sending along e-mails about concert or event tickets, or mailing good books you've finished is a great way to build common, safe territory with in-laws. Doing so shows your respect for your in-laws' independent personalities, and also reflects well on your own taste for coming across the things in the first place.

- **VOLUNTEER . . . STRATEGICALLY.** When your in-laws announce that they're traveling, get in touch to ask if there's anything you can do, from watering their plants to dog sitting. You can even help out from miles away by asking friends for hotel recommendations in the area or offering up your corporate rental car discount. Gestures like this show you to be attentive, interested, and responsible—always a good quality to highlight as someone who's married their son or daughter—and require little to no actual interaction with the in-laws on your end. Genius!

# [L]

# Sibling Rivalry

In-laws don't start and stop at MIL and FIL. Sometimes the most divisive relationships in a marriage can be those between a spouse and his or her siblings. Because they're closer to your own age, it can be even easier to hold a spouse's brother or sister to the same standards of behavior that you ask of yourself.

## COMMON FIGHTS

- "He just needs a little loan" vs. "We need to be saving for our retirement, not helping pay your brother's rent!"

- "Your little sister just wants to visit because you let her get away with stuff, and then your parents will blame me" vs. "Aw, c'mon, she's just a teenager."

- "Your parents paid for your sister's law school. I don't understand why you won't ask them to help with our down payment!" vs. "Look, I just don't want to burden them more."

## HOW TO DEAL

- **Tame the triangle.** A sibling's presence in your marriage can put people in an awkward triangle of figuring out what they "should" do for a family member versus what they'd like to do for their spouse. Understanding this dynamic will help you each take the offending spouse's behavior less personally. (It's not that he wants to give away your hard-earned money or wake up to his brother on the couch every weekend, it's that he feels it's his obligation.) There's no way around it: Bloodlines run deep.

- **Admit the larger issues.** Successful resolutions come when couples hunker down for a twosome talk and figure out how they feel about themselves, instead of making it about the particular issue. Often the conflict has nothing to do with the sibling: It might not be the sister-in-law's cursing that really offends you, it's the fact that her being there so much means less time with your spouse; or perhaps you resent when your brother-in-law asks about your job because you secretly don't feel successful enough.

- **Dig up the family dynamics.** Marriage doesn't magically make our pasts disappear. Whether your partner in crime was the favored son, the responsible older sister, the middle child, or the baby in the family, their established relationships with their kin will continue to come into play. As always, it's better not to psychoanalyze your mate and use it against them in an argument— but a little pop psych analysis may help you understand their actions.

- **Make rules for unruly relatives.** Accommodating, yes. A spot on your couch for the next six months, no. Don't hesitate to demand some definitive action if a sibling-in-law is fundamentally disrupting your relationship. Don't make the rules—or have the discussion—yourself. As with all family matters, to each his own.

# Thank-you rules

*Q. Is it okay to send thank-you notes via e-mail?*

A. Although the handwritten note is still the preferred method, e-mailing a thank-you note is better than not sending one at all. Send an e-mail to acknowledge a small gift or gesture, but make it as heartfelt as you would a handwritten card. Don't use Web abbreviations (LOL, BTW, etc.), and be sure to sign your name at the end. However, when it comes to wedding and shower gifts, a handwritten card is a must!

friend had to follow your rules. Of course you'd give that tactic a last go and "forbid" her to leave the state!

**DEAL WITH THE DISCOMFORT, GRACEFULLY.** Since you're the newest major element of your spouse's life, it can be easy for them to associate the move with you (or, as you experience it, to blame you). The good news is, you're an adult and your spouse is an adult. That means you're hardwired with the ability to make your own decisions—even the ones that mean choosing something different from what your mom and dad would want for you. It also means that even if you're upset by another person's decision (and we're talking about MIL and FIL now), you've got the capacity to get over it and adjust.

## RELIGION

**Why it's an issue:** There's no topic touchier and less negotiable for many families than religion. By definition, most people think that their religion is the one way. How you practice as a couple can be a huge sticking point if you and your spouse were raised with different values.

### Saving-grace solutions

**DEFINE YOUR FAITH.** You and your spouse need to decide together how religion will play out in your lives. Whether one of you is converting, you're both joining a more moderate church, or your spouse is devout and you're practicing watching Sunday-morning cartoons, you have to put away your own religious differences or the in-laws will use it as an opening to press their own arguments.

**BE FORTHRIGHT.** Talk it over as thoroughly as you can so that when you or your partner say, "We've decided to explore our respective religions separately for now," or

# Coping with a Major Loss

When you get the news that an in-law, no matter how distant, has passed away, here's how to help your mate.

**BECOME A DRIVING FORCE.** No one ever really knows how to act when someone they love dies, but since your spouse is even closer to the situation than you are, he or she may be paralyzed. It's really helpful for you to step in and take over, even if you don't feel certain you're doing the right thing (don't worry, it's hard to do the wrong thing in a situation like this). Snap into action, finding out as much information as you can. Call his relatives to learn things like when services will be held and whether it would be helpful for them to have you guys there for an extra day or two. Ask them if *they* need help making arrangements or notifying other friends and family. If they do, they'll tell you, and then what you can do is obvious. Finally, make travel arrangements and help pack (if you two are that kind of couple).

**LISTEN.** Grief is unpredictable, and a spouse who seems unfazed may break down months later at the sight of something that reminds him or her of the departed. It's okay to ask questions like, "What do you miss most about so-and-so?" and "When do you find yourself thinking about so-and-so?" These open-ended questions are always appropriate and will help your partner feel he or she can talk about the loved one without being morbid or a downer. Also, understand that men and women talk about their sadness differently. Men may have fewer words, and women may sound like they want advice when really they're venting. It's important to be open and not try to "solve" issues of death for your spouse, since there are no easy answers.

**REMEMBER THE PERSON.** Create unique ways to honor the memory of your loved one as a couple and family, whether it's by celebrating a birthday, saying a mass, or another fitting tribute.

**ASK FOR HELP YOURSELF.** If the relative was someone also close to you, you'll be dealing with your own emotions surrounding the death. Talking with friends who've been through similar situations can be cathartic, and it keeps the pressure of your grief off of your spouse, who's probably too emotional to be able to provide substantial support.

# Religious Riff

Q. I didn't grow up with a connection to any particular religon, but my husband and his family were really involved in their church, so he thinks I should just go with him to keep the peace. I feel like a hypocrite attending every week and saying things I don't necessarily believe. What should I do?

A. This is an area where you always need to be gentle, but also upfront with your husband. Tell him if you're open to exploring their religon, but aren't ready to make a full-on commitment (no need to let them think your attendence on Sunday has sealed the deal) and think about making an appointment to talk to the clerics or going to a new-member class to see what this church is all about. If you know religon will never play a big role in your life, be honest about that, too. Tell your husband and his family in a way that let's everyone know that you respect their beliefs even if you don't share them. You might be able to participate in church-related events that aren't actually religious (cookouts, wine and cheese parties, volunteer projects, etc.). This way, you'll get to support your husband's beliefs and spend time with his family doing things they care about while still being true to yourrself.

"We're both very spiritual and appreciate the lessons from that church, but we're practicing in our own way," it sounds honest. "She wants me to go to her church" is passing the buck for the most personal and important of decisions and may encourage in-laws to blame you for steering their baby onto the path of damnation—hardly the right message you want to send.

FIND COMMON GROUND. Being honest and unwavering is your best bet in the situation, but there are other ways you can go about letting the in-laws know that your decision isn't made out of disrespect. You can make an effort to read or learn about their religion and join them in their services while you're a guest in their home.

If they do bring up the subject of religion, ask why it means so much to them, and then share your own experiences of how your chosen brand of religion honors those same virtues (whether you're Anglican, Wiccan, or anything in between, most religions promote being kind to other people, giving thanks for what you've got, and trying to be a good person—hardly radical, huh?).

GO TO CHURCH. And if your parents really keep pushing, go old-school and do something they can understand, setting up a meeting with the four of you and your pastor. A pastor's built-in authority tends to appeal to parent types, and he or she has the experience to answer any questions unflappably and to assuage any doubts they may have. At the very least, letting them see you in a religious space will help them realize that your new choice of church isn't an excuse to get away from them, but a real place where you do worship.

Once a couple gets to the bottom of how they want and need to be treated by each other's families, they can make sure to nurture the parts of the relationship that are being tested; *and* they will be more likely to anticipate when they need to draw boundaries with their *own* siblings and parents.

## . . . . AND OTHER UNSOLICITED ADVICE

**Why it's an issue:** You marry into this family of strangers and all of a sudden they know what's best for you (you should get that hangnail surgically removed, you should drive forty miles on a Saturday morning to check out some bargain basement, you should switch to organic soap so your clothes don't smell so flowery). Yes, from financial investments to which grocery store you frequent, your in-laws are going to be chock full of "helpful" tidbits.

**Saving-grace solutions**

You have three options when their subtle suggestions become oppressive:

DO EVERYTHING THEY SAY and continue to beat yourself up when, no matter how hard you try to be perfect, they still find something new you "should" do.

IGNORE ALL THEIR SUGGESTIONS and risk having them think you don't respect their experience or insights (and look snobby).

OR REALIZE THAT THEY'VE GOT DECADES MORE LIFE EXPERIENCE and set personalities and are probably just as "helpful" to their friends, priests, and the checkout girl. That's right, meddling advice is usually not an attack on you but a way for your in-laws to feel useful and smart and make conversation. And if they do go from helpful to harping on a particular topic, you should already have the skills from earlier in this chapter to thank them gracefully but assure them you have the situation under control.

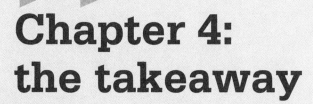

# Chapter 4:
# the takeaway

Three steps you can take right away to smoothly navigate the dangerous waters of in-law discord:

**Promise to never side with an in-law against your mate.** No matter how rough things are between your spouse and your parent, the one thing that will make it a million times worse if is you go along with a parent's criticism of your spouse. Read more rules to remember on page 135.

**Understand how your families are different.** He may never comprehend why your mom has to check in with you every day; you may never understand why his father insists on rearranging all your furniture. Stop taking it personally and realize that your families are set in their ways. See more VIP family secrets on page 136.

**Take turns calling dibs on holidays.** It's hard telling *any* family member that you're not going to be there for Thanksgiving/Christmas/Flag Day, and it gets worse if your family feels they're competing with your spouse's for rights to your smiling faces. To make it fair for both of you—and give you an unassailable excuse to use with the in-laws—simply alternate which of you is in charge of big holidays. Find out how to tackle other big controversies on page 146.

# [ sex ]

**How great is being married?** You get to have a best friend with benefits—forever. But staying on the same page in the bedroom department is not as easy as it seems, no matter how in sync you feel now. Issues arise. And keeping that lovin' feelin' alive long after your first anniversary can be one of the biggest challenges to connubial bliss. Your insurance policy? Making sex a pet project.

## the nest test:
# your sex secrets

The quickest way to better sex? Confessions. So ask each other these questions. Hint: It might be a good idea to do this before bed.

## 1. What do you consider great sex?

**2. What do you love most about our sex life?**

**3. Fess up: your ultimate sex fantasy?**

**4. In a perfect world, how often would you want to do it?**

**5. Ever feel insecure about yourself in bed?**

## 6. Anything I do that you wish I didn't?

**7. Whips? Costumes? What won't you try?**

# let's talk about sex

If you had to choose one thing to focus on in your relationship, it should be communication. It's not just talking that's important, it's *how* you talk and what you say—you have to be able to tell your partner if you're not pleased, feel unequal, or are having a physical problem in bed.

Still, even the best communicators have trouble talking about "it." Sex is a sticky subject. Even the most liberal individuals don't chat much about things like foreplay. At the other end of the spectrum, plenty of people are still raised to believe sex is an inappropriate topic for conversation and saying any related words out loud makes them embarrassed. Lastly, there's the common misconception that sex is just too sensitive a topic to bring up; it's better to suffer in silence than risk hurting your mate's feelings.

Many people assume that if their partner *could* please them, they would have by now, right? Well, we want to flip that notion on its head: Instead of thinking it's an insult to tell your spouse what you want, we say it's an insult *not* to. After all, this person has pledged to spend the rest of his or her life making you happy—do you really think your mate will refuse to give you what you want if he or she knows what it is?! We're going to tell you exactly how to say it.

## BRINGING UP THE BIG ISSUES

When it comes to topics like sexual dysfunction, trying new things, or comparing notes on libidos, it's smart to do it outside of an intimate encounter. Whether you're dropping the "I haven't had an orgasm in two years" bomb or just want to suggest new uses for those leather restraints left over from your rodeo days, approach the topic anywhere but the bedroom. You don't want any confrontational associations with the actual sex act. Remember that and these other talking tips.

**Make it about you.** Reassure him or her before you suggest any sort of disenchantment so there are no defensive feelings. Compare how you'd feel if someone said, "You have some sort of problem climaxing—you should see a doctor," vs. "I love you, I love having sex with you, I love when you come. I'm concerned that you're not, lately, though—what can I do to help?" Always broach the topic with a question that makes it clear you consider it an issue for you both to work on—not one person alone.

# Remember the Romance

Sensuality isn't fluff or made-up fairy-tale expectations: Fueling your love life with romance is a key factor in feeling close . . . and frisky. Here, our quickie ways to getting romantic—minus the cheese factor.

PLAN AHEAD TO PLAY HOOKY. Call your honey's boss and schedule a day off for him or her. When that day rolls around, surprise your spouse with the no-work news and a day's worth of things you plan to do . . . together.

IT'S SHOWTIME. Find out when your mate's favorite band is coming to town and preorder tix. If the nearest show is in another city, make a weekend out of it—double the romantic impact.

SEND A MESSAGE. Flowers are an easy fallback, but with a coded message they become part of an intriguing seduction. Plan to send flowers every Thursday for one month; with the first, enclose a card with the start of your sentence: "I can't wait to see you in . . ." The next arrangement will arrive with a note that says: "the bedroom wearing . . ." You get the point.

TURN BACK THE PAGE. Find a page in your journal from when you first met. Photocopy it, send it via snail mail, or have it framed.

ROLE REVERSAL. He bakes cookies; she brings him chocolates. Being caught off-guard can be supremely sensual in its own right.

YOUNG AT HEART (AND OTHER PARTS). Think back to decades past: When you were young and didn't go all the way, you sure did whatever you could to get any kind of action, right? Try pulling out all those same stops and you'll wind up with cute ways to bond that don't involve anything that would get you grounded.

Also, confess your feelings: "I hate when you fall asleep on the couch" can sound like a nag, while "I know it's crazy, but I feel rejected and like you aren't interested in me sexually when you don't come to bed." That makes it clear you're not just picking a fight; you're responding to your feelings, and it gives your mate a share of the responsibility in finding a solution.

**Do it when you're in a good mood.** Sex can be an emotional topic, and talking about it when you're frustrated or, worse, already fighting, means the conversation's more likely to dissolve into accusations or an argument. The last thing you want your honey to think is that you're *blaming* him or her because of a sexual problem (even if it's true); it'll create a self-defeating cycle of anger and distance, not the closeness you want.

**Put some booty behind it!** After you've had a serious talk, always end it on a light-hearted note and reassure your mate you're happy to just be talking about it. If you have the chance, it can't hurt to go for a round later that day, just so there's no misinterpretation that you're not interested in it anymore. It lets your spouse know that while you may want to better a certain part of your partnership, you're far from unhappy with it as is.

## Time Out

# Toy Shop

**Don't let saving your sex life be a chore. Here's how to get giggling again:**

Take an afternoon and wander with your honey through a sex store. Look at different toys, from ones you're secretly curious about to ones you never knew existed. It's a fun way to find out whether you may have some shared fantasies, and it'll rev you up to be surrounded by sexaphanalia—just wait until you get home! Too shy for the store? There are plenty of sites online, including Drugstore.com, that will discreetly mail you your novelties.

## TALKING ABOUT BED *IN* BED

Regardless of your own communication style or that of your partner, there are ways to communicate in bed about immediate, intimate topics.

Sailor-mouthed spouses may have no trouble yelling out their desires, but it can come across as bossy to a partner. On the other hand, if a shy guy or gal thinks that moans of pleasure mean, "Keep doing that!" while the other thinks someone's getting sore, neither of you will get what you want. Our "best ways" (below), are clear and direct enough to make your point, as well as loving and discreet enough to avoid horrible embarrassment to the faint of heart. Of course, if you two are superverbal, you can up the intensity of your sex talk as needed.

### Finding Out What Your Lover Likes

Bossy way: "What do you want me to do now?"

Bashful way: "Mmmmmmmmmmmm?" [Hummed to the tune of "Is that what you wanted?"]

Best way: "I love making you happy—show me exactly where you want my hands and mouth right now."

### Asking for Something You Want

Bossy way: "Blank my blank."

Bashful way: "Hmmmm." [Keeps repositioning self in hopes that the partner will get the hint.]

Best way: "Oh that feels so amazing—I'd love it if you put your blank right blank my blank."

### Telling Your Partner You Don't Want Something

Bossy way: "Gross. No way."

Bashful way: [Squirms away.]

Best way: "I'm not totally sure I'm ready for that; I might need some coaxing."

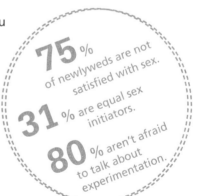

### Saying It Feels Good

Bossy way: "Finally, something works!"

Bashful way: [Silence, hoping if you don't say or do anything, your mate will keep on trucking.]

Best way: "Don't stop." It's verbal encouragement that not only gets your point across, but gives your partner a major ego boost.

# the nest married sex strategy

How do you keep sex at the top of your to-do list? In a counterintuitively unromantic way. You need to create your own personal sex plan. Together. Think of it as your sex schedule—your way of ensuring sex is a priority and as good (and frequent) as it should be. Hey, studies show sex declines in the first two years of marriage. If you don't want to join them, beat them.

## STEP 1: LAY OUT YOUR CARDS

**Frequency:** If your spouse wants it five times a week but you know good and well you're too busy, come up with a number. Start gradually—say, one or two more times a week than you're currently doing it, then build up. Realistic goals guarantee you don't fall short your first week and give up.

**Vary your location:** No married couple is going to have swinging-from-the-foyer-chandelier sex seven days a week, so make your goals practical: "For every four times in the bedroom, we'll hook up one time somewhere else."

**Timing it right:** Does one of you snore through late-night routines? Does the other stay half-asleep during prework quickies? Figure out what your own weak spots are, and then create a sex goal about the time of day.

**Foreplay:** Does every session feel the same? Make it a goal to engage in foreplay for fifteen minutes before going all the way. The extra time will guarantee you don't just go through your motions. Challenge yourself to add variety any time you create a new goal; for example, for every half-hour of fore-play, try to have one quickie another time during the week. (It also makes cajoling your buddy into it easier if he or she knows there's instant gratification in it for both of you.)

**Positions:** Promise one another you'll have oral sex at least once a week, or vow to alternate who's on top—whatever you need to break out of your patterns.

> "I used to laugh when I read those statistics that said the average couple has sex once a week. Not me, I swore. Now try once a month."
> —MrMomOH

## tip
Studies show the more you have sex, the more you want to have sex, and the more satisfied you'll be.

## STEP 2: NAME YOUR PLAN

Use a shared sex-talk vocabulary to create a fun name for your sex project. That way you can write "Operation Daily Show" in his planner or talk about "The Moo Shoo

(continues on page 176)

# [?] Quiz
# is your sex life in sync?

Take this quiz together and find out if life between the sheets needs a tweak.

### 1. What's your idea of sexy lingerie?

**a.** A silk chemise.

**b.** Flannel pj bottoms with a tank top.

**c.** Something latex.

### 2. Your idea of an exciting new sex toy is:

**a.** A piece of chocolate passed back and forth between your mouths as you kiss.

**b.** Your spouse.

**c.** Something that most people wouldn't even think of as a sex toy!

### 3. Paging through *The Joy of Sex*, you see a position that strikes your fancy. What would you do about it?

**a.** I'd stick a note on the page and leave it on my honey's bedside table.

**b.** Like I'd really be reading that!

**c.** I've already tried everything in *The Joy of Sex*. Twice!

4. Let's say your new bed hasn't been delivered yet, but you've tossed the old one. Where will you do it in the meantime?

   **a.** In the guest room—so we can pretend we're at a bed-and-breakfast.

   **b.** This is so inconvenient, I don't know.

   **c.** In the car—the police might come at any moment!

5. What's the sexiest thing about you?

   **a.** My overactive brain and the things it comes up with.

   **b.** My smile.

   **c.** My collection of naughty DVDs.

6. If your sex drive were an animal, it'd be:

   **a.** A lion—prowling and pouncing.

   **b.** A deer—elusive but magical.

   **c.** A monkey—up for anything and utterly crazy!

7. Your spouse suggests you make love with a mirror next to the bed. What's your reaction?

   **a.** My partner can look, but I think I'll just concentrate on how things feel.

   **b.** Oh, sure—as long as the reflective side is facing the wall!

   **c.** I'll see your mirror and raise you a video camera!

(continued on next page)

**8. When do you like to make love?**

a. When I'm awake.

b. When my partner suggests it.

c. If I could figure out how to do it when asleep, I'd do that, too!

**9. How often do you try to switch things up in the sack?**

a. I stick with what works, but am open to suggestions.

b. Switch up? Switch up what?!

c. I rarely do it the same way twice.

**10. When it comes to talking dirty, what's your policy?**

a. I like it rated PG-13.

b. Never! Feel stupid doing it, feel icky hearing it.

c. Your ears would melt if you heard what comes out of my mouth.

**11. If you found out your partner had some naughty magazines or movies, what would you do?**

a. Accept it as something she/he likes and suggest using them for inspiration.

b. Pretend I'd never seen them and probably feel a little weird about it.

c. Jump with joy and suggest we combine our libraries.

# individual results

## mostly **as**
### True Romantic
You're comfortable balancing common sense with your coy side, so you can pull out the oh-so-steamy stops when you or your partner really want it, but you don't try to get hot and heavy when you can tell the time's not right.

## mostly **bs**
### Reserved Romantic
You're not that into the spectacle of sex. This doesn't mean you don't love sex—you just don't need novelty positions, exclamations of dirty talk, and public ickiness to express your libido.

## mostly **Cs**
### Sexed-up Spouse
Getting horizontal (and vertical, backward, and inside-out) with your partner is still one of your favorite ways to spend time together.

- - - - - - - - - - - - - - - - - - - - - - - - - - - - - - - -

# your couple combo

## a&a: Normal Nuzzlers
Sometimes one of you wants it, sometimes the other one does. The biggest lesson to learn is that if your partner seems tired or uninterested, it doesn't mean he or she doesn't want you—he or she just needs to be turned on first. Keep exploring your partner's pleasure buttons like you did when you first got together and you'll not only get the sex you want, but you'll also build a stronger bond.

## a&b: Driven Duo
As a couple, you've got the drive to have a satisfying sex life, but syncing up your libidos is another story. If you're the partner who wants it more, remember that while your mate may be just as happy not to do it, that doesn't mean he or she is rejecting *you*. If you're the more low-key spouse, be supportive when you put off your partner's advances. Instead of saying "not now," specify *when* would be better, and don't be afraid to detail what you need to be in the mood (in a nice way of course).

## a&C: Peppy Paramours
You've both got the desire for an active, ongoing sex life, and with the wild one's imagination, making that come true should be a breeze. The libidinous lover can take the lead, making sure to be sensitive to the more middle-ground one's needs and roadblocks. If you're the less lusty spouse, show your honey how much you appreciate his or her nonstop action by planning (or at least initiating) some nookie yourself.

## b&b: Cool Couple
You're far from frigid—you're just not sex obsessed. Of course, sex is an important element in any permanent partnership, and the truth is, if you're both totally passive about passing out once your heads hit the pillows, you could see your sex life dwindle away entirely. Just make sure your schedule leaves you at least a few minutes a week when you'll have the energy to work up some good old-fashioned lust.

## b&C: Attractive Opposites
Caution: Sometimes you feel like the world's last remaining idealists/realists. He or she won't always be as in the mood (or not) as you, and you can't take it personally when your spouse needs prep time. The high-libido one can help the other infuse sex into daily life; the low-libido one can show their partner other ways of expressing intimacy.

## C&C: Steamy Sweeties
Let the neighbors know nobody's being hurt! You're both super in touch with your sexuality, so trying new things or convincing the other to do it is never a problem. But realize that there may come a time when your partner wants to just—gasp—snuggle, and it won't be a reflection on you. Put as much importance on your life outside the sheets as you do between the sheets, and you two are set for life!

(continued from page 171)

Plan" out loud on the phone. Nobody else will know what you're talking about, but the words alone will give you a sexual thrill that will increase the energy between you two once your actual encounter starts.

## STEP 3: PRIORITIZE YOUR PASSION

In other words, how often will you do it? You have to work late. The house is a mess. Your favorite show is on. These may sound like reasons for relegating sex to the bottom of the to-do list, but they're not. Think of sex as being as essential to your health as oral hygiene. Agree to set aside time for sex on a regular basis, to be mutually agreed upon, then schedule it like you would any other commitment.

## STEP 4: STAY ON TRACK

What good is all this planning if you forget about it two weeks later? Not much.

**Be goal-oriented.** Just aiming for "more sex" won't necessarily improve things—setting specifics about what kind of sex you want or where will guarantee you get what you want. And once you hit your targets, switch your targets. Whether it's increasing the frequency by one or subbing "kitchen-table sex" for "morning quickie," changing your plan monthly helps ensure you won't fall into another boring pattern.

**28.1** minutes is the length of the average sex session in America. **17.2** minutes is the global average.

**Plan to put effort into it.** As that fabulous New Year's weight-loss plan you immediately shelved may have proved, you can't declare you're going on a program and assume results will follow. Having better sex is going to require time, both for the execution and the planning. Sure, you may not have as many hours to spend prepping for book club or to work out, but with all the calories you'll be burning in the bedroom, you won't care.

**Take turns keeping score.** If only one of you is in charge of making sure you make every "appointment," the other partner can get big complexes—like "Geez, I must be a terrible spouse if she has to nag for sex," "Oh here we go, checking another shag off the list," or "Well, we have to make sure you get what *you* want, huh?" Skip these worries completely by having one of you create a list of goals for two weeks and having the other make sure you reach all the aims. The second half of the month, switch.

This kind of shared responsibility shows that you both care about the other's feelings and that you're serious about making sure you each get what you want.

**Repeat a mantra.** A pro-you slogan that only you know can help get you in the mood when you're feeling too tired to bother with sex. Just come up with a sentence that describes your ideal sex life and how working for it makes you feel: "I'm a sexy devil and I *deserve* sex as often as I want it!" or "I'm still so in love with my mate that I can't keep my hands off [him or her]." Whether it's demure or dirty, just thinking the words in the middle of the workday will instantly amp you up and get you reexcited about your sex life.

**Re-create your routine.** As you experiment, you're going to rediscover the sexual pleasures that you love. Whether it's doing it in the shower or on Monday mornings before the workweek, try to incorporate anything you enjoy into your everyday life—even if it's not written into your "plan." You stopped having sex because you got into the habit of not doing it—if you get into the habit of having it as much as you want it, soon you won't need a reminder!

## Mr. & Mrs. Manners

# Hiding Porn?

Q. I walked in on my husband surfing porn sites. He assured me that it was no big deal, but then, a couple days later, I went online and "noticed" that he had been on them again. Should I be worried?

A. You should definitely speak up. When couples keep secrets from each other, especially sex secrets, it only hurts the relationship. He may be afraid of hurting you, so tell him that you're okay with his interest in porn, you're just uncomfortable with the lying. Assure him that there's nothing to hide. If your sex life is good, you should *never* take your husband's porn tastes to be a reflection on you (i.e., "He's got a mag called *Big Rack City* and I'm an A-cup!"). And consider your find a blessing—now you know what he fantasizes about, which is just part of knowing your man inside and out!

# getting birth under control

Even if you've been on the pill for eight years, once it's official that you're STD free, you can reassess your birth control method and see if a new one is right for the two of you.

## BARRIER METHODS

**Male condoms** Most of us have used them before and know the drill. Condoms come in many varieties—from mint flavored to lubricated, from latex to natural skin, from "Magnums" to "ribbed for her pleasure."

PRESCRIPTION NEEDED: No

EFFECTIVENESS: 85 to 98 percent (when used correctly and consistently every time)

UPSIDE: Doesn't play with hormone levels. Plus, they're the only birth control method that wards off sexually transmitted diseases.

DOWNSIDE: May not feel as good.

WHY COUPLES MAKE THE SWITCH: Many women choose to go off the pill in preparation for trying to get pregnant, while condoms are a low-cost way to make sure she stays without child until she's definitely ready.

**Female condoms** The female condom looks like a jumbo male condom, but it lines the vagina and stays in place with a diaphragmlike ring that fits over the cervix. Note: Female condoms should not be used at the same time as a male condom because the friction between the two may cause them both to break.

PRESCRIPTION NEEDED: No

EFFECTIVENESS: 79 to 95 percent (when used correctly and consistently every time)

UPSIDE: Allows for more spontaneity in sex—it can be inserted a few hours before.

DRAWBACK: The outer ring is visible outside the vagina.

WHY COUPLES MAKE THE SWITCH: If they're married to the idea of a condom but annoyed by not having one on hand, the pre-sex insertion makes this a favorite.

**Diaphragms** Soft, latex, bowl-shaped devices that slip into the vagina to cover the cervix and are usually used with spermicide. The cost varies but is in the $20 to $30 range plus the cost of the exam and the spermicide; can be used for up to three years.

PRESCRIPTION NEEDED: Yes

EFFECTIVENESS: 84 to 94 percent

UPSIDE: Like the female condom, it doesn't interrupt your "moment"—it can be inserted hours ahead of time.

DOWNSIDE: May cause a woman to develop frequent bladder infections.

WHY COUPLES MAKE THE SWITCH: It's a low-effort, no-hormone method with condom-level effectiveness rates.

**Cervical caps** Similar in method and price to diaphragms, sailor's hat–shaped cervical caps come in silicone and in several sizes. They go over the cervix and are to be used with spermicide.

PRESCRIPTION NEEDED: Yes

EFFECTIVENESS: 71 to 86 percent

## Time to Get Tested

The scariest part of STDs (sexually transmitted diseases) is that they can lie dormant for years undetected or undiagnosed. That's why, if you haven't already, you and your spouse should check in with the doctor. Both men and women should get tested for HIV and other STDs, including herpes, hepatitis B, gonorrhea, chlamydia, syphilis, and HPV (human papilloma virus, also known as genital warts), which affects 75 percent of sexually active people, and if left untreated, can lead to cervical cancer and may cause complications during pregnancy.

UPSIDE: Can be kept in place and maintain effectiveness for up to two days.

DOWNSIDE: Might dislodge from the cervix during sex.

WHY COUPLES MAKE THE SWITCH: Once they've been together, couples aren't as embarrassed about talking about having to go put it in—it's still a bit inconvenient, but sensation-wise, it's a big step up from the condom.

**Vaginal spermicides** Spermicides come in several forms, including foams, creams, jellies, suppositories, and films, and are often used with the sponge, condoms, diaphragms, or cervical caps. Most contain nonoxynol-9 and all are inserted into the vagina before sex.

PRESCRIPTION NEEDED: No

EFFECTIVENESS: About 71 to 85 percent for spermicide alone, but they're best used with another method like condoms, diaphragms, or cervical caps.

UPSIDE: They're a good back-up method in the case of missed pills or the condom breaking.

DOWNSIDE: Some people are allergic to benzalkonium chloride, nonoxynol-9, or octoxynol-9, which are commonly found in most spermicides.

WHY COUPLES MAKE THE SWITCH: It's an unusual choice for long-term couples, but can be effective when condoms are disliked.

# Topic:
# what's your best sex advice?

**HAVE SEX DURING THE DAY**—and not just in the bedroom. —stellasmom

# Sleep naked.
—uncannycanuck

# Keep things fresh and new.
—malepointofview

**HAVE YOU TRIED WATCHING DIRTY MOVIES?** It helps us sometimes.
—lovinlife430

# Don't compare yourselves to other couples.
,,
—Maybride2

''

I think it's necessary to be able to laugh at yourselves and not take yourselves too seriously.
—ABowden4Life

**DON'T BE AFRAID TO TRY NEW THINGS** —THEY MIGHT FEEL GREAT AND YOU MIGHT LOVE THEM. —Mrs.Ian

**nest note:** Nowhere is it written that a healthy marriage requires x amount of sex per week. Everyone's preferences are different, so do what works best for you and your spouse.

## HORMONE-BASED METHODS

The pill and similar birth control methods rack up some of the highest effectiveness ratings around. But these methods don't protect against STDs, so make sure you both have been tested.

**Oral contraceptives** Also known as the pill. This method usually combines two hormones, similar to estrogen and progesterone (in various amounts), to stop ovulation entirely.

PRESCRIPTION NEEDED: Yes

EFFECTIVENESS: 92 to 99 percent

UPSIDE: Less cramping during menstruation, lower benign-breast-disease rates, and, sometimes, clearer skin.

DOWNSIDE: Weight gain and a lessened libido. Can cause rare but potentially fatal blood clots.

WHY COUPLES MAKE THE SWITCH: Once they're monogamous, many people prefer taking one pill each day to fumbling around with a barrier method during each encounter.

**Vaginal rings** This small ring (about 2 inches in diameter) is inserted into the vagina and left in for three weeks—a good option for those who have trouble remembering to take a daily pill. It releases a slow and constant stream of hormones to prevent pregnancy. It's removed for a week during the menstrual period, and then a new ring is used.

PRESCRIPTION NEEDED: Yes

## Mr. & Mrs. Manners

# Sex at the In-laws'

Q: The thought of her parents hearing us at it is a huge turn-off for me—but she doesn't seem to care. Is it really appropriate to fornicate in her father's house?

A: While it can be a rush—taking you back to high school and possibly getting caught by your parents—you are adults now. How uncomfortable would it be for your spouse's parents to catch you in the act? Why not skip it altogether and wait till after your visit? Having a few days with a between-the-sheets separation will fill you with anticipation and make the sex better when you get home.

EFFECTIVENESS: 99 percent

UPSIDE: Good for those who have trouble remembering to take a daily pill.

DOWNSIDE: It can be removed for up to three hours, but any more than that and you'll have to use another form of birth control for a week after reinserting the ring.

WHY COUPLES MAKE THE SWITCH: It's a fairly new development, which some couples might only learn about when they're reexploring their options.

**The patch** Works just like the pill but a patch is put on the stomach, back, arm, or rear. It's changed once a week for three weeks, and then removed during a woman's period.

PRESCRIPTION NEEDED: Yes

EFFECTIVENESS: Up to 99.7 percent

UPSIDE: Another option for forgetful ones.

DOWNSIDE: May not be as effective for obese women.

WHY COUPLES MAKE THE SWITCH: It requires less remembering than the pill and may work for women who have tried several types of pill and been unhappy with the side effects.

**tip**
If you're thinking bambinos are in your future, you might want to make sure your gynecologist also practices obstetrics so you can build your rapport with the doc before your pregnancy.

**Contraceptive injection** This contraceptive is a slow-releasing, long-acting shot injected into your booty or upper arm. It's effective for three months and costs about $30 per shot, plus the OB/GYN visit.

PRESCRIPTION NEEDED: Yes, a doctor injects the shot.

EFFECTIVENESS: 97 to 99.7 percent

UPSIDE: Just progestin—good for women who can't take estrogen.

DOWNSIDE: It's not immediately reversible. You must wait until the three-month supply is out of your system before toasting a bun in the oven. Plus, can cause spotting.

WHY COUPLES MAKE THE SWITCH: It's reliable like the pill but you only have to think about it four times a year instead of twenty-one times a month.

**Intrauterine device (IUD)** Studies show that today's IUDs are safer and more effective than their predecessors and have one of the highest long-term satisfaction rates among different types of contraceptives. A small piece of plastic is placed into the uterus and makes the lining less receptive to fertilized eggs. Some slowly release hormones; other copper ones prevent implantation—but researchers aren't sure how. Recommended for women who have at least one child.

PRESCRIPTION NEEDED: A health-care provider fits the device.

# Tricks Every Couple Should Try

**And remember, if you haven't done it in the last year or two, it counts as new to you! (Well, sort of . . . )**

**TAKE IT OUTSIDE.** It doesn't matter whether you're isolated in the middle of the woods or sneaking out on your balcony at midnight, being partially exposed will take you back to the thrill of your early encounters.

**HAVE SOME LONG-DISTANCE FOREPLAY.** Whether your significant other is calling you on a cell phone from the grocery store two blocks away or e-mailing you from a business trip across the country, it's a turn-on for you both to remember just how hot you make each other. A little dirty talk or just an out-of-the-blue, "Remember last night when you had my leg around your neck? That was fun," will give him an unexpected thrill.

**TOUCH YOURSELF.** Taking turns masturbating in front of each other gives you a rare distanced view of what turns your spouse on, and it's also wildly arousing just watching your partner get off. Not to mention that you both know you'll get touched exactly how you want.

**STAND UP.** In real life, vertical sex rarely goes as seamlessly as it does in movies, but there's still something irresistible about this gotta-have-you-here-and-now position. Brace yourself against a wall as he enters you to make sure you're both stabilized before attempting anything more acrobatic.

**TRY A TOY OR TWO.** It doesn't matter if it's a silly pink feather or a purple twelve-inch vibrating god-knows-what, you can always accessorize. Even trying a flavored or warming lube makes for hotter play. If it goes over well, upgrade to something more daring next time.

EFFECTIVENESS: 99 percent

UPSIDE: A hormone IUD can last up to five years; a copper IUD lasts up to twelve years.

DOWNSIDE: Copper IUDs may cause an increase in cramps and heavier and longer periods.

WHY COUPLES MAKE THE SWITCH: If a couple's certain they don't want to get pregnant for a few years, this is a one-stop device that requires little to no maintenance.

## "NATURAL" BIRTH CONTROL

**Rhythm** Watch the calendar and avoid sex when you think the woman is most fertile. One product that can make counting days easier is CycleBeads, a color-coded string of beads that helps track fertility during the month.

EFFECTIVENESS: 75 to 99 percent effective—but it requires expert training and no cheating.

UPSIDE: Less expensive.

DOWNSIDE: Abstinence for nine or more days per cycle, which can be a real drag if you two are hot and horny newlyweds (also, women are generally most horny during their fertile periods).

WHY COUPLES MAKE THE SWITCH: Religious couples who don't believe in birth control pioneered it, but it's also popular among couples who have stopped having frequent sex or who are trying to do it organic style and hormone-free.

"Sure I often wish that we had sex more often and envy the girls who claim to have it every other day. But most days we just don't have the energy, and I think that sex would feel like a chore if we 'made' ourselves do it. So I'm okay with that." —May2C010

**Withdrawal** Also known by its fancier Latin name, *coitus interruptus,* withdrawal is exactly that—withdrawing before ejaculation.

EFFECTIVENESS: 73 to 96 percent

UPSIDE: Won't cost a dime.

DOWNSIDE: Requires you to stop right when he's about to really enjoy himself; timing is key.

WHY COUPLES MAKE THE SWITCH: It's cheap and doesn't have the physical side effects of other birth controls.

## EMERGENCY CONTRACEPTION

So, you got carried away last night (or you forgot your pills or the condom broke or . . .). There is an after-the-fact contraceptive option, which usually consists of several birth control pills.

HOW IT WORKS: Taken within seventy-two hours of the sexual encounter, the pills reduce the risk of pregnancy by 75 percent. Don't confuse them with RU 486 (the

# Preventing Post-Sex Distress

One in five women will suffer from urinary tract infections (UTI) in their lives—and for many the infections are recurring. According to the National Institutes of Health, 20 percent of women who have a UTI will have another. Here's what you need to know about dealing with them.

**WHAT THEY ARE:** UTIs are bacterial infections that start at the urethra (where urine comes out) and develop along the tract to the bladder.

**HOW YOU GET THEM:** Any behavior that allows bacteria to get in contact with the urethra can up the incidence of UTIs. Engaging in anal-to-vaginal sex is a huge risk, but even vigorous thrusting or wiping from back to front can cause UTIs. People with diabetes, women who use diaphragms, and women whose partners use condoms with spermicidal foam have also been found to get more UTIs. And if you're dehydrated, you're not washing the germs out of your body as you otherwise might, and you're more at risk for getting one.

**WHY THEY MATTER:** They're uncomfortable, and an unchecked infection can spread to the kidneys and, in rare cases, cause kidney failure.

**tip**
Antibiotics can affect your birth control pill, the patch, and a vaginal ring's effectiveness, so make sure to use backup during the time you're on antibiotics and in the weeks after.

**HOW YOU KNOW YOU HAVE ONE:** A sensation of burning when you're peeing and the constant feeling that you have to go—even when nothing comes out—are two of the most aggravating and common symptoms. You might even feel tired, shaky, and exhausted all day long. Weird-looking or –smelling urine is a red flag that something's wrong. A fever, nausea, pain in the lower back, or vomiting could indicate that the infection has reached the kidneys. A doctor can run a simple test to diagnose a UTI, and women with recurrent infections often get test strips they can use at home.

**HOW TO TREAT THEM:** A simple course of antibiotics usually wipes out the infection.

**HOW TO PREVENT THEM:** The goal—and the way nature designed our bodies to work anyway—is to keep a steady stream of sterile urine flowing out of the body and flushing away anything bad. You can aid that process by drinking tons of water, peeing after sex, taking showers instead of baths, getting lots of vitamin C (increasing the acid in your body makes bacteria less able to grow), wearing cotton undies that let your body breathe down there (that's right—camel toe is a health risk), and, yes, drinking cranberry juice (doctors aren't sure why, but it helps). Don't use douches or vaginal deodorant sprays, as they can irritate the area—as can some lotions, lubes, and bubble bath–type products. Some frequent sufferers take acidophilus or start their day with yogurt, a source of "good" bacteria.

"abortion pill"). They can't end a pregnancy that's already occurred (in fact, you'll take a pregnancy test before pills are prescribed).

**WHERE TO FIND IT:** Planned Parenthood, many health providers, or possibly your doctor.

**PRESCRIPTION NEEDED:** It's recommended to see a doctor instead of self-prescribing.

There are more permanent options for couples who don't want to have children. Tubal ligation or vasectomies are two surgical procedures that prevent pregnancy. However, in some cases, these procedures can be reversed.

From gag reflexes to strange bumps, we've got your answer. Go to: thenest.com/sexqa

# your sex problems . . . explained

There are tons of underlying issues that can contribute to either sexual dysfunction or total lack of drive altogether. No matter what the cause, though, rest assured that you're not alone. Universities have paid mountains of cash to fund studies that, time after time, prove what you already know: after the first few months or years of marriage, couples have less sex. We've divvied up reasons into three categories. These factors are the ones you need to work on as a couple:

Physical factors are directly linked to your bodies—they're either caused by a condition or a physical side effect of something else.

Psychological factors, even mild depression, can have a huge impact on sex life (and most people will suffer some form of mental illness at some point in their lifetime).

Romantic factors—it's no secret that as you two get more and more used to spending twenty-four hours a day together, you're going to spend less time on the wine-and-roses action and more time fuming about the dang toothpaste cap being off again. Without that stream of input, the sex drive can die down.

While some of these factors will need the help and input of a professional and are not self-inflicted, there are other sex suppressors that you can, and should, avoid if libido is flagging:

**Alcohol and other drugs:** While many drugs, including alcohol, can initially make users feel more in the mood, we've all experienced the lethargy that comes at the end of a long night of partying. Not only is excessive partying likely to leave you tired (especially if it's habitual), but since alcohol is a depressant, it numbs your nerve endings, making both men and women less likely to achieve an orgasm. Other drugs like cocaine seriously inhibit male performance. SEX SAVER: Decrease your intake (it's a healthy move, anyway).

**Anger:** Problems in your relationship can be a nasty sex-drive drainer. Maybe you're constantly fighting about your in-laws; or you're feeling unappreciated by your mate. Maybe he canceled date night *again*. Whatever your issue, anger toward your spouse is taking over your emotional state—and the last thing you want to do is something pleasurable with *this* person. SEX SAVER: You need to diffuse the anger. Pinpoint exactly what is making you so mad, and try to work it out with your spouse—calmly and rationally. (Skip to Chapter 7 for solid communication tips.) If you still can't get over the anger, consider seeing a couples counselor for professional help.

**Band-aid sex:** For couples who are bad at talking about their feelings, sex is a common way for them to reconnect, reassure each other after a rocky situation, or just prove that they're still really into each other. As time goes on, sex can become less useful as a temperature-taking tool, and that's a good thing, as long as it's replaced by more mature ways of feeding the relationship (like, er, talking). But if the issues are being left untouched and the sex is no longer used to demonstrate that the issue's been solved, those issues are likely to fester and affect your relationship altogether. SEX SAVER: When you feel inclined to cuddle away any issues that arise, don't wait to see if your partner is game. Instead, use that as your cue to yourself to say, "Listen, I know I was really mad earlier, but I think I

## Finding a Good MD

The best ones are always booked or don't take your health plan (or any insurance at all). Once again, ask friends, family, and coworkers for the scoop (and your spouse's coworkers and even their spouses). First check in with your health plan for leads in your 'hood. You can also consult Web services such as the American Medical Association (AMA-Assn.org) or WebMD.com for references and suggestions.

just wanted to get that out. I'm fine with what we resolved—do you have any more concerns about it?" (if it was a little fight) or, "I'm so happy we're married" (if it's just your lazy way of showing it).

**Body image:** The newlywed weight gain is an unspoken given, and its impact in the bedroom is twofold: First, most of us *feel* more self-conscious and less sexy if our weight is spiraling out of control, and second, new heft actually impacts the ability to perform. And it's a cycle: The less satisfied you are in bed, the more likely you are to drown your sorrows in ice cream. SEX SAVER: Work out. You don't have to aim for supermodel measurements, but just expending energy will not only help you burn extra calories but give you extra energy for things like, well, sex. Try it together—if you're not having sex, at least you'll become more intimate and comfortable with each other's bodies.

**Boring sex:** Most of us get into some lazy habits: hand goes here, legs go here, lick here, and done. But when your body just goes through the motions, your mind zones out, and you both feel unsatisfied. That's because the romantic element of the sex is gone. SEX SAVER: Forget missionary at 10:35 P.M. in the bedroom. Before setting the sexual goals from earlier in this chapter, spend one week doing it in every different way imaginable just to break out of the rut.

**Depression:** One of the physical manifestations of a depression—which, it should be noted, often has *nothing* to do with a patient's current circumstances—is a loss of interest in sex. With about 18.8 million adults suffering from the condition in any given one-year period, it's hardly unthinkable that a sudden bout could waylay your sex life. The good news is that depression is treatable, and the resultant low libido isn't permanent. SEX SAVER: See a doc—most family physicians can screen for depression, but since they don't see you every day, you'll need to ask them to check.

**Low libido:** All these factors listed affect your sex drive, but having a low libido could be a condition in itself. In the medical realm, there are several reasons why a woman may have a decreased libido, including the natural decline in the hormones of desire: estrogen and testosterone. SEX SAVER: Talk to your doctor. He or she may be able to prescribe low doses of these hormones. Also, there are some medications to improve a woman's sexual desire that are currently being studied and are undergoing the clinical trial process.

**Medication side effects:** The most talked-about libido-squashing side effects are from antidepressants, but they're far from the only ones: Meds for birth control, epilepsy, heart disease, prostate, high blood pressure, cholesterol, stomach problems,

# Get in Shape—Side by Side

**EXERCISE AS A DUO.** Research shows that you're more likely to stick to a workout regime if you're doing it with a buddy. Take a walk after dinner instead of watching TV, go for a bike ride on Saturday mornings instead of sleeping in, or join a softball league. Not only are you getting healthy—you're gaining valuable couple-time, too.

**TAKE A COOKING CLASS.** Learn how to cook healthy meals together, and make it a point to do the food shopping and meal prep as a team.

**BE DARING.** Pick activities that you might have been hesitant to tackle before, like going rollerblading or learning how to salsa. Tackling the "scary" stuff together can be a great bonding experience.

**GET A DOG!** Research shows that people who regularly walk their dogs are able to shed pounds and keep them off—just another reason to love man's best friend.

**BE EACH OTHER'S CHEERLEADER.** Make sure you compliment each other on even the smallest accomplishments—he lost three pounds, she made it two miles on the treadmill. Remember, that encouragement goes a long way in motivating you to stick with the program.

**INDULGE (SOMETIMES).** You can't deprive yourselves of the stuff you love 24/7, or one of you is bound to fall off the wagon. Once a week, reward yourselves with a treat. A great choice: dark chocolate. It's high in flavanoids, which have been shown to decrease LDL cholesterol and possibly protect you from some forms of cancer.

and insomnia have all been linked to sexual problems. Even over-the-counter allergy meds can affect your sex life—the same ingredients that dry out your sinuses can also decrease lubrication down there, making you not want to bother. SEX SAVER: If you suspect your medicine cabinet is interfering in the bedroom (either lowering your libido or causing physical problems like erectile dysfunction), ask your doctor to suggest some alternatives.

**Medical problems:** Inhibited sexual performance is often psychological, but changes, particularly sudden and dramatic ones, could indicate that something else is at play. Cancers, tissue damage, diabetes, high blood pressure, allergies, and thyroid disorders can all impact your ability to do it like you used to. SEX SAVER: Head to your respective doctors and report the big change—that'll help determine what the causes may be and prompt questions about any other symptoms that may help with a diagnosis.

**Stress:** Stress, depression, and fatigue are often linked, but when you're stressed, you're too preoccupied—with the problems you're having at work, in your personal life, with money—to focus enough to enjoy sex. You may feel unable to connect with your partner, or too upset about a perceived failure to feel worthy of sexual attention. SEX SAVER: Figure out what's got you so upset. Even if it's not something you can fix or control, you can at least get a handle on what you need to manage your own emotions—look for help from your buddies, your spouse, a personal coach, or a therapist.

## tip

It's hard to count how many things can affect someone's sex drive: stress, fatigue, intimacy issues, meds. We've even heard guys with decreased sex drives say it's because they love their partner too much—that the excitement of sex has been completely replaced by the romantic nature of the act (which isn't such a bad thing, but if he's feeling like that, talk about ways you can experiment). The advice here is good: Communicate with your mate and seek advice from an expert if necessary (remember to ask about prescription side effects). Bottom line, sex drives can come in waves but you want to make the effort to keep it on the upswing.

### NEED A LITTLE HELP?

When sexual problems arise, the first place many couples go isn't to each other—it's to the free-spirited friend who'll talk about anything or to a medical website to look up the possible causes for it. The first question everyone has, no matter what the problem is "Is this normal?" We're here to tell you the answer: YES. But just knowing it happens

# Topic: no sex drive

**Lately, we have sex once every 3–4 weeks. Any suggestions?**

—Marie&Brad

## Just do it!

—mike626

Try a **little extra foreplay** or a back rub. —kozigirl

Take a hot shower, light some candles, and listen to some good music.

—Tessaann

SOMETIMES YOU HAVE TO JUST 'MAKE' YOURSELF. Nine times out of 10 I end up getting into it and being glad I did! —newportbride715

**If he says no, I say 'that's too bad' and tackle him to the ground!**

—july16thbride

Maybe you guys can do a **date night** or something to rekindle those flames.

—ChattyCathy

### nest note:

When you come home from work exhausted, it's easy to slip into some comfy sweats and hit the hay. But putting more effort into what you wear to bed (this is for the women *and* men) can help give your sex life a real boost. After all, if you look sexy, you're bound to feel sexy, too.

isn't always enough. Here are some common routes couples (or individuals) take when they're looking to improve on intimacy.

### The Helping Hand: Your Friends

THE PROS: Running a scenario by a more sexually adventurous friend can help you feel better about issues like "Have *you* ever been with a guy who wouldn't come?" or "How do I tell her I hate it when she blows in my ear after years of letting her do it?" Your friends know and love you, so you can be sure that their advice will be well intentioned and, in many cases, exactly what you need to know.

THE CONS: Your friends know and love you, so their advice may be tailored to what you want to hear rather than what you need to know to fix the situation. And then there's the trust issue: If you're at all worried that your spouse will flip out if he or she learns that you've told someone else about his or her problem, it may be worth going to one of the other sources below first.

# Foreplay Refresher

Put the play back in foreplay with these guaranteed sex starters.

KISSING: Play a no-touching game with your spouse. Start by kissing, but neither of you is allowed to touch the other one with your hands or any other part of your body. The first one who does has to be the slave of the person who "wins" (don't tell, but you actually both win). You'll build serious sexual tension trying not to touch and also remember what it was like back when it was all foreplay, all the time.

TOUCHING: You have access to every inch of each other's bodies, but can let only your fingers do the walking. Guys: linger at her chest. Girls: Gently scratch his upper thighs. Tickle and tease her until you can't take it anymore.

ORAL SEX: Make it a pact to not penetrate. A night of mutual oral sex is always a treat (not to mention, most women reach orgasm easier this way). Want to drive your lady crazy? Use your tongue to spell the alphabet. Going down on your guy? Pretend you're licking an ice-cream cone on a sweltering summer day.

### The Helping Hand: A Topic-Targeted Book

THE PROS: Whether it's a hipster guide to introducing S&M into your 1BR or a tome for seniors on herbal remedies for a flagging sex drive, there's a book for every problem and every sufferer out there. Find one that addresses sex in a way you're comfortable with.

THE CONS: Finding the right book. If you're shy, a dominatrix-penned guide to better sex may scare you; a clinical discussion on the psychology of talking dirty may put you to sleep. Read reviews and excerpts online for a sense of it before you purchase.

### The Helping Hand: The Internet and Message Boards

THE PROS: It's anonymous, it's endless, and you can do it from the privacy of your own home. Top searches on Internet health boards routinely turn up sex-related topics, from herpes to pregnancy. If it's a health question you have, look for doctor-advised sites like Yahoo! Health, WebMD, and the Centers for Disease Control and Prevention site at CDC.gov. Sexuality topics are handled by a variety of hosts, from columnists to sex therapists. The advice column at the women-run sex shop Toys in Babeland at Babeland.com and Columbia University's GoAskAlice.com are good (read: free of porn pop-ups) places to start.

THE CONS: Sites can be useful for diagnosing a problem, but they don't always go the extra step and offer detailed, practical advice for solving it. Make sure you've got a network you can turn to once the Web points you in the right direction.

### The Helping Hand: Sex Seminars

THE PROS: Like personal trainers of sex, sexuality instructors are becoming more common and can give you one-on-one advice in a still-professional (and discreet) forum. Think of Andy Dick's character from *Old School* but not a total freak: These experts often give workshops in large cities, or will do home visits for couples or a group of female friends (hello, bachelorette-party idea). Worried about frauds? Try online directories or a Google search for sexuality workshops in your city—that should at least get you a list of possible speakers you could consult about a specialized program.

THE CONS: Like a real personal trainer, these instructors' services can be costly. Depending on your mortification level, learning the female anatomy through a toy in front of friends may be unsettling, too.

### The Helping Hand: Therapists

THE PROS: A therapist will work through your relationship issues and help you quickly ascertain if it's a psychological block or a physical problem. Even if it's a physical issue, talking to an unbiased and nonjudgmental source about your issues can never hurt.

THE CONS: If it's a physical problem, they may not be much help. They'll probably recommend a sex therapist in addition to their services, which is certainly going to cost you.

# How to Hire . . . a Sex Therapist

Paging Dr. Ruth . . . If one or both of you are experiencing major sexual difficulties, like having trouble reaching climax, or really want to change your sexual habits (in either a more kinky direction or the opposite), then a sex therapist might be for you. Keep in mind:

- Sex therapists focus strictly on sexual issues and may not take other relationship factors into account, so a relationship therapist (whether a holder of a PhD or MSW or an MD who can dispense meds) might be a better starting point.

- When you look for one, go to your family physician, gynecologist, or urologist for references. This isn't the kind of practitioner you want to find on the Web.

- Once you call, don't say, "Hey, we have a problem . . ." Instead, ask for the professional's specialty, experience, fees, and what a typical session is like. You want to make sure you know what you're getting into.

- You can also check credentials with the American Association of Marriage and Family Therapy or the American Association of Sex Educators.

### The Helping Hand: Sex Therapists

THE PROS: Sex therapists are a highly trained group—some are psychologists (also called sexologists) and affiliated with major hospitals and universities. Sessions with a sex therapist focus solely on the sexual issue, but may do so by examining the relationship as a whole. By the way, sex therapists do *not* have sexual contact with their clients . . . ever.

THE CONS: This kind of treatment is the most comprehensive and professional—and so the most expensive (one estimate puts the average course, which consists of several appointments with the therapist, at between $600 and $2,300). Some health insurance plans cover some costs of sex therapy, particularly if your therapist is a psychologist or psychiatrist. The clinical setting can be a huge mental block to many couples. After all, by actually venturing into a doctor or other professional's office, you're fully admitting there's an issue. But if you think that's not sexy, try ignoring the problem and waiting for it to fix itself—that's an invitation into a lifetime of unsexy.

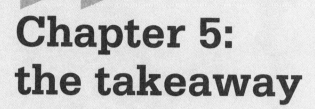

# Chapter 5:
# the takeaway

**Make sex a priority.** Promising yourselves you'll do it means that you'll both carve out enough time and energy for the act, which already means it's going to be better than it's been when you're sneaking it in just before sleep on Saturdays. Learn how to personalize your own sex plan on page 171.

**When things aren't right, talk about them.** Challenge yourself to speak up when all's not well in the bedroom or you're sentencing your love life to all sorts of resentment and frustration that—we guarantee—*will* come out in other ways. Go to page 167 for talking tips.

**Try something new tonight.** So you've been doing this a certain way for so many years that you'd be a jerk to try that, right? Wrong. Your sex life shouldn't stop evolving when you walk down the aisle. Find out ways to keep it fresh on page 183.

# [ kids ]

Fact is, love, marriage, and the baby carriage walk hand in hand. But whether you know you want children right away, later, or not at all, you still need to deal with baby pressure at the same time you're getting on the same page as your spouse. Our advice: Give yourselves at least a year postwedding before you throw out the birth control, and revel in this responsibility-free time together.

# the nest test:
# your parental plans

Get your baby brains on the same wavelength.

1. **How many children do you see yourself having?**

2. **How old is too old to have a baby?**

3. **Who's going to take care of our kids?**

## 4. If we got pregnant next month, would you think "yay!" or "yikes!"?

5. **What should we say when people ask about our baby plans?**

6. **Anything you desperately want to accomplish before we become a trio?**

7. **Do daddies do diapers?**

8. **Who would be the first person you'd tell?**

9. **What lifestyle changes do you expect to make when you become a parent?**

# your family plan

Chances are you had your first baby talk *before* you got married, when you shared your future dreams: two kids, big house, cute dog. Now that you're official, the conversation needs to take a more specific turn. We're not talking baby names yet; but you do need to agree on when you want to start "trying" and how many members you want in your clan.

"I know that you can't ever be completely ready for a baby, but last night we decided to save $50 out of each of my paychecks and set it aside in an account for the basics we'll need for our baby."
—FabulousMrs.P

## CHECKING EACH OTHER'S CLOCK

Just because you know you want kids doesn't mean you'll know exactly when. Getting pregnant because your spouse wants to or all your friends are doing it is *not* the right way to approach baby-making. Instead, enjoy your alone time as marrieds and use it to really research when you want to get pregnant. Then start setting goals based on the following factors.

**Goals:** Is one of you still in school, or thinking of applying to a postgraduate program? Consider the financial and time-management implications. Sleepless nights probably won't help your GPA.

**Your career:** Your twenties aren't just prime time for baby-making (fertility's thought to start to decline at 27), but they're also the years when you're establishing yourself at work and busting your butt to achieve professional goals that can impact the rest of your working life. The good news? Wanting to have both a baby and a career is no longer a pipe dream. Over half of all women who've given birth return to work within a year; for women with a college degree, it's over three-quarters. And you aren't alone if you decide to focus on your career now and really get yourself situated before starting to have babies. The birth rate for women in their 40s is increasing every year—for women 40 to 44, it's gone up 51 percent since just 1990 and it's more than doubled during that time for women 45 to 49.*

*No, we didin't do the research ourselves. Here are the links: http://www.census.gov/prod/2005pubs/p20-555.pdf; http://www.cdc.gov/nchs/data/nvsr/nvsr52/nvsr52_10.pdf

# Baby Talk Tactics

Three subtle ways to get the conversation started

WHEN: After you've seen other people's children, when you observe your mate around kids—especially if your spouse is good with children—is a great time to broach the topic.

WHAT TO SAY: "Where did you learn those baby skills? You're a real natural with kids."

FOLLOW UP WITH: "Are you looking forward to starting a family or do you think we should wait a while?"

WHEN: There's a baby reference on TV. In fact, schedule your viewing habits to catch a show with a pregnant woman or a functional family with lots of kids. Hint: Don't watch HBO.

WHAT TO SAY: "Wow, what a great-looking pregnant woman. Wonder what it'll be like when I'm/you're pregnant? I hope equally amazing."

FOLLOW UP WITH: "When were you thinking about having kids?"

WHEN: If your spouse makes a particularly negative comment about kids.

WHAT TO SAY: "So-and-so's kids are such brats. We're going to have to make a better effort to keep our kids from turning out like that."

FOLLOW UP WITH: "Starting a family is a major commitment. But I'd like to start thinking about it. What's your feeling? You can be honest."

**Conception concerns:** No matter how well we know our bodies, most of us have no idea about a fundamental aspect of our health—our ability to conceive—until we actually start to try. Worrying that it could take several months, even years, to become pregnant can make you anxious to jump into the baby ring. But you shouldn't start trying until you'd be ready to be a parent in nine months—plenty of people get pregnant on their first try.

**Your friends:** Are you one of the few marrieds in your circle? Or have you lost all your pals to parenthood? Having a baby will definitely change your standing Saturday-night party plans, but just because Sam and Anna are ready doesn't mean *your* twosome is ready for an addition.

**Your relationship:** Being married isn't easy, but it's easy to think a baby will make your life a fairy tale. Don't make the mistake of expecting a baby to fill a void in your marriage, or use the idea of starting a family as a quick fix for your relationship. Instead, work on the two of you, and remember all the fabulous reasons you got together in the first place—then make room for baby.

**Space:** Think about square footage, especially in metropolitan areas where it's at a premium. When you have kids, you might not be able to make do with the tiny apartment—and the really cheap rent—after your child turns two. You'll either need to make enough money to upgrade or move to a less expensive locale.

**tip**
You should also both think about genetic testing that may be determined by your ethnicity, e.g., Jewish people of Eastern European descent should test for the Tay-Sachs gene, a devastating disease of the central nervous system. Your doctor can help you decide if testing's necessary.

## FACING YOUR FEARS

If you're nervous about becoming a parent, that's okay. It's a big decision—the *biggest*. But if the object is to reduce the pressure on you, then ignoring it is only going to make things worse. First, figure out what your concerns really are. Are you worried about what will happen to your freedom, your sex life, or whether you'll be a good parent? Then communicate them to your partner, and ask about his or her hopes and fears as well. You have to deal with it like you probably did your engagement: Find out why there's a rush and reassure him or her you have the same goals. By sharing your deepest feelings, rather than erecting a wall, you will strengthen your emotional intimacy as a couple and will find it easier to negotiate on this issue.

flip

Need to find a therapist? See our step-by-step sidebar on page 235.

## WHEN YOU DON'T AGREE

So you're married to a person who has a different idea about raising kids—here are four rules for coping, whether the difference is in number of kids, when to have them, or whether to have them at all.

**Don't use pressure or guilt.** Give yourselves time to accept the differences about each another, and come back to the topic later when you may have had time to consider

# Topic:
# when only one of you is ready

> "
>
> Maybe if you have a timeline in mind it will make both of you feel more at ease.
>
> —sarahkelly

After a mutual decision to wait a while, I am now ready to start our family. **My husband, on the other hand, isn't because he has so many great dreams that he'd like to fulfill before 'settling down'** with children. Does anyone have advice about how to handle or approach this issue?
—Ravenswood

My DH said the same thing. So I asked, **WHAT IS IT YOU WANT TO DO BEFORE HAVING A BABY?** Turns out he only wanted to get a big screen TV. He thought we would not be able to afford it afterwards.
—alyadams

**You need to wait because your DH is not ready.** You'll do far more harm than good by dragging him down the baby trail before he's ready.
—akaNicole

ASK HIM TO DEFINE HIS RELUCTANCE in starting a family. Some men are just really, really scared of having to 'give up' their own childhood to become a 'real' man by having a baby.
—Karen-MOB

**What exactly does he want to 'do' before you have kids?** My DH said the same thing . . . turned out he only wanted one more big vacation (which we are taking in 2 weeks, when I will be 7 weeks pg).
—Jennn

### nest note:

Many men and women worry that becoming parents means the beginning of huge responsibilities . . . and the end of fun. If that's the case, talk to friends and siblings who already have kids, and ask them to be honest about their experiences. Sure, jetting off to Paris on a moment's notice won't be so easy once junior's around, but that doesn't mean there aren't plenty of good times ahead.

compromises. Marriage is a big change that overwhelms many people and your spouse may not be fully ready to consider another change right away. Pressure doesn't work—ever—so try again later on your own terms before getting frustrated.

**Be open and honest.** Under no circumstances should you attempt to get your way by "forgetting" your birth control and figuring your spouse will adapt if you *do* wind up pregnant. Tricking someone else into a lifelong decision is a manipulation that gets your entire marriage and parenting partnership off on the wrong foot. You want your spouse to welcome your child, not resent you for having it.

**Talk it over with a third party.** If your disagreement is too big to bridge or is seeping over into other areas of your marriage, make an appointment with a marriage counselor to help you work through the issues together and find an acceptable solution.

**Relax.** If your disagreement is about how many kids to have, don't worry. Things change, multiple births occur, and that first child may make you *both* rethink how you feel about adding to the family. Start with your first baby and take it from there.

> "When I was 20 I said my cutoff was 32. I'll be 36 on Saturday and we are just now TTC. So my cutoff is when I hit menopause."
> —morgan2004

## PLANNING AHEAD

Before you rush into parenthood, make sure you've done pre-pregnancy prep work and agreed with your spouse on the following topics.

**Get financially stable.** Few can really *afford* to have kids—the cost of raising a baby from birth to age seventeen is estimated at more than a quarter of a million dollars for families making $70K or more per year. And this number doesn't include heavy medical bills or ritzy private schools—or the cost of college. But hey, you get the tax deduction, right? In all seriousness, finances (or lack thereof) will influence your decision to conceive. And you *should* organize your married money before you even think of banishing birth control. But don't wait till you've saved that $250K—you may be in a rocking chair by then. Just use our budgeting tools in Chapter 1 to work up a modified, fit-to-be-parents plan for yourselves. Knowing what to expect—and evaluating how kid-friendly your career is—will help you prepare for the future.

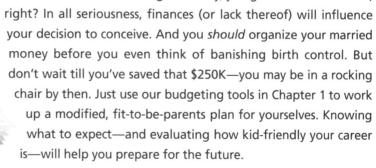

# Fur Babies—A Parenting Prep Course

Getting a pet is a fun and common way to dip your toe in the parenting pool without getting in over your head. Taking care of your "fur baby" will bring lots of your parenting styles and skills (or lack thereof) to light. You'll see how you each nurture, maintain, and discipline a completely dependant, and completely devoted, member of the family. Find out if you and your honey are up to the challenge by answering yes or no to the following questions.

- Is one or both of us always able to come home after working just 8 hours?
- Does one of us have a job that doesn't require travel?
- Do we always plan our vacations well in advance?
- Can we afford veterinary care, food, and other costs of a pet?
- Is there enough room in our house/apartment for a pet?
- Are we both on the same page as to how we'll divvy up things like walking, feeding, and grooming the pet?

If you answered yes to four or more questions, you're ready for a pet. It's time to start picking out names and anticipating the pitter-patter of little paws around your home.

If you answered no to four or more questions, you're not there yet. Don't worry—it's not a bad thing. But pets take a lot of time, energy, money, and love, so if you're not 100 percent sure you can do it, it's best to wait before making the commitment.

## Best Reasons to Get a Fur Baby

UNCONDITIONAL LOVE. We'll bet that you won't find anyone—not even dear old Mom—who is going to greet you at the door with as much enthusiasm as your pet. And no matter what your mood is, s/he will always want to be around you.

PETS DESENSITIZE YOU TO GROSSNESS. Diapers and burp cloths really will feel like child's play once you've paper-trained Rover and dealt with Fluffy's furballs.

YOU'LL FORM A DISCIPLINARY STYLE. Are you guys equally likely to enforce the "no pets on the couch" rule? Are you more of a good cop/bad cop team? You'll see your natural tendencies and be able to come up with approaches that work for all of you.

BASIC RESPONSIBILITY. It's one thing to forget to pick up each other's dry cleaning—there's something to wear in the closet—but you and DH need to get used to providing for another's needs when it comes to basics like food, water, medicine, and attention.

**Figure out whose career comes first.** Children come with added responsibilities that, no matter how little you need to sleep, will tend to take away from at least one of your careers. How long will the wife stay home after giving birth—and how long will the husband take off? Who will stay home when your baby has strep?

**Have a childcare plan.** If you both work, you'll need it. There are many options, from grandparents playing primary caretakers to a group daycare situation, with nannies and sitters in between. And it's going to cost you. The price of childcare varies with type and location: a spot in a daycare center can cost from $6,000 to $10,000 per year. A full-time nanny or sitter can require a salary equal to that of an executive assistant ($15,000 to $36,000 per year). Relatives are often a more cost-effective option, though some couples either compensate or offer to compensate family members who lend a hand.

**Sync up your parenting styles.** When it comes to childrearing, family differences will definitely rear their ugly heads. You should both try to strategize about what kind of parents you'd like to be. (Tip: Make a list of all the good—and bad—things about your parents. Better tip: Make sure they never see it.) Topics you must tackle are: gender roles (who's staying home, who's changing diapers, who's making decisions, etc.); parenting styles (what time to put kids in bed, warnings vs. time-outs, etc.); lifestyle (travel with kids vs. focusing on familyhood and putting kids first). Your thoughts might change over time, but it is always better to have these discussions prior to having a baby in the house because the pressure is off and you can have a really helpful theoretical discussion rather than feeling your disagreements are personal.

## WHAT'S YOUR LUCKY NUMBER?

Ask your partner how many kids he or she wants and the reasons behind the number (your spouse was one of eight and felt lost in the shuffle; he or she couldn't imagine not having a big family; or maybe your mate just wants to retire young). Remember, circumstances always change (and accidents happen). The important thing is to understand each other's general expectations for your future family. This will also help you determine when you might want to start having babies—if it's seven or bust, you best get moving.

Is the 2.2 child national average right for you? Experts say the factors that contribute to your number choice relate to career (especially for women trying to combine family with work), finances, family backgrounds, and age. Here, we help you understand the pros and cons of the numbers.

### The Only Child

STAT: 17 percent of couples have just one.

ADVANTAGES: You can indulge one child financially more than you can multiple children. You can spend more one-on-one time with an only child as well.

DISADVANTAGES: Only children miss out on the bonding that happens with siblings. Also, having one child is sometimes psychologically distressing because you put all your emotional time and energy into him or her, which can put a lot of pressure on your kid. Then there's the possibility of sibling rivalry . . . with a pet.

### Two for Two

STAT: 35 percent choose two.

ADVANTAGES: Follow the 1950s standard and have two children. Your kids won't have to worry about only-child or middle-child syndrome; plus you've already starting raising one—why waste the skill set?

DISADVANTAGES: Sibling rivalry can become an issue. The more children you have, the less you can provide each child. Your attempt at democracy won't work: Family votes will always even out (two kids say yes; two parents say no).

### The Fantastic Five

STAT: 20 percent of couples opt for three kids.

ADVANTAGES: A crew to help with household chores eventually and a support network for one another.

DISADVANTAGES: With three, the often-discussed middle child syndrome (where one parent is most closely bonded with one child, one parent with another, and the "middle" child feels left out) can become an issue. Space becomes a problem and it's much harder to find a table at a restaurant.

### A Caravan of Kids

STAT: 15 percent of couples have four kids or more.

ADVANTAGES: Older siblings can serve as mentors to younger ones. The probability of having that coveted girl (or boy) is slightly higher.

DISADVANTAGES: It can be difficult to pay attention to all those kids, let alone pay for them. With the price of college averaging more than $100K, you do the math. Plus, you're way outnumbered.

# Topic:
# the baby question

**I HAPPEN TO BE THE ONLY MARRIED WOMAN IN THE OFFICE WHO DOESN'T HAVE CHILDREN, SO I GET THE 'YOU'RE NEXT!' LINE A LOT.** I always politely say that DH and I aren't having kids for at least 4 or 5 years, but one of my coworkers loves to say, 'Well, you just never know. When it's time to have a baby, it's time.' I told her to back off and now she's not speaking to me.

—redheadAya

**I hate that 'are you trying' question** the most —it's like asking if I had sex last night. I usually answer, 'Well, we're trying to prevent it, but we had sex xx times at xx hours since you're asking' just to make them feel uncomfortable.     —dana92504

If I'm in a snippy mood I generally respond with, **'That's kind of a personal question**—why would you like to know?' That generally shuts them up!     —PittTexan

**I immediately change the subject to *their* kids, so they never get an answer from me.**     —crsd99

**IT'S NO ONE'S BUSINESS!** —njbride

My favorite from my mom and MIL is **'I AM READY TO BE A GRAND-MOTHER!'** Well, WE aren't ready to take that step. —trishaggie01

## nest note:

Not all baby questions are malintentioned, just to play devil's advocate for a second. But when a coworker, a friend, or even your mom doesn't understand your reasons for waiting, set the record straight (politely) and say that everyone has their own timeline. What worked for them may not be right for your relationship. Stay poised, and remember, it's your life. You don't have to prove anything to anybody.

# Quiz
## is it time to try?

**There's no formula that can definitively** tell you the right or wrong time to have a baby. This quiz should just give you a reality check before you hop on the baby bandwagon. Choose the best answer for each question, and then read the key to see where you are on the Baby Meter.

## 1. You live in a:

**a.** Studio apartment.

**b.** Two-bedroom co-op.

**c.** Starter home with a backyard.

## 2. The wife is:

**a.** In college.

**b.** In her mid-to-late twenties.

**c.** Well into her third decade.

## 3. The husband is:

**a.** In college.

**b.** In his mid-to-late twenties.

**c.** Well into his third or fourth decade.

## 4. Your ideal number of kids is:

**a.** One.

**b.** Two to three.

**c.** Four and up.

## 5. You'd like your kids to be:

**a.** One year apart.

**b.** In the same school.

**c.** In different generations.

## 6. Your finances:

**a.** Are riddled with debt.

**b.** Could be better, but you break even.

**c.** Are solid, complete with a 401K and investments.

## 7. Your friends:

**a.** Go out every night.

**b.** Are all married.

**c.** Have their own buns baking.

## 8. One career:

**a.** Is going nowhere.

**b.** Is more like a good job.

**c.** Is on the up-and-up.

- - - - - - - - - - - - - - - - - - - - - - -

# results

## mostly **a**s

This year is probably not the best time for you to conceive. We suggest waiting two years, and in the meantime, start getting your finances and priorities in order.

## mostly **b**s

Wait a year. But don't stress about the decision; let it happen naturally.

## mostly **C**s

Go for it. Right now. Drop everything, slip into something comfortable, and start having that elusive birth control–free sex.

# making babies

Some couples refuse to become slaves to an ovulation clock and let nature take its course when trying to get pregnant. Seventy-five to 85 percent of couples get pregnant within a year, but some couples get pregnant on their first try! Even so, there's a lot you should know about fertility, pregnancy myths, and what to do if conceiving takes you longer than you'd like.

## HOW TO GET PREGNANT

We hope (by now) you know the basics: The egg is fertilized by sperm, implants in the uterus, and nine months later (40 weeks, actually) a baby is born. Yet getting pregnant in the real, nonfilmstrip world is a little more complex. Sperm survives in your uterus for two to three days, but your egg can live no more than twenty-four hours after ovulation. So there are actually only one to four days per cycle when a woman can become pregnant: the one to two days before ovulation—when your egg is released from your ovary—the day *of* ovulation, and the twenty-four hours after. Many women can tell they are ovulating because they have lower abdominal pain, breast tenderness, or vaginal discharge. Around this egg-dropping time, have sex every other day to increase your chances—it helps keep sperm concentrated and in tip-top shape.

> **click** Create a free ovulation chart at MyMonthlyCycles.com

Besides having lots and lots of sex, there are other things you must do to help the pregnancy process.

**Have the right sex.** It's missionary or man on top. These positions have been shown to increase the odds of getting PG. To really up your chances, place a small pillow under the woman's hips afterward so the cervix is covered by semen for about twenty minutes. It helps the little guys swim up. Avoid straddling, woman on top, sitting, or standing positions, because sperm are fighting an uphill battle.

## Three Things Every Dad-to-Be Should Know

1. Don't take your wife's mood swings personally. It's probably the hormones.
2. Read pregnancy books. Her body is doing some wacky things, and she'll feel less alone if you understand what's going on inside.
3. Have as much fun as you can now. Your social life will never be the same.

# Ovulation Predicting Options

**Here, some different ways to figure out exactly when you're ovulating.**

**MUCUS ANALYSIS:** You know the slimy stuff inside your vagina when you're not on your period? It's called cervical mucus, and right before you ovulate, it changes. You'll have more of it, and find it's extra clear, slippery, and thin. Testing your vaginal mucus by feeling discharge with your fingers can give you a good idea of when you're ready to ovulate. As soon as the egg is released, the mucus tends to dry up very quickly.

**OVULATION CALCULATOR:** Since figuring out your ovulation date is pretty much a numbers issue, an ovulation calculator does the math for you. Enter in the start date of your last period and how long your cycle is, and you'll come out with a range of days you're most likely to be fertile. There are plenty of these on the Web—we trust the March of Dimes (MarchofDimes.com), an organization specializing in prenatal health!

**TEMPERATURE TRACKING:** Ask your gyno about the best ways for making use of a special temperature-taker known as the basal body thermometer. Each morning before you get out of bed, you check your temp. When you notice the number's gone up about two-tenths of a degree, you've already ovulated.

**HOME PREDICTION KIT:** Home tests let you pee onto a test strip the same way you would in a pregnancy test. You test your urine at the same time every day (or even twice a day). Right before you ovulate, there's an LH surge—a huge increase of the luteinizing hormone, and it's that peak in LH that the test will reveal. Soon after you detect the LH surge, you'll likely ovulate.

**HIGH-TECH HELP:** Another method is a handheld computer that each day measures and stores the levels of electrolytes in your saliva. The machine then lets you know when you're most likely to ovulate based on the chemical makeup of your saliva.

# Pregnancy Myths Busted

**HAVING SEX WHILE STANDING UP INCREASES YOUR CHANCES OF HAVING A BOY.** There are tons of urban legends out there along the same lines. Our favorite: Lie down after sex and stay there for a while. Supposedly that gives the boy sperm a chance to beat the girl sperm to the egg.

**IF YOUR FACE STARTS TO CHANGE (LIKE GET UGLY), YOU'RE HAVING A GIRL.** There is an old wives' tale that your baby girl "steals" your beauty. But there's no truth to this myth. Being pregnant does not have to compromise your appearance (at least not above the belly), but you do need to be smart. While there is a theoretical risk associated with coloring your hair (chemicals being absorbed through the scalp), studies have not shown anything conclusive. Avoid dye for at least the first trimester, when the baby's organs are forming. Relieve worries by opting for a natural vegetable dye over a semipermanent or permanent product.

**HOW YOU CARRY INDICATES THE BABY'S GENDER.** No matter how many times your great aunt swears she can predict a baby's sex by how the mother is carrying, there's no scientific evidence that backs up this method. The shape and height of a woman's body during pregnancy is determined by things like her muscle tone and the position of her baby and uterus.

**NEVER RAISE YOUR ARMS OVER YOUR HEAD.** Raising your arms will not put a kink in the umbilical cord or choke the baby. As a matter of fact, nothing you do can cause kinks or tangles in the cord. Fetal movement is what causes cords to sometimes get twisted up. If it's comfortable for you to put your arms up, reach for the sky.

**EXCESSIVE HEARTBURN MEANS A BABY WITH A FULL HEAD OF HAIR.** Unfortunately, frequent heartburn is a common occurrence during many pregnancies, not just for moms who give birth to babies with Donald Trumpian locks.

**YOUR JET-SET DAYS MUST BE PUT ON HIATUS.** It's perfectly safe for pregnant women who are not experiencing complications to fly in a plane until about the last six weeks of their pregnancy, though morning sickness and a general dip in your energy level in the first trimester might make flying then a pain. Of course, before you finalize your trip, it's a good idea to let your ob-gyn know your plans so he or she can make doubly sure you're not at risk for things like blood clots, high blood pressure, or other complications. If you're going to fly when you're preggers, get an aisle seat so you can move around frequently, bring your medical records on board, drink one liter of water for every two hours in the air, and fasten your seatbelt low around your hips, not your belly.

# You Don't Want Kids?

Years of diapers and playdates may not be on everyone's to-do list. Many (13 percent!) couples see themselves as forever kid-free. Why? A fear of raising children, fertility issues, the simple notion that they can live their lives more fully alone. Seeing your best friends' lives go from fabulous couple to diaper-changing duo in nine months flat might be enough to defer your admission into the baby club. Here is advice on taking the non-parent path.

**MAKE THE DECISION TOGETHER.** The two of you should look at your lifestyle and relationship to figure out what's right for you. It's vital that you and your mate are in total agreement. Above all, you must be open and honest with each other about your expectations. It's not fair to keep your partner waiting years for a bundle, hoping you will change the no-baby law. It may be difficult to bear right now, but it's better than discovering your differences ten years down the road.

**SPREAD THE WORD.** No matter how evolved we like to think our community is, the notion of choosing not to have children is still pretty unconventional. But done delicately, you can tell your parents, siblings, and closest friends your plan without facing too much backlash. *Don't* be negative: Say, "Actually, we've decided not to have kids." *Don't* disparage: Rather than pointing out how loud kids are, say, "We totally respect other people's decision to *have* kids." Do stay positive, personal, and nonjudgmental: "We've really thought about this and have decided we envision our future as just the two of us." Tell the inner circle (your parents, siblings, closest friends) individually. Great times include during dinner at a restaurant—emotions need to stay in check to avoid a scene—or during a nonholiday, low-key, family or friend weekend. And do it in person because, let's face it, everything sounds better face to face.

> "We love kids, and love being an aunt/uncle, but we do not want our own children. People just can't understand it."
> —finally:)

**PREPARE FOR BACKLASH.** Don't be surprised if your parents (or siblings) are disappointed by your decision. Don't be afraid to acknowledge how they're feeling. Say, "I can completely understand that you're upset; this means you won't have any grandchildren from us." Then, let them experience the emotions.

**KNOW YOU CAN CHANGE YOUR MIND.** Remember: Baby-free living equals a certain level of freedom to have a constantly changing outlook and lifestyle. While you might be a little embarrassed to announce your plans for a baby after expounding on the limitations of parenthood, you'll make it through. Because it is your decision to begin with, changing your mind is also your prerogative.

# Baby Shower Basics

**Chances are that if you're thinking about babies, your friends are bound to be having them. Time to brush up on your baby shower etiquette.**

**TIME IT RIGHT.** It's a good idea to hold the shower later in the mom-to-be's pregnancy—some time in the last trimester months.

**GET THE WORD OUT EARLY.** Send out your invites six to eight weeks before the event—you want to make sure all the VIPs can make it. Remember to include directions as well as a phone number and/or e-mail address so guests can RSVP or contact you with any questions.

**BE CREATIVE.** Work a specific theme (tea party, the nursery's décor, etc.) or color into your planning—from the invites and decorations to the food and drink.

**CHOOSE MEANINGFUL GIFTS.** Besides getting gifts off the registry, you can also work a theme into smaller presents. For example, ask each guest to bring a special gift celebrating all the "firsts" the mom-to-be will be sharing with her little one, such as baby's first bath, first steps, first day at the beach, and the like.

**MAKE IT FUN.** Come up with activities that will guarantee your guests have a good time, such as a mini-spa experience with onsite manicures, pedicures, and massages. Or if you're really good with a needle and thread, have guests personalize quilt squares beforehand (you can send them out with the invites) and then sew them together to present as a gift to the guest of honor.

# Pregnant Pause

Q. I'm pregnant! I want to tell everyone, but a close friend has been trying for years to conceive and isn't having much luck. I don't want to seem like I'm rubbing my good news in her face—should I wait to tell her?

A. Absolutely not—leaving her out of the loop will only send a message to your friend that you felt uncomfortable sharing your good news with her, or that you feel sorry for her. Either way, it's not going to make her feel good. So whether you're making the announcement via e-mail, on the phone, or in person, include her. But stay away from following up your announcement with something like, "Don't worry—I'm sure it'll be your turn soon!" Although you might just want to offer your friend some words of encouragement, bringing up her fertility issues will only make her uncomfortable. Besides, this is your moment in the spotlight, and if she's a true friend, she won't want to take anything away from it.

**Go off the pill.** Fertility can return almost immediately but sometimes takes up to six months. It depends on dosage; with lower dosage pills your fertility usually comes back quicker.

**Know your cycle.** You ovulate on the fourteenth day before your period begins. So it's important to know if you have a twenty-eight-, thirty-two-, or even a twenty-four-day cycle (or some entirely different schedule).

**Eat a well-balanced diet and take vitamins with folic acid.** This will help prevent birth defects.

**See a doctor (both of you).** Before pregnancy, make sure you get any pre-conception tests done, such as genetic testing, or immunizations to diseases like chicken pox and measles, which can be harmful to the fetus. Also ask your doctor about any preexisting medical conditions that might impede your chances of getting pregnant.

**Quit partying (both of you).** Drinking, drugs, and smoking can all affect an unborn fetus and can affect sperm's motility. It's best to cut down on or eliminate these vices while trying to get pregnant.

## PROBLEMS WITH THE PROCESS

When you're trying to get pregnant, a few issues—such as problems with fertility and baby-making becoming more of a chore than a pleasure—can arise. Sex on demand, high-pressure, baby-making sex is not hot sexy spontaneous sex. It's about timing and testing body fluids and consulting checklists. It's important to prepare for the emotional impact.

Frustrated trying to get pregnant? Not sure about eating lunch meat? Our Nesters are a supportive bunch (plus, most have been there). Visit TheNest.com/babytalk

click

At times, men can even find it hard to perform. You *will* get stressed. Sex will *not* be as fun anymore. That's why you have to make time for romance apart from sex. Corny as it sounds, make an effort to do nice things for each other (even something as simple as ordering your mate's favorite dish—the one you hate—or leaving a cute note). Also, you must talk about what you're going through. How easy is it to just ignore bad or uncomfortable things? That only makes it worse in the long run.

## Infertility

What if you're doing everything right—the charts, the schedule, the romance—but there's still no baby? Infertility is a problem that affects more than six million couples in the United States. That's about 10 percent of people of reproductive age. If you're under thirty-five and haven't conceived in a year, see a fertility specialist. If you're over thirty-five, wait only six months. The causes of infertility range from irregular cycles to more serious conditions such as endometriosis, in which the uterine lining doesn't shed properly during menstruation. Even extreme stress can affect normal ovulation and sperm production. Our advice: Relax, make a schedule, relax, give it a whirl, relax some more. Don't get discouraged or feel inadequate—chances are, there's an explanation.

## Miscarriage Miseries

A surprisingly high number of pregnancies end in miscarriage. (We've heard as many as one in six.) Most happen before you even know you're pregnant. As your doctor will surely tell you, an early miscarriage or two is no reason for alarm. Most women go on to have plenty of happy, healthy pregnancies. One of the reasons to keep your pregnancy news to yourself until the twelve-week mark is to spare yourself the emotional strain of having to tell other people who check in about your "good news" that there's a sad coda. But even if you have a miscarriage, don't worry. Be upbeat, try again, and consider your false alarm a practice run. If, however, you miscarried after trying particularly hard or it was late in the pregnancy, don't deny your grief or try to make yourself "get over it." Many parents-to-be feel the loss as deeply as they would the death of a family member. Consider talking to a counselor if your sadness continues and don't rush into a "makeup" pregnancy.

# How to Hire . . . an Ob-Gyn

We're assuming (or hoping) that you see a gynecologist annually. If you like him or her, when you start trying to get pregnant, ask if your doctor practices obstetrics (these days, some don't). If the answer's no, ask your gynecologist or primary care physician for a recommendation. You might also want to ask friends or relatives who have recently given birth.

Once you're pregnant (or before, if your medical condition means you'll likely have complications) you should visit several doctors before making a final decision (this is your baby we're talking about) and set up an OB consultation with each. Assess these key factors:

- **LOCATION.** When you're pregnant, you need to schedule monthly visits. Will this office be convenient for you? Hint: The closer to work, the better.

- **GENDER.** Some women feel more comfortable with a female doctor, some with a male doctor.

- **BEDSIDE MANNER.** You want a doctor who you feel comfortable with and who communicates well.

- **MEDICAL NATURE (I.E., OLD-SCHOOL OR HIGH-TECH).** Ask some basic questions about epidurals, C-sections, and midwives, such as how often he or she uses them, and gauge the doctor's attitude toward them and other potential issues. There's no right answer here, you just need to find a good match for your feelings on the topic.

Still at a loss? Go to the American College of Obstetricians and Gynecologists website to find a physician in your area. (ACOG.com)

click

# Think You're Pregnant?

**The first three things to do when you sense you have a bun in the oven.**

TAKE A TEST . . . TOGETHER. It's not as much fun to find out this news when one of you is away on a business trip or just got home from a really bad day. Decide together when to take the test if you have an inkling, and leave yourselves time to celebrate if the news is good. Don't do it before you go to work—even though many tests say to take them in the morning—wait until Saturday morning if you're feeling formal. You can't be expected to care about the 9:30 planning meeting when you just got the biggest news of your life!

DON'T TELL ANYONE—YET. This is a huge secret for you to revel in together. Share your secret for a few days—or weeks. Decide on a plan for letting the parents know and when. It is best to wait until you're at least several weeks in to let your family in on it. Make sure you roll out the info to both sets of in-laws equally to minimize hurt feelings. And make a plan to let your friends know once you've passed the twelve-week mark.

SEE YOUR DOCTOR. Chances are the test was correct and all is perfectly well, but seeing your ob-gyn is an important step. Call for an appointment as soon as you know, explain that you just found out you're probably pregnant, and ask what he or she recommends timing-wise for getting you in there. Your doctor will take good care of you and make sure that you and baby are fully ready for your nine exciting months together.

# Five Ways to Hide Your Pregnancy

**Being pregnant is nothing to be ashamed of. But because complications are so common in the first trimester, it's advisable to resist the temptation to tell everyone you know (moms and dads are, of course, okay). Wait until you're in the clear—and have completely absorbed the exciting info!**

1. Complain to your coworkers that you're getting fat and you have no time to work out.

2. Curb your cravings. Dying for a pickle covered in peanut butter? Besides being plain gross, it's gonna raise some eyebrows.

3. Put a lime in anything you drink (clear beverages and watered down cranberry juice work great) so it looks like a cocktail.

4. Save the maternity clothes for when you really need them.

5. Don't have too many "doctor's appointments." Think of something clever, like you need to wait for the plumber/electrician/cable guy/etc.

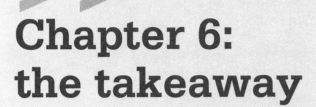

# Chapter 6:
# the takeaway

## Starting a New Family

**Agree on a timetable.** If you have decided to try for a mini-me, be fair and honest with your partner about when you'll be ready to start. Constantly putting it off or saying, "Maybe after [insert life or work milestone here]," can build resentment, because there's always going to be some goal you can say you need to hit first. Find more conversation techniques on page 200.

**Talk about the numbers.** Money aside (no one ever feels like they're financially ready to take on a dependent), discuss what size family you want. It will affect when you start, and how much to put away in the bank now. Check out our breakdown on page 206.

**Start practicing!** You can't make an omelet without breaking a few eggs. (You know what we mean.) Our pregnancy primer starts on page 210.

CHAPTER

7

# [ making it all click ]

**Bottom line: If you can communicate**
—even if it's fighting—you can get through anything. Regardless of what Mars and Venus claim,
you have to personalize your communication universe to work within your orbits. Diplomat and drill
sergeant, lover and fighter, you must find the
means to a happily-ever-after end.

## the nest test:
# your future together

Quiz each other with these questions over a nice big glass of wine. Listen carefully.

1. **What's the nicest thing I've ever done for you?**

2. **What habit of mine do you hate most?**

## 3. What are the three traits about me you love most?

4. **Do we fight too much?**

5. **Name three big things you must do in this lifetime.**

6. **If you're grumpy, do you want to be left alone, or do you want me to try to make you feel better?**

7. **What aspect of your parents' relationship do you most admire? Despise?**

8. **What do you want our life to look like five years from now?**

# can we talk?

You've dated, fallen in love, and committed to spending the rest of your lives together. You feel confident that you know each other inside and out, right? (Well, except for that incident in Mexico when you were twenty-one. But that's *ancient* history!) Your brains are in tune, but are your communication styles? How you handle the ups and downs of married life depends on this synchronization.

## FIVE COUPLE TYPES—WHICH ARE YOU?

Forget food: You are what you speak. Unless you married after dating for just two weeks, you probably have fallen into specific couple behaviors. Some good (he cooks, she cleans) and some bad (he sulks, she nags). While there's some comfort in preestablished styles, you might be selling yourselves short when it comes to growing your relationship.

It's time to pinpoint your couple personality and learn to work within who you are—communication quirks included—to make your marriage thrive. We've illustrated some typical partner types and the role ruts unique to each. Now these styles are pretty stereotypical, but even if you don't see yourselves there, do take away the overall message: You can't change who people are (and you shouldn't want to). But you can appreciate and try to work with what you've got.

*"I have got to learn to communicate more effectively. I take an awful lot of comments or situations that irritate the heck out of me and don't say anything. I think I am being a doormat."*
—mmg

### The Old Schoolers

It's almost like you stepped back into the '50s: The guy brings home the bacon and the gal cooks it. Or he takes care of the finances and she takes care of the housework. (It doesn't matter that she has a full-time job, too!) On the communication front: He talks, she listens.

Pitfalls: Even if you're traditionalists, being so rigid in your roles can only lead to resentment. Even if you aren't officially bringing home a paycheck, you still should get a voice in how money is spent.

## tip

He seemed like the ultimate modern man before you got married, and now he keeps referencing the way things are in "the old country." Cultural differences often become more extreme post-wedding when everyone is trying to figure out how to play "husband" and "wife." Don't flip out immediately, but don't let it go on too long. Traditional roles can be habit-forming.

# That's So Annoying!

Q. The quirks that were once cute are now killing me. What can I do?

A. Whether your partner snaps gum or shouts out game show answers, the fact is *everyone* has traits others might find irritating. And although these little quirks get on your nerves, they are just that— *little*. Take a look at the bigger traits. If your spouse is kind, loving, and dependable, maybe you can overlook the negative habits. However, if it's gotten to the point where you can't even be in the same room whenever *Jeopardy!* comes on, then bring the subject up gently and with a bit of humor, but prefacing it with some of his positive attributes. For example, "Honey, you are *so* smart for knowing the answer was 'photosynthesis'! And I'm sure Alex Trebek would be impressed, but the constant shouting really gets on my nerves. Do you think you could try toning it down, please?"

Key to Success: Make sure there's enough give and take to allow either of you to switch up the roles a bit. Sit down and really dig into what each of you likes and dislikes about this style. Believe it or not, he may resent her lack of an opinion, and she may love running the family finances.

Be careful: Even if everyone agrees on making a change, the first few times a previously deferential person chimes in with an opinion might not go over so well. Traditional habits—particularly those handed down for generations—die hard.

### The Bickersons

One of you is always playing devil's advocate, and you can never seem to agree on anything . . . except to disagree. Your passion for debate keeps things pretty hot in the bedroom, but it makes outsiders witnessing the fighting uncomfortable.

Pitfalls: Studies show fighting can be healthy, but not when it's a pastime. Fighting more times a week than you, say, have sex, starts training you that arguing is a normal way to live. But the increased stress is actually bad for you—not just your marriage, but your physical health!

Key to Success: Learn to pick your battles. Even if you know it takes twenty minutes to get to the mall, not thirty, bite your tongue and ask yourself if this one's really worth elevating your blood pressure.

### The Hand-holders

You share the same interests and, more important, you dislike the same things. Whether you're at home or out with friends at a bar, you're always by one another's side. You are so in sync, you complete each other's sentences and sometimes feel no need to talk at all.

Pitfalls: Losing your identity . . . and your friends . . . and your deep connection with one another. It's wonderful that you want to spend every waking moment together, but being joined at the hip doesn't guarantee your relationship will remain deep. Unless you have different experiences to share, you'll never evolve together. Besides, his friends may start to get resentful if she's always there to watch the big game, and her friends may groan if he's intruding on girl talk once again.

Key to Success: Maintain some independence by designating one night a week to be alone or "with my friends." Time apart from each other is as vitally important as togetherness because it allows each person to grow as an individual, to develop new interests, to be an "I" as well as part of a "we." Plus, it gives you something to talk about over your Wheaties.

### The Dissectors

You've spent a lot of time in the self-help section and know what the experts say makes a relationship work. Yet you overanalyze every eye roll, every spat, every decision to be made.

Pitfalls: Overtalking can lead to frustration and relationship paralysis where you fear any change will lead to another talk. Non-issues can also become issues when too many questions are asked. "Were you bothered by that?" "Why, should I have been?" "No, I

## Battle of the Sexes

Husbands communicate differently from wives. We know it sounds like a line ripped out of *Men Are from Mars, Women Are from Venus*, but it's true. Being aware of these differences can help you find a gender-bending middle ground.

HUSBAND M.O.: Facts, logic, structure. Men like to know how things work.

WIFE M.O.: Feelings, senses, meaning. Women like to know why things work.

YOUR NEWLYWED M.O.: Describe emotions in a factual way, and give concrete examples/solutions that contribute to the conversation. ("I'm angry because you made other plans; I shouldn't assume you're always available, but next time, can you check with me before accepting an invitation?")

was just wondering, because it might have bothered me." "Why on earth would something like that bother you? And are you saying that I'm competely insensitive because it didn't?" You get the point.

**Key to Success:** Stop overanalyzing! Make a pact that if something bothers one of you, you'll discuss. Otherwise, start enjoying your relationship.

## TALKING POINTS

Our best advice, no matter what kind of couple you are, is to learn how to communicate effectively and to consciously make the effort to keep the communication lines open. In the first years of marriage—and throughout your lives together—there are so many decisions to be made. And, because no matter how close you are you don't share a brain, you can never assume

you know what the other is thinking. You need to talk. A good percentage of the time, you'll have differences of opinion. But don't worry, every time you disagree—or even get mad at one another—it does not mean you're heading for a divorce. You're allowed to argue. What's not allowed? Throwing unwarranted hissy fits, never speaking up for yourself, and going to your pals instead of dealing with each other. Better communication will help prevent (and resolve) conflicts. Follow these rules:

**Think before you speak.** Figure out what you want to say before you bring up a touchy topic so you can stay diplomatic. Ask yourself, Is it about the incident at hand, or is that a symptom of a bigger issue? You don't want to argue about your mate not treating your niece nicely when it is really about a perceived lack of interest in having children. Consider mapping out one or two talking points ahead of time.

**Timing is everything.** Don't try to have an important conversation when the other person is really tired (read: cranky) or preparing for a big day at work. Stress and exhaustion can help turn a seemingly harmless talk into a full-blown battle. Make sure you have his or her undivided attention—TV off, cell phone on vibrate. You will not be heard if your listener's mind is elsewhere. If necessary,

**tip**
Choosing an inappropriate time to talk, like at 2 a.m., is a passive-aggressive move—either to cause additional conflict, or to "prove" that the person doesn't want to deal.

schedule a time to talk that's good for both of you (but don't put it off indefinitely—chances are the issue will only grow bigger).

**Make a physical connection.** Show that you're listening with positive body language: Maintain eye contact, nod, and don't cross your arms. Being sexual can sometimes be a tactic to distract the other person, to avoid the conflict. This is not a good idea. The issue won't go away just because you offer your services.

**Time Out**

# Go for the Gold

Take out your aggression in a fun way: friendly competition. Create a bedroom Olympics tournament with games like mattress gymnastics, pillow wrestling, and lamp hurdles.

**Listen up.** This one's obvious but essential. Listen to your partner without judging or making assumptions, and you will have a much more productive conversation. Better-listening tip: Ask frequent questions (without interrupting) to make sure you understand what your partner is trying to say (minus the sarcastic "So let me understand"). Let your mate finish the thought, even if you think it might kill you. Try not to refute what your partner just said. You must clarify how you're feeling, not defend yourself. If you tend to be the talker in the couple, it's a good idea to let your significant other speak after your monologue.

**Give and take.** Make sure you're being heard, too. To clear up any miscommunication —or reading between the lines—on the spot, ask if your spouse really understands what you said. (Try, "Am I making sense? I'm so upset I want to make sure I am being clear.") To be understood you first must truly understand yourself. Before you start talking about something contentious, jot down what you need to communicate. Putting your thoughts on paper will force you to make sure that you are not muddying the discussion with other agendas.

**Look at every angle.** Try to flip the situation in your mind and empathize with your partner. (Note: Empathy and sympathy are not the same thing. Sympathy is feeling bad for someone who's upset. Empathy is being upset right along with them.) Feel what they're feeling and let them know that you've taken notice (e.g., "I understand that you're feeling upset.

"There's no such thing as too much talking. Ask how the other person is feeling and ask about their day. Volunteer information about your day if they 'forget to ask.'"
—MrsOctBride

# Password Protection

**Q. Now that we're married, I think we should know each other's passwords for e-mail and online financial stuff, but my wife disagrees. Who's right?**

A. When you signed your marriage certificate, you didn't sign away your rights to any sort of private life, so it's totally legit for your wife to want to keep her e-mail account for her eyes only. When it comes to money matters, however, your individual financial decisions affect your joint future, so there's no reason you each shouldn't have access to the other's accounts. However, if this is a problem, it's clear that passwords aren't the real issue, and you need to examine why you need access to every corner of her online existence, and why she's so reluctant to share it.

Tell me why."). If after really listening and trying to put yourself in their place you just can't get as worked up as your spouse is, then just keep listening as they deal with their emotions. Sometimes a sounding board is all another person needs. And remember, the upside to empathy is that when your mate is having a great day, so are you!

**Understand your mate.** While some right-brained individuals turn on the emotional talk like a faucet, others have to be prodded into sharing how they really feel—they may feel bad for wishing you'd do something differently or resentful from waiting so long to speak up. If honest communication is difficult for your partner, take baby steps. Ask if he or she would be more comfortable discussing these topics via e-mail or by actually writing letters to each other.

## THE TRUTH ABOUT THE HONESTY POLICY

Sure, your parents and teachers taught you to never tell a lie—unfortunately, life isn't that simple once you're an adult. The simple truth is that there are going to be details of your past (or present) that your partner doesn't need to know about. Figuring out what to reveal—and what to keep under wraps—can be tricky. Here's a breakdown on the three most common types of "lies," and how to decide if you need to come clean.

**Skeletons in Your Closet** The simple guideline is this: If the issue from the past could affect your current life (i.e., "I have a son from a high school girlfriend"), it's better that your mate know now rather than when a shy sixteen-year-old shows up on your doorstep. If it's just going to hurt someone's mood and create new anxieties (i.e., "I once cheated on my boyfriend"), then trust the gut instinct that kept your lips sealed this long. Couples can love each other for who they truly are without knowing every sordid detail about their partners' pasts. What's of greater concern is that this long-lost issue is starting to creep into your mind. You need to do some self-evaluation to figure out why: Are you feeling guilty about a certain topic that's come up in your life again? Are you regretting how you treated someone in your past? Are you trying to test your partner's unconditional love for you? Work these out on your own, and your relationship will benefit without having to suffer the unnecessary drama of your self-compelled confession.

## tip

Some couples simply don't argue. Whether it's pure bliss, or, more likely, fear of conflict, they both withdraw from the threat of confrontation. A fight-free relationship isn't always healthy: Differences tend to be repressed or ignored. And when they erupt, look out. If this is you, let it out in measured doses. A good fight (even if it's over something as contrived as dishes in the sink) is good for the soul.

**Lying by Omission** Leaving out that one tricky part from an otherwise harmless story seems like an easy way to avoid a potential argument—like when you go out for drinks with some college friends but fail to mention that your ex-girlfriend was there too, or you go shopping for your mom's birthday, and don't tell your hubby that you also bought yourself a new handbag. In fact, some often debate whether this is actually lying since you are simply "forgetting" to add in a few details here and there. Since your spouse probably won't accept this logic, think about this: Would I be upset if my partner hid this from me? Will my partner find out—either through my own slipup or another person's innocent mention? Will finding out cause my partner to lose trust in me? Then behave accordingly. In many instances, it's not the actual behavior you chose to hide that would cause a fight, but the fact that you chose to be deceptive.

**Little White Lies** These small fibs—telling your wife you had a salad for lunch today even though you really inhaled a Big Mac and fries, or claiming you couldn't call DH's mom back because your cell phone died—rarely cause any real damage. You might even push the truth aside in an effort to protect your mate's feelings (i.e., telling him that you just love the hot pink stretch pants he got you for Christmas). For the most part, a little white lie every now and then isn't going to do any harm to your relationship. But if you find yourself constantly falling back on this tactic, you've got to start

# Topic:
# why do you fight?

WE DON'T REALLY EVER FIGHT BUT WE CERTAINLY BICKER. Lately it's about the house and decorating–we have different opinions on colors, etc., and he always thinks he is right.

—dekesgril

Probably it is the tone in our voices. Not necessarily the subject at hand, but just when I act annoyed or impatient it reflects in my manner of speaking, and he CANNOT handle that. We fight about our communication styles.

—wondercat04

How laid back he is....sometimes things don't get done because my sense of urgency is more intense than his. —JoonBug

**MONEY & CHORES**...although he has been helping lately with chores and we are still trying to work on the combined finances w/ money. Again all of this is part of the first year of marriage especially since we did not live with each other before. —aly81475

asking yourself why you feel compelled to lie so often. Are you afraid of his or her temper? Is your spouse too controlling? Or are you passive-aggressively trying to exert your independence (i.e., "She's not going to tell me what to eat for lunch!")? After you've thought about it on your own, calmly address any of these issues with your spouse. If necessary, talk to a marriage counselor, who can help you improve your communication skills.

## JOIN THE FIGHT CLUB

All relationships have conflict. And all couples deal with it differently: Some refuse to go to bed mad, others slam doors. Learning how to calm down and read between the lines is the ticket to turning destructive battles into constructive bonding.

**Fight Right.** Our secret to a fair fight: Know what is really going on. Nine times out of ten what you are yelling about is not what you are fighting about. If someone feels strongly enough to get into a serious argument, it is because they are either afraid or hurt—not because they actually care about your working late/dirty dishes/whatever it was you forgot to pick up on your way home. Once you turn on your emotional x-ray, you'll be able to quickly defuse the immediate problem and spend your time dealing with what's really causing tension.

**Survey the scene.** Don't underestimate the power of external circumstances. Are you stressed, tired, or angry about something else? Think about whether you're being affected by other factors.

# Fight Club

**You're completely normal if you fight about . .**

**MONEY:** Spending habits, uncontrollable debt, planning for the future (and, yikes!, retirement). No matter how much you have, money will cause angst.

**CAREER:** Unless you both do exactly the same job, for exactly the same amount of money, for exactly the same amount of hours, there will be job strife in your life. So long as there's an imbalance, there'll be battling.

**SEX:** Mismatched libidos are a main source of frustration. Sex lives tend to fizzle unless you both make a gallant effort to reignite the proverbial spark.

**FAMILY:** Overinvolved in-laws, sycophant siblings, who gets what holidays. You can't pick your family —but you can pick your fight.

**RELIGION:** If you are of different faiths, this conflict, which probably started with the wedding ceremony, will come back in a big way—often from relatives—when you start thinking about kids.

**Be self-aware.** Are you arguing because there's something you're avoiding, such as apologizing, compromising, or forgiving? Make sure you're not fighting to protect your pride. Being able to own up to your mistakes and say "I'm sorry" is a lesson well learned.

**Watch your habits.** Do you tend to slip into behaving like a child—sulking, blaming, or being obstinate? Or do you become like a critical parent, condescending, criticizing, or punishing? Identify your style and take it down a notch.

**Bend a bit.** It's impossible to make your partner change, but if you change your own behavior, he or she will almost certainly react differently. Your feelings may not be under your control, but your actions—and reactions—are. If you're angry, say, "I'm angry because . . . ," not, "You made me angry."

**Assume the best.** Don't let unjustifiable suspicions slip into your psyche. Unless you have evidence to the contrary, your partner is innocent until proven guilty.

**Don't hold a grudge.** It's difficult, but you have to forgive *and* forget. Revisiting old arguments (or even combining them with new conflicts) will send the message that there will never be an end to the debate.

## ANGER MANAGEMENT

Some couples tend to argue about the same thing over and over again. The reason? Your personality influences your fighting habits, and you can't change who you are. The plan? Identify your personal conflict styles and figure out how you need to act to get to the make-up session faster.

### The pacifist

You're a lover, not a fighter. When someone's voice gets a little louder than normal, you see it as your duty to play peacekeeper and work things out asap—even if this means admitting you're wrong when you're not.

HOW TO EVEN OUT: Take a time-out to let your mate cool off. Then, calmly state your point. Tell him or her that you can't have a discussion while tempers are flared.

> **click**
>
> Test your partner comprehension skills with our quiz (and don't worry—we've got plenty of expert advice to help you untangle anything that might get lost in translation): TheNest.com/communication

# Project: Resolution

**Get to the finish line faster with these four mottos.**

1. **DON'T LET IT ESCALATE.**

2. **RESOLVE TO RESOLVE.** "Forget it" is one of the most frustrating phrases ever said in fight land. (And when paired with walking out of the room, driving away, or looking back down at your book, it's practically a death wish.) Moves like these will only make your opponent want to prove you wrong even more, so when you're battling, everyone needs to feel that both parties are 100 percent committed to finding a resolution. If there is a deadline—your parents are arriving in five minutes—table the discussion in a way that shows you are still connected. Agree on a time and place to pick it up again and find a way to say "I love you"—just uttering the words can bring you to a point where you could dream of apologizing. The same strategy works with fights that are dragging on until 3 A.M. Even though the old adage says never go to bed angry, the consequences of fighting all night could do far more damage to your relationship. Instead, wake up early and resolve the issue then.

3. **RESPECT EACH OTHER'S RECOVERY PERIOD.** Some people can snap right back and snuggle on the couch immediately after the "I'm sorrys" are said. Others need to take some time to calm themselves down and put their emotions to rest (which can be disheartening to the quick recoverer). Don't let this difference in style drive you into another round, though. Try to determine each other's coping mechanisms and learn to deal.

4. **SAY YES TO MAKEUP SEX.** No, you are not alone—the sex after a knock-down, drag-out fight is much steamier. Both of you are at your most vulnerable and the desire to reconnect can create an intense charge. Just make sure the fight is over before you begin.

**tip**

No sleeping on the couch. Turn your backs to each other on opposites sides of the king-size mattress if need be, but always spend the night in the same room. And always say good night.

### The defense lawyer

You believe that the more decisively you strike, the better. You're no stranger to threats ("It's me or the pooch. . . . What's it going to be?"). Your sharp tactics tend not to work, and even when they do, you're left wondering if you said something you're going to regret.

HOW TO EVEN OUT: Listen first and think before you speak. You have a lifetime to finish this argument.

### The pushover

You don't like to speak up when something's wrong, and instead wait for your partner to react to your cold-shoulder treatment (or constant sighing). You open up eventually, but it's a slow and exhausting process.

HOW TO EVEN OUT: Make your partner aware of your style and shift the burden to him or her to open up the dialogue. For your part, agree to participate in the conversation when it *is* brought up. Also, you want to clue your partner in to signs that you're not upset, so he or she will know.

### The know-it-all

There's a little bit of this one in all of us. You think you're right—even if you're wrong. And you'll fight to the death to prove it.

HOW TO EVEN OUT: Can't you both be right? Find something that's accurate that the other person said (even if it's that the sky is blue) and allow them to do the same for you; go from there.

### The diplomat

You (calmly) listen to your spouse's side, then (eloquently) express your own opinion. You (considerately) try to find a compromise that suits both viewpoints and both people.

HOW TO EVEN OUT: Your impressive (and mature) conflict-management skills could become bothersome to an agitated mate. Sometimes you need to put up a good fight to let off steam.

# How to Hire . . . a Marriage Counselor

You may be thinking, we're newlyweds—there's no way we need counseling. But therapy doesn't signify the end. Talking out your problems with an experienced mediator may help you understand your partner—and your marriage—a little better. Think of it as preventive medicine.

- Check your insurance plan. Many times, the therapist will have to submit some sort of diagnosis to the insurance company in order for the treatment to be covered. Some insurance companies require referrals from primary care physicians. If this is the case, the person would have to see his or her primary doctor to be evaluated and referred to a therapist.

- Get referrals. Ask for recommendations from friends/family members who have gone to therapy. Most therapists are reluctant to work with two people who have close relationships (like your brother or mother), but that doctor should be able to refer you to someone else. Check the websites of various professional associations like APA.org or NASWDC.org. Insurance company websites also have doctor locators that will help you find the type of doctor/therapist you're looking for, and that way you'll know the person is definitely covered by your insurance.

- Real qualifications. Therapy is a really gray profession and can be practiced in so many different ways (MD vs. PsyD vs. PhD vs. Family Counselor vs. Certified Social Worker vs. anyone, in some states, who calls himself a counselor). Briefly: An MD went to med school, a PsyD has a doctorate in psychology, a PhD has gotten a doctorate in something (check on it—might not be psychology or family relations at all), a family counselor has received special training in the field of family relations (but might not have an advanced degree), an LCSW may have studied assessment and psychotherapy within a broader context—possibly by getting an undergraduate degree. For couples therapy, it's important to find someone with an MFT certification, because these are the people who are specially trained to facilitate communication and they're very solution-focused.

- Interviews. Ways of interacting with patients vary, so it's important to meet your candidates face to face. The type of therapist to choose varies for everyone. There's nothing wrong with shopping around to find the one you like best and whose methods of treatment are most effective for you (just remember, you'll be charged for each meeting!).

## tip

Once you've found a therapist, make a pact to go for, say, ten sessions and then reevaluate. (Make sure to let your therapist know, too, in case he or she has a different timeline for your work.) Knowing the process won't go on forever can make it more palatable and may actually increase your focus on getting results—not just talking it out.

# making the effort

-------------------------------------------------------------------------------

When you first met, every date filled you with the thrill of anticipation. Now that you're always together, you start to take each other for granted. After all, no reason to write a cute limerick e-mail inviting your mate to a special dinner tonight—he or she is gonna be there when you get home anyway (possibly splayed out on the couch, zonked from a long day of work).

When the flowers and fanfare die down, it's easy to worry that something is wrong with your relationship. You may even find yourself having postnuptial cold feet. We have two words: Stop it. Just because the romance has started to wane doesn't mean your feelings have at all. The truth is, part of the wining and dining romance of those early days came from the idea that this very special person might just be perfect for you, and you needed to make the effort to hold on to them. Now, it's not that you were wrong, but when you're sharing the mundane details of daily life like flossing and filling out tax forms, it can be hard to step back and see that person as the ideal mate you once dreamed about. But your perfect partner is exactly that—someone you can rely on to degrout the tub, help baby-sit your demonic niece, and not laugh when your attempt to make salmon fails miserably.

## ROMANTIC EXPECTATIONS

Just like with any other issue along the winding road of marriage, communication is the key to finding a romantic balance. Romantic types must express their need for sweet nothings to emotionally challenged spouses. Stoic types need to make known how deep (or shallow) their capability for cuteness runs. How? Ask specific questions. Start with the yes/no variety like, "Does it make you unhappy when I do this?" "Do you wish I'd do [this or that] more often?" "Would you like me to plan more of our time together?"

"It sounds funny, but DH and I both seem to have higher standards for ourselves and each other since we got married. He prides himself more on making sure I have what I need, and I take more responsibility for the house and looking after him. We see each other as partners now."
—lizzie&chris

Then, pay attention to your partner's response to everything, from how much PDA they want to whether they'd rather get a lap dance or a library card on a date night. Figuring out where your opinions differ the most will tell you the first place you can start working on compromises and setting goals that will make you both feel absolutely adored. Here's how to make it work.

### For the Romantic Partner

Talking about how much romance you like to give and receive doesn't take the magic out of it. Look at it this way: Say your number one dream is to get flowers on your birthday, and you don't. If you assume that "My spouse would do this for me if he or she could or wanted to," you're pretty much guaranteeing that you're not going to get flowers on your next birthday, and your poor spouse is going to go around thinking you're perfectly happy. It's only by talking about your deepest, dreamiest, fairy-tale wishes that you have any chance of seeing them come true in your day-to-day marriage.

Focus on the positive things that you miss from before you got married. Explaining why a particular gesture or behavior was such a turn-on will likely make your partner want to do it again right away—it may even have been something he or she didn't do consciously. And when your partner does come through on those promises to try and be more romantic, don't forget to say thank you for it. When romantic gestures are met with silence, it's easy for the active partner to assume it's not worth wasting time on it. Then *you* think they don't care about *you* anymore. Avoid this catch-22 by being generous with both your romantic gestures and your appreciation for your partner's.

### For the Less-Romantic Partner

Being romantic in the "right" way also requires work, precisely because it is such a personal, undefineable quality. We've all gone out with someone who pouted because we didn't hold hands during the movies, then pouted when we did, because "You're only doing that to make me happy!" It takes time to create a romantic persona that blends both sincerity and your own personality. Just like when you learn a new language, you're not going to sound totally confident your first few

# Topic:
# date ideas

"

For our anniversary I'm giving my husband a box of 52 date ideas (1 for each week). I'm trying to keep them inexpensive, but lots of fun. Any suggestions?

—gryphonchild

Carnivals, mini golfing, going for a walk.

—MrsBostonBride

**TRIP TO A BUTTERFLY GARDEN**, stay in and make cookies, watch the stars, go to the circus, **buy some kites** and fly them on a windy day.

—JeffAnEm

**Some ideas:** Blockbuster night, a picnic, museums, botanical gardens, aquariums.

"

—celinaonline

**Couple massages at a spa. Cooking classes.** —michelleinaz

GET TICKETS TO SEE A BAND THAT WAS POPULAR WHEN YOU WERE GROWING UP, go rollerskating, challenge him to invent a new ice cream sundae, go on a morning jog (to burn off your taste-testing calories).

—Carra

### nest note:
Make sure you each get a chance to plan date nights so that no one can complain about not getting to choose. But be fair—if your wife hates football, don't force her to spend the day watching it with you, and if your husband can't stand the opera, it's probably best not to choose that for your big night out. Remember, this should be fun for *both* of you.

times saying it out loud. With enough practice, though, you'll become fluent in being able to give your lover the right input and reading his or her response.

If your partner is überromantic and you're not, enlist his or her help to plan dates and outings. It will show you're really trying. Your spouse can plan the day ("We'll go canoeing and then stargazing!") while you carry out specific tasks ("Can you pack a picnic lunch with [this, this, and that], and also call around to find out where we can rent canoes and print out the map of how to get there?").

## KEEPING THE ROMANCE ALIVE

Besides basic date nights, make sure you're putting enough romance fuel into your daily life. We've pulled together four things just-marrieds say (on TheNest.com message boards) they miss from the old days of their courtship: communicating "just because," little gifts, physical affection, and compliments. If they sound familiar, it's because they're the same things you've probably been doing with and for your honey since high school! That should tell you a couple of things: they're simple, they'll feel intuitive once you pick them back up as habits, and they're also likely to set off hormonal urges—maybe not to the degree you had when you were sixteen, but more than you otherwise might at the end of a long workweek.

### Communicating "Just Because"

If you've got access to your e-mail from the beginning of your relationship, an interesting experiment is to open it up and reread old notes. You may be surprised by the frequency or length of early e-mails, since now they usually begin and end with, for example, "ok that I asked Tom to come by for dinner?" When you have all day and all night to talk about stuff, you forget about the flirtatious excitement of answering a call at work from your dearest or the thrill of seeing a new message from his account.

**Get It Back**

- Start by writing one e-mail or making one phone call per week that's "hello-plus"— saying hi and filling in your honey on the events of your day.
- Add to your reminder notes. Follow up "Make sure to drop off files at the accountant," with something unnecessarily mushy, like "And also remember that I love you very much and am happy every day to be married to such an amazing individual."
- Go way back in time and pass notes. Tuck a Post-it in your spouse's pocket or purse to find later. You don't even have to be all Shakespeare—a simple happy face or heart signed with your initials will send an unmistakable, low-maintenance message.

# Free Love

Here are 20 sweet things you can do for each other that don't entail a credit card, taking your clothes off, or a vacation day.

1. Put toothpaste on her toothbrush before she even gets to the sink.

2. Load a surprise playlist on her iPod.

3. Take care of one item on his to-do list (making a dentist appointment, picking up his mom's birthday gift, finding an intramural soccer league).

4. E-mail an interesting link to her friend who you barely get along with.

5. Invite five friends over for a surprise half-birthday cake.

6. Leave a pack of his favorite gum in his bag with a note that says "pucker up."

7. Subscribe to news clippings on some of her favorite topics. Being interested in each other's interests makes dinner conversation ten times more interactive.

8. Let him read the front section of the paper first.

9. Buy a picture frame for her to bring to work and put her favorite snapshot in it.

10. Hand him his towel as he's getting out of the shower.

11. Rent the movie you know she has been dying to see, but you could live without watching.

12. Send a card in the mail, despite the fact you see each other every day.

13. Hand her a big glass of water and a reminder to stay healthy.

14. Buy her a single truffle from a gourmet chocolate store.

15. Sit down for a half hour with a blank notebook and recount five of your favorite memories of each other. This will come in very handy on your tenth, twentieth, and fiftieth anniversaries.

16. Call, e-mail, or text during the workday just to say "Love you. Can't wait to see you." It's faster, and it feels like kids passing notes in class, if you come up with an acronym like LYCWTSY.

17. TiVo the game if the fan can't be home to catch it.

18. Rub his shoulders for fifteen minutes after a stressful day at work.

19. Wear her favorite shirt of yours, and when she compliments you, say thanks and tell her you were thinking of her when you pulled it from the closet.

20. Fold down the corners of magazines and catalogs if you think he'll be interested in what's on the page.

**Little Gifts**

When you were dating, picking up little presents for your honey was an easy way to show affection: the chintzy figurine in the shape of a childhood nickname, a book by his or her favorite author from the dollar rack, a pint of ice cream because you knew you'd be having dinner, a sweet flower arrangement after a great date.

Of course, now that you're married, you don't have to prove your attraction anymore—you've both got rings that make that fact perfectly clear. Plus, you already share grocery-stocking and house-cleaning duties, so you know very well that you don't need more "junk" sitting around. But that doesn't mean it's not still fun and arousing for your partner to get a little present, no matter how silly.

**Get It Back**

- Put an earmarked ten-dollar bill in your purse, wallet, or money clip, and make that your "mushy-gift fund." The next time you see a small item that makes you think of your spouse, you won't have to think about its practicality—you'll know that's exactly what your fund is for.

- Every time you take a trip, even if it's just two towns over for work, bring back something. It can be sentimental or silly, but says, "I was thinking of you." (This works doubly well in the heartmelt department if you pick up something while you're on a trip together and then give it to your spouse once you're back in your day-to-day life.)

**Physical Affection**

We're not nuts—we realize that if you spent every second together holding hands, no one would ever clean the bathroom. But when you intersperse tender touches into your daily routine, it reminds you that you're more than just roommates or names on a marriage license—you're two people with a bond that no one else could ever understand. Hugs and caresses have long-term results: Every time you reach out and touch your partner, even in passing, you're stimulating their body and mind to think about you, which is only going to get them thinking more about you when you're not there.

**Get It Back**

- Make it your goal to touch your partner one extra time every day—a kiss on the head before you leave for work, a quick neck rub while they're straining at the computer, a hand on the thigh under the dinner table, or a loving pinch to the bum while they're brushing their teeth.

# Dangerous Habits

**Stay vigilant and steer clear of these five seemingly harmless behaviors that quietly scream you don't care . . .**

**SKIPPING HELLOS AND GOOD-BYES.** When your significant other arrives in the house or walks into a room, you must stop what you are doing for a second and greet them. You don't need to get up from the couch and escort them in royal style, but you do need to make eye contact, say hello, and ask how they are. Same goes for good-byes. No one likes to get out of the shower and realize they are alone – it makes you feel invisible. Long kisses are not required, just a quick moment of connection.

**MAKING JOKES AT YOUR SPOUSE'S EXPENSE.** We all like to be funny, but when you start teasing the love of your life in front of your friends or family, it sends out a very weird message. So many truths are said in jest that even if your comment is innocent and purely for fun, it will probably raise some eyebrows and sting your so-called best friend.

**REVEALING SECRETS TO OUTSIDERS.** Soul mates need the security of knowing that if they've gone out on a limb and exposed their inner self, their secrets are safe with their spouse. Even if you are talking only to a close friend or a parent, even if you are sharing good news (like a pregnancy), even if you've sworn your audience to secrecy and you believe you are speaking in complete confidence, it is still wrong. You can't unilaterally change the boundaries of privacy on behalf of your twosome. Ask first. Chances are your spouse will understand your need to have an outside sounding board. If not, out of respect, keep the matter private.

**FORGETTING.** Yes, everyone is busy and overwhelmed, but forgetting your darling's birthday, or pretending you have a present delayed in the mail when in reality you didn't shop till the last minute, is a sure sign you are taking each other for granted. While not of the same magnitude, neglecting to remember critical information about your significant other's interests (the big pitch meeting she has on Tuesday, the fact that the Final Four starts on Friday, the day his mom is scheduled to go in for surgery) implies that you are either not listening—or not interested—in the matters that make them tick.

**BEING TOO CASUAL.** Don't confuse being comfortable—or being equals—with being rude. The day your partner lets a door swing shut in your face as you try to walk in behind, you need to have a sit-down. Common courtesies (saying please and thank you, offering a soda when you pour one for yourself, opening the car door, carrying some of his or her bags) are tiny threads of love that keep the whole relationship tied together.

- Once you've reached that goal, make it twice a day, and keep increasing it. Soon you'll be feeling so back in love that you'll forget to count your little contacts.

## Compliments

When you live with a person, their wake-up face can start to blend with the I'm-all-dressed-up face. Soon, you barely notice what they're wearing unless they show up at the breakfast table in black-tie attire. But compliments were the building blocks for many couples, from hearing "You look great" at the beginning of a date, to whispering something grateful during sex, to saying "You must be awesome at work to have gotten that meeting with your boss—wow!" When compliments start being forgotten, people start to feel undervalued. You can nip that in the bud by laying it on thick—and sincerely.

### Get It Back

- Say something nice about the person every day. Physical appearance is an easy one, but many people feel more truly touched when you compliment something less obvious, such as telling your spouse how great his laugh is or admiring how well she handled negotiating with the realtor.
- Start giving a compliment any time you're about to say "Thanks." "Did you call the plumber today? Thanks," becomes "Did you call the plumber today? Thanks—you're so good at taking care of all the house stuff that I'd be lost if anything happened while you were out of town." "Pass the pepper. Thanks," becomes "Pass the pepper. Thanks—wow, your hands are really soft today." Your spouse will not only get an ego boost, but will associate those good feelings with being around you. Double win!

# **Your Anniversary**

**Every year when you make it to the big day, you need to celebrate! You've successfully waded through the ups and downs of married life for another twelve months. Be sure to plan something special: that expensive restaurant you've been dying to try, a weekend spa getaway, breakfast in bed. You get the idea.**

### GET SERIOUS ABOUT CELEBRATING

Planning an anniversary is not something you do the night before: Start four weeks out—or even four months out if you're considering an anniversary vacation. Your first step is figuring out who is responsible for the idea and the execution. We like the idea of rotating—she takes odd anniversaries (one, three, five), he takes even (two, four, six). This way both parties get to be indulged . . . or even surprised.

### MAKE IT EASY ON YOURSELVES.

Don't like the pressure of coming up with new ideas every year? Always go to the restaurant where you got engaged. Or every five years take a trip to a new spot in Mexico or wherever you spent your honeymoon. Honoring this event shouldn't cause more tension in your lives.

### CONSIDER FETING WITH FRIENDS.

If going out to a nice restaurant is nothing special to you, make your anniversary an excuse to throw a big dinner with friends. Pick a Caribbean restaurant if you honeymooned in the Bahamas, and have your photo album out. (You might want to wait until the third, fourth, or fifth anniversary because close pals may have seen enough of your wedding for a while.)

## The etiquette of anniversary gifts

Unless you take pleasure in a 1950s traditionalist approach to life, you should both give each other a gift. Set a loose budget guideline so that on your "paper" anniversary one person doesn't give stationery while the other pulls out first-class tickets to Paris. Try to hide the exact cost from each another, so use cash or your personal credit card. It is less romantic when the bill-payer has to make payments on her own diamond earrings. Another good idea: Go in on a gift for the two of you. Buy yourselves a wine refrigerator, a six-week cooking class, or a day of couples treatments at the city's best spa.

The only rule is that your gift to your relationship should feel indulgent. (No matter how much you need one, a new vacuum cleaner—even the fancy $900 kind—is *not* a good anniversary gift.)

And honestly, if money is an issue, you don't need to buy each other gifts at all, but both parties need to know about—and agree on—that plan. Recite five things you adore about each other.

## NEW GIFT IDEAS

Let's face it, anniversary traditions are a bit . . . traditional. While some symbols can be easily translated into a thoughtful or even sexy gift, others (like iron) are a bit more obscure. To bring these customs into the twenty-first century, we've compiled a gifting array that spans both the classic and the modern.

1. **Paper**

   CLASSIC: Monogrammed stationery

   MODERN: Floral origami; watercolor or charcoal artwork; a highway billboard announcing your anniversary and proclaiming your undying love

2. **Cotton**

   CLASSIC: High thread count sheets

   MODERN: Plantation-inn stay; nineteenth-century tapestry; fabulous designer shirt

3. **Leather**

   CLASSIC: Monogrammed attaché case or great designer bag

   MODERN: Those wing tips or stilettos you've seen him or her eyeing

4. **Flowers**

   CLASSIC: A year's worth of flowers delivered once a month

   MODERN: Plant a tree in your yard and watch its progress over the coming years

5. **Wood**

   CLASSIC: A wood desk

   MODERN: Chessboard, billiards table; a secluded weeklong vacation at a log cabin

6. **Iron**

   CLASSIC: Wrought-iron bed frame

   MODERN: His or her own golf club engraved with a romantic message; ironclad promise for a weekend of sensual massage

7. **Wool**

   CLASSIC: Cashmere scarves; sweaters; bedding

   MODERN: Knitting lessons; trip to the Shetland Islands in Scotland or to Cashmere, Washington

8. **Bronze**

   CLASSIC: Bronze household-fixture upgrades

   MODERN: Statue; bookends; sundial

9. **Pottery**

   CLASSIC: Bake-your-own clay pot; raku vase

   MODERN: Moroccan tagine (with heavy stew inside)

10. **Tin**

    CLASSIC: High-performance luxury sedan; pressed-tin ceiling

    MODERN: Trip to Tinseltown; Grand Canyon tour via ultralight aircraft

flip

Keep a log of your anniversary celebrations using our worksheet on page 283.

# Topic: the best part of being married

**Always having someone to come home to.**

Even when you're not involved in a conversation, the room just feels **WARMER AND COZIER** with your spouse in it.

**Cooking for two** is so much more fun than cooking for one.

Knowing that, for the rest of my life, **I AM GUARANTEED TO LAUGH—A LOT.**

We'd been together forever, but after the marriage certificate was signed, I started to think, 'That's my husband—he's so cute/adorable/amazing/sexy.' **I have never been more lovestruck in my life!**

**A warm bed.**

**Splitting dessert—it saves me some calories.**

I think my heart grew bigger and filled up with love when we said 'I do.'

The sense of calm that comes with knowing you're together—forever.

**Sharing knowing looks** with her from across the room when we're at my crazy parents' house.

# finding your future

By now you realize that your (wonderful) wedding wasn't the culmination of your relationship, but the beginning of a whole new love story between you and your spouse. Over the past chapters, we've given you specific tools for carving out a successful partnership in everything from decorating together to decoding your in-laws' weird behaviors. But the real key to success is your own willingness to see marriage as a flexible, fluid journey between two dynamic people who love each other.

## YOU VS. THE TWO OF YOU

Ages ago, when you first realized that the other had serious potential as a life partner, you were probably drawn to the things that you added to each other's lives—she opened your eyes to scuba diving, he could diffuse tense situations and still get to the bottom of things. Now that you're permanently paired up, it's still important for each of you to evolve—and to allow your twosome to evolve.

### Pursue Yourselves

Each of you needs to continue pursuing your passions, maintaining friendships, and just generally growing so that you each continually have something new and exciting to bring to the marriage. This is easy if both parties are engaged in their own interests and careers. It becomes more complicated when one person feels lost or relies on the relationship to be their entire sense of purpose. Your spouse should be your biggest supporter, but not the legs you stand on.

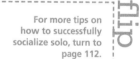

For more tips on how to successfully socialize solo, turn to page 112.

### Accept the Space

No matter how close and connected two people are, they will forever be separate—this is a fact not only to accept, but to delight in. If you desperately try to close that distance by convincing your spouse to think you way you do, forcing him to tone down his quirks, or asking her to give up the things that take time away from you, the relationship will be flat, or even worse, claustrophobic. Nurture your mate to be who they are—not who you want them to be—and learn to love each other's uniqueness.

# Career vs. Couplehood

**It can be difficult balancing the two, but it's not impossible. Here, the five most common scenarios—and how to not let them take over your marriage.**

### One of you is always working late.

While one of you is usually home for dinner, the other frequently pulls in long hours to make the boss happy. After a while, the waiting spouse might start to feel like second best.

**KEY TO SUCCESS:** No one expects you to give up your career once you get married, but you also need to remember that now there is a person at home anticipating your return. If possible, try to give him or her a heads-up on your work schedule the weekend before ("I know I have to work late Tuesday and Thursday"). This way, your spouse can feel free to make dinner plans with friends. Of course, there are times you might have to work late unexpectedly—when that happens, be sure to call home so there's no need for your honey to worry.

### One of you is unhappy with your job.

Since most of us spend the majority of our time at work, hating your job can really take its toll—both personally and professionally. After all, it's hard to put on a smiley face at night or on the weekend when you have work stress hanging over your head. As for the other spouse, seeing your sweetie unhappy can stress you out, too—not to mention sometimes having to walk on eggshells because your significant other's mood swings are out of control.

**KEY TO SUCCESS:** If you're the unhappy camper, try to come up with solutions to your problems: Can you transfer departments or find a similar position at another company? Would you be happier switching careers or going back to school? Coming up with possible answers to your problem will at the very least make you feel like you're taking control of the situation.

If you're the spouse, be supportive. We know it can get annoying listening to the same list of complaints over and over, but being that ear to listen or shoulder to cry on is what you signed on for when you said "I do." If he or she asks for your opinion, by all means feel free to throw in your two cents. If they don't, it's probably best to keep quiet. Oftentimes your spouse just needs to vent and isn't looking for you to fix the problem.

**One of you gets offered a great new job—in another state.**

Which career is more important? If the other person doesn't like their job, would rather stay home with the kids, or makes significantly less money, this could be an easy question. But if both your careers are on the upswing, the other person might not be so enthusiastic about this new opportunity.

KEY TO SUCCESS: Don't take it personally. If you're the one with the great opportunity, don't get offended if your spouse doesn't automatically volunteer to give up his or her job. And the same goes in reverse—if you're the spouse being asked to move, don't assume that your sweetie is insinuating that your career is less important. Part of married life is figuring out what works best for the two of you as a couple, not as individuals. So sit down calmly and talk over the pros and cons, each of your fears, etc. Then make a decision together.

**You both work late.**

While you don't have to worry about your spouse complaining that you're never home, this scenario definitely cuts into your couple time. A few stolen moments in the morning and late at night won't help you in the romance department, and pretty soon you both might start taking each other for granted.

KEY TO SUCCESS: You can have a successful career and marriage—all it takes is some organization. Both of you can try getting into the office an hour earlier a few days a week so you can be home in time for dinner together. And try to keep work on the weekends a minimum since you'll want to use that time to reconnect.

**You work together.**

You get to spend plenty of time together during the week, which can be a real catch-22 (hey, everyone needs some space). Work stress can seep into your relationship outside the office, and some couples even get overly competitive with each other—especially if one of you is higher up on the company ladder.

> Dish about all aspects of your work life on our boards: TheNest.com/9to5talk.
>
> click

KEY TO SUCCESS: Make it a point not to discuss work-related issues at home. This can be tough—especially if you're running a business together—but make a real effort. Your time outside the office should be all about having fun with each another, so pick activities that you both enjoy that have absolutely nothing to do with work, like taking a cooking class, dancing lessons, or joining a book club. This way, you'll have more to talk about over the dinner table than just business.

### Prepare for Being on the Outs

The ebb and flow of a relationship doesn't stop when things are official. There will be times when you will feel like two juicy peas in a warm and cozy pod, and there will be other times when it feels like your words are echoing across a canyon between the two of you. It is a frightening feeling, but one you'll need to learn to face—candidly and without blame. Couples who have been married a while learn to articulate the issue, and that in itself brings them closer: "Wow, we aren't really connecting right now, are we?" Or even, "Man, we're going through a tough time! I just want you to know that even though I don't really like you that much this week—I really do love you." Being this honest requires a tremendous amount of confidence in yourselves and in the strength of your commitment—so take it slow.

**tip**
Dinner conversation getting a little drab? Don't turn on the TV. Instead, make the effort to bring up two or three new topics—an article you saw, a political debate, even a previously untold story from your childhood.

## SIDE BY SIDE, IN THE SAME DIRECTION

Whether it's an age thing, or the sense that you've taken one huge step toward the "real" rest of your life, marriage all of a sudden becomes the gateway to your future and the countless bumps in the road. In the best relationships, couples learn to adapt and evolve together. They accept that change—be it someone wanting to go back to school, or give up a career to become a full-time mom, or head off for six months to care for an aging parent—is an essential part of coexistence and they support each other, for better or for worse. But while life can be a long and very winding road, having a shared sense of direction—where you see yourselves in five, ten, fifty years—will make the overall journey that much more enjoyable.

### What Do You Want?

You've got the most important thing in life: a 24/7 loving teammate. But what else is on your list? Are there places you'd like to live? Cities you must visit? A language/skill/dance style you'd like to learn? Kids and career goals are also musts for the list. Think short-term (things you'd like to do next year) and long-term (things you'd like to do before you die). Once you've both got your top twenty to-dos, it's time to trade papers. Share why you'd like to achieve these things. What does it satisfy? Is it security, popularity, or your own satisfaction? When we talk about our dreams and ambitions, we're sharing things that have shaped us and who we hope to become. We're saying something about our personal values and priorities.

### Planning Your Route

Making your priorities parallel so you can take on the world together is the real secret to happily ever after. To do this, you'll need a game plan. Brace—and pace—yourselves. This isn't an on-the-phone-at-work, what's-for-dinner kind of conversation. You need to sit down and dig into the details of your life plan. It's not as scary as it sounds—you've probably discussed all these things at some point in your relationship anyway. You know he's always wanted a dog; he knows you're spoiled by your parents' beach house and want your own someday. Now you need to reassess and turn these assumptions into future facts.

Ask some specific questions and make a list. Some points to ponder: Do you need to stay near your families or should you angle to live abroad for a while? Do you want kids a year from now, five years, ten? When do you want to buy a house? What do you need to do financially to make that possible? What are you working for—or toward? Are you the retiring types? If one of you dreams of devoting your life to the arts, how can you make that possible? Any luxuries (a boat, a cottage in the country, one month in Spain each summer) that you need to be happy?

Once you've thought about all that and more, look at your list and make a plan. Which dreams are the most important? What can we make happen this year and next? What will we have to leave on the list until we are sixty? Which ones contradict each other? But this isn't a swap meet: You both need to feel that your goals are reflected in your future plans so you can be equally invested in making them come true. Revisit the list yearly to see if you still want the same things. Be thrilled if you hit half the spots you expected to visit on your lifelong road trip together, and make certain to be open to surprises.

### Ready, Set . . . Go.

What comes next isn't a science. All the worksheets or self-help books or family histories in the world can't predict how your romance will evolve over the next years and decades you spend together. And you know we'd be lying if we promised you that it'd be a picnic every day. But you've got the power to learn from each stage of your relationship—about taking care of yourself, your spouse, and your marriage (which can be three very different things).

If you make your marriage a priority in your life—not an obsession, but not an afterthought—we truly believe that you can enjoy (nearly) every minute of the experience. Your first responsibility? Relax. Don't try to put everything we've laid out for you on your immediate to-do list—at least not all at once. Put down this book, think about the parts that spoke to you, and keep it somewhere handy so you can refer back to it when you start dealing with some of the issues that seemed totally foreign to you when you read about them. A marriage isn't about planning, lists, or plotting, even if those can help along the way. It's about loving that fact that you get to live every day with an amazing person who—lucky for you—loves you, too. So get up, give each other a big squeeze, and head out into the world. Your future is waiting.

**tip**

Maybe it's a little dorky, but we guarantee you'll be glad you did it: Keep a "marriage time capsule" of wish lists, yearly goals, and plans—a secret box that only the two of you know about. Make a tradition of opening it every New Year's Day to remind yourselves of all you've accomplished together.

# Chapter 7:
# the takeaway

**Fight right.** The best couples aren't the ones who agree on everything—they're the ones who know how to pick their battles, work through them, change their own behavior when needed, and learn something more about their relationship from the process. Tips start on page 231.

**Appreciate one another (we're serious).** When you were first dating your partner, out-of-nowhere gifts, compliments, cuddles, and communications didn't just seem like relationship perks, they actually made you love the person more. And guess what—those techniques still work. Find inspiration on page 236.

**Get excited for your future together.** Part of the power of being in a couple is having a teammate and supporter for all your future plans and dreams. It can feel corny to talk about them, but your long-range goals are going to be directly impacted by your partner, and have an effect on his or her life, too. Turn the page to get started.

# [the nest]
## Newlywed Worksheets

We all know how hard it is to organize oneself, but put another person in the mix, and it's a rather daunting task. Use these worksheets to get your newlywed life in line—you'll have everything in one place when it's time to fill out paperwork or look up something.

### tip
You can always fill these pages out right in this book, but you can also photocopy them and put them in a binder, or post them in key places like on the fridge or file cabinet.

 # Our 411

Keep this list somewhere secure—you two need to be able to access it, but no one else should!

## HIS

Legal Name _____

Date of Birth _____

Driver's License # _____

Social Security # _____

Place of Birth _____

Phone (cell) _____

Phone (work) _____

E-mail Address _____

E-mail Address 2 _____

IM Name _____

Mom _____

Dad _____

Address _____

_____

Phone _____

Mom's work # _____

Mom's cell # _____

Dad's work # _____

Dad's cell # _____

Manager _____

Phone _____

E-mail _____

Work Address _____

_____

Office emergency # _____

Siblings/Friends _____

_____

_____

_____

_____

_____

## HERS

Legal Name _____

Date of Birth _____

Driver's License # _____

Social Security # _____

Place of Birth _____

Phone (cell) _____

Phone (work) _____

E-mail Address _____

E-mail Address 2 _____

IM Name _____

Mom _____

Dad _____

Address _____

_____

Phone _____

Mom's work # _____

Mom's cell # _____

Dad's work # _____

Dad's cell # _____

Manager _____

Phone _____

E-mail _____

Work Address _____

_____

Office emergency # _____

Siblings/Friends _____

_____

_____

_____

_____

_____

# Our Health Sheet

## HIS

GENERAL PRACTITIONER: _____

**Name** _____

**Address** _____

_____

**Office #** _____

**Pager (cell)** _____

SPECIALIST _____

**Name** _____

**Address** _____

_____

**Office #** _____

**Pager (cell)** _____

SPECIALIST _____

**Name** _____

**Address** _____

_____

**Office #** _____

**Pager (cell)** _____

**Food Allergies** _____

_____

**Medical Allergies** _____

_____

**Last Tetanus Shot** _____

**Blood Type** _____

**Medical History** _____

_____

**Insurance** _____

**Policy #** _____

**Group #** _____

## HERS

GENERAL PRACTITIONER _____

**Name** _____

**Address** _____

_____

**Office #** _____

**Pager (cell)** _____

SPECIALIST _____

**Name** _____

**Address** _____

_____

**Office #** _____

**Pager (cell)** _____

SPECIALIST _____

**Name** _____

**Address** _____

_____

**Office #** _____

**Pager (cell)** _____

**Food Allergies** _____

_____

**Medical Allergies** _____

_____

**Last Tetanus Shot** _____

**Blood Type** _____

**Medical History** _____

_____

**Insurance** _____

**Policy #** _____

**Group #** _____

While you're both grownups capable of caring for yourselves, who couldn't use reminders every now and then? Use this list to check in on checkups.

# Checkup Checklist

## For Both of You:

[ ] **Routine Physical Exam: every two years or as directed by doc**

[ ] **Complete Blood Count: Annually**

[ ] **Skin Exams: Every 3 years (ages 20 to 40)**

[ ] **Blood Pressure: Every 2 years**

[ ] **Cholesterol: At least every 5 years**

[ ] **Dental Exam and Cleaning: 1 to 2 time(s)/year**

[ ] **Eye Exams: 3 to 5 years if no vision problems present**

[ ] **Hearing: Every decade, if no problems**

[ ] **Tetanus Booster Vaccine: Every 10 years**

## For Her:

[ ] **Breast Self-Exam: Monthly (7 to 10 days from start of period)**

[ ] **Professional Breast Exam: Annually**

[ ] **Pap Smear: Annually, or as directed by physician**

[ ] **Pelvic Exam: Annually**

## For Him:

[ ] **Professional Genital Exam for Testicular Cancer: Every 3 to 5 years**

[ ] **Self Genital Exams: Monthly**

# ✚ Our Emergency 911

Nearest Hospital_____
_____
_____

Local Police_____

Local Fire_____

Poison Control_____

Neighbors_____
_____
_____

Lawyer_____
_____

Insurance_____

Accountant_____

Plumber_____

## Our Emergency Plan:

_____
_____
_____
_____
_____
_____
_____
_____

**tip:**

Be prepared for an emergency. Hopefully, you'll never have to worry about a fire, medical emergency, or natural disaster, but it's a good idea to have a plan of action just in case. Sit down with your spouse and go over all the basics: Where are the important documents (insurance forms, social security cards, etc.) kept? If you're separated during the event, where will you meet up (your mom's house, a friend's place)? And know who to call *if* something comes up—keep doctor, pharmacy, and health insurance numbers in your wallet at all times so they're always on hand.

# Our Documents

Hard-to-replace originals (think anything with an official stamp) should be kept in a safety-deposit box or fireproof safe. Make copies of the others for your files.

| | HAVE | NEED | WHERE KEPT: |
|---|---|---|---|
| Marriage License | [ ] | [ ] | _____ |
| Birth Certificates | [ ] | [ ] | _____ |
| Social Security Cards | [ ] | [ ] | _____ |
| Passports | [ ] | [ ] | _____ |
| Immigration Papers/Visas | [ ] | [ ] | _____ |
| Will | [ ] | [ ] | _____ |
| Living Will | [ ] | [ ] | _____ |
| Power(s) of Attorney | [ ] | [ ] | _____ |
| Mortgage Documents/Apt. Lease | [ ] | [ ] | _____ |
| Deed | [ ] | [ ] | _____ |
| Property Tax Statements | [ ] | [ ] | _____ |
| Car Registration | [ ] | [ ] | _____ |
| Car Lease | [ ] | [ ] | _____ |
| Income Tax Returns (previous two years) | [ ] | [ ] | _____ |
| Health Insurance Cards | [ ] | [ ] | _____ |
| Record of Immunizations | [ ] | [ ] | _____ |

 **Our Utilities**

[  ] **Electric bill**

Company _____

Mailing Address _____

Account # _____

Customer Service _____

[  ] **Heating Bill**

Company _____

Mailing Address _____

Account # _____

Customer Service _____

[  ] **Gas Bill**

Company _____

Mailing Address _____

Account # _____

Customer Service _____

[  ] **Water Bill**

Company _____

Mailing Address _____

Account # _____

Customer Service _____

[  ] **Home Phone Bill**

Company _____

Mailing Address _____

Account # _____

Customer Service _____

[  ] **Cell Phone Bills**

Company _____

Mailing Address _____

Account # _____

Customer Service _____

Company _____

Mailing Address _____

Account # _____

Customer Service _____

[  ] **Cable Bill**

Company _____

Mailing Address _____

Account # _____

Customer Service _____

[  ] **Internet Connection**

Company _____

Mailing Address _____

Account # _____

Customer Service _____

[  ] **Garbage Collection**

Company _____

Mailing Address _____

Account # _____

Customer Service _____

[  ] _____

_____

# [$] Our Budget Worksheet

Start by finding out your joint monthly income. The use the chart below to track everything the two of you spend in a month (either write it all down or use cancelled checks, debit payments, and ATM withdrawals to add up what you spend). If the outflow is more than the income, make adjustments. If not, make sure you keep up the good work. The numbers in parentheses represent national recommendations by the Consumer Credit Counseling Bureau for the percentage of your income that should be spent on these goods and services.

## Housing (20 to 30%)

| | |
|---|---|
| Housing Cost | $ _____ |
| Real Estate Taxes | $ _____ |

## Utilities (4 to 7%)

| | |
|---|---|
| Gas Bill | $ _____ |
| Electric Bill | $ _____ |
| Home Phone Bill | $ _____ |
| Telephone (and cell phone) Bill | $ _____ |
| Cable/DSL Bill(s) | $ _____ |
| Home or Renters' Insurance | $ _____ |

## Transportation (6 to 20%)

| | |
|---|---|
| Car Payments | $ _____ |
| Car Insurance | $ _____ |
| Car Maintenance/Gas | $ _____ |
| Parking | $ _____ |
| Tolls | $ _____ |
| Public Transportation | $ _____ |

## Medical (2 to 8%)

| | |
|---|---|
| Dependent Care | $ _____ |
| Health Care | $ _____ |

## Clothing (2 to 4%)  $ _____

## Investment/Savings (5 to 10%) $ _____

## Debt Management (15 to 20%)

| | |
|---|---|
| Loan Payment | $ _____ |
| Credit Card Payments | $ _____ |

## The Small Stuff (5 to 10%)

| | |
|---|---|
| Cleaning Service | $ _____ |
| Pet Care | $ _____ |
| Groceries | $ _____ |
| Cleaning Supplies | $ _____ |
| Restaurants | $ _____ |
| Bars | $ _____ |
| Takeout | $ _____ |
| Breakfast at Work | $ _____ |
| Lunch at Work | $ _____ |
| Vices (e.g., cigarettes) | $ _____ |
| Random Home Items | $ _____ |
| Grooming | $ _____ |
| Laundry/Dry Cleaning | $ _____ |
| Gym Membership | $ _____ |
| Drug Store Products | $ _____ |
| Gifts | $ _____ |
| Movies/DVD Rentals | $ _____ |
| Magazine Subscriptions | $ _____ |
| Other | $ _____ |

## Monthly Income:

| | |
|---|---|
| After-tax Income (1) | $ _____ |
| After-tax Income (2) | $ _____ |
| Interest/Other Income | $ _____ |

## Total:   $ _____

---

Income $ _____ - Expenses $ _____ = Money to savings or splurges $ _____

# [$] Our Accounts: Banks

## Savings

**Account Type** _____

**Bank** _____

**Account Owner** _____

**Account Number** _____

**Customer Service** _____

**Website** _____

**Login Information** _____

## Checking

**Account Type** _____

**Bank** _____

**Account Owner** _____

**Account Number** _____

**Customer Service** _____

**Website** _____

**Login Information** _____

## Money Market

**Account Type** _____

**Bank** _____

**Account Owner** _____

**Account Number** _____

**Customer Service** _____

**Website** _____

**Login Information** _____

# [$] Our Accounts: Investments

## 401k/IRA

Account Type _____

Company _____

Account Owner _____

Account Number _____

Customer Service _____

Website _____

Login Information _____

## Brokerage

Account Type _____

Company _____

Account Owner _____

Account Number _____

Customer Service _____

Website _____

Login Information _____

## CDs

Account Type _____

Company _____

Account Owner _____

Account Number _____

Customer Service _____

Website _____

Login Information _____

# [$] Our Accounts: Loans

## Mortgage

**Bank** _____

**Account Owner** _____

**Account Number** _____

**Interest Rate** _____

**Customer Service** _____

**Website** _____

**Login Information** _____

## Student Loans

**Bank** _____

**Account Owner** _____

**Account Number** _____

**Interest Rate** _____

**Customer Service** _____

**Website** _____

**Login Information** _____

## Car Loans

**Bank** _____

**Account Owner** _____

**Account Number** _____

**Interest Rate** _____

**Customer Service** _____

**Website** _____

**Login Information** _____

# [$] Our Accounts: Credit Cards

## Credit Card 1

**Company** _____

**Account Owner** _____

**Account Number** _____

**Interest Rate** _____

**Customer Service** _____

**Website** _____

**Login Information** _____

## Credit Card 2

**Company** _____

**Account Owner** _____

**Account Number** _____

**Interest Rate** _____

**Customer Service** _____

**Website** _____

**Login Information** _____

## Credit Card 3

**Company** _____

**Account Owner** _____

**Account Number** _____

**Interest Rate** _____

**Customer Service** _____

**Website** _____

**Login Information** _____

## Other

Account Type _____

Company _____

Account Owner _____

Account Number _____

Customer Service _____

Website _____

Login Information _____

## Other

Account Type _____

Company _____

Account Owner _____

Account Number _____

Customer Service _____

Website _____

Login Information _____

## Other

Account Type _____

Company _____

Account Owner _____

Account Number _____

Customer Service _____

Website _____

Login Information _____

# [$] Our Insurance

## Property Insurance

**Firm Name** _____

**Name of Policy Holder** _____

**Account Number** _____

**Type of Policy** _____

**Claims Phone #** _____

**Coverage Period** _____

**Website** _____

## Renters' Insurance

**Firm Name** _____

**Name of Policy Holder** _____

**Account Number** _____

**Type of Policy** _____

**Claims Phone #** _____

**Coverage Period** _____

**Website** _____

## Auto Insurance

**Firm Name** _____

**Name of Policy Holder** _____

**Account Number** _____

**Type of Policy** _____

**Claims Phone #** _____

**Coverage Period** _____

**Website** _____

## Life Insurance

Firm Name _____

Name of Policy Holder _____

Account Numbers _____

Type of Policy _____

Claims Phone # _____

Coverage Period _____

Website _____

## Health Insurance

Firm Name _____

Name of Policy Holder _____

Account Numbers _____

Type of Policy _____

Claims Phone # _____

Coverage Period _____

Website _____

## Disability

Firm Name _____

Name of Policy Holder _____

Account Numbers _____

Type of Policy _____

Claims Phone # _____

Coverage Period _____

Website _____

# Our Home Inventory

The best thing you can do to recoup your material losses in case of a fire, flood, or other act of God is have a photo inventory of your goods. Every six months or so, take a picture of your apartment, print it out, and file it away.

[image here]

**Item Name**

**Description**

**Cost/Value**

**Quantity**

**Date/Place Purchased**

**Make**

**Model**

**Serial Number**

**Receipt/Appraisal**

[image here]

**Item Name**

**Description**

**Cost/Value**

**Quantity**

**Date/Place Purchased**

**Make**

**Model**

**Serial Number**

**Receipt/Appraisal**

[image here]

**Item Name**

**Description**

**Cost/Value**

**Quantity**

**Date/Place Purchased**

**Make**

**Model**

**Serial Number**

**Receipt/Appraisal**

[image here]

Item Name

Description

Cost/Value

Quantity

Date/Place Purchased

Make

Model

Serial Number

Receipt/Appraisal

[image here]

Item Name

Description

Cost/Value

Quantity

Date/Place Purchased

Make

Model

Serial Number

Receipt/Appraisal

[image here]

Item Name

Description

Cost/Value

Quantity

Date/Place Purchased

Make

Model

Serial Number

Receipt/Appraisal

[image here]

Item Name

Description

Cost/Value

Quantity

Date/Place Purchased

Make

Model

Serial Number

Receipt/Appraisal

[image here]

Item Name

Description

Cost/Value

Quantity

Date/Place Purchased

Make

Model

Serial Number

Receipt/Appraisal

[image here]

Item Name

Description

Cost/Value

Quantity

Date/Place Purchased

Make

Model

Serial Number

Receipt/Appraisal

# Our Moving Checklist

## Month Before (or earlier)

[ ] Hire mover

[ ] Have mover visit home to assess needs and firm up moving fee

[ ] Sign agreement with mover, making sure to note their liability for damages

[ ] If moving to or from an apartment, make arrangements with building to reserve move-in/move-out date

## Week Before

[ ] Confirm pick-up and delivery date with moviers

[ ] Pay all local bills

[ ] Initiate all utilities in new location

[ ] Return cable box and remote

**If moving long distance**

[ ] Transfer your bank accounts and empty safe-deposit box

[ ] Get final shots/treatments for pets

[ ] Get your prescriptions for the next month and fill them

[ ] Confirm travel reservations

**Pack personal items and valuables you'd prefer to handle yourselves:**

[ ] Documents: passports, SS cards, birth certificates, etc.

[ ] Fine jewelry

[ ] Irreplaceable family photographs

[ ] Sentimental items

[ ] Prescription medication

[ ] Move-related paperwork

[ ] Laptop

[ ] PDAs

[ ] Computer file backup

## Day Before

[ ] Confirm mover arrival time

**Perform one last walk-through of your old home**

[ ] Drain gas from all engines (i.e., from lawn mower)

[ ] Drain all hoses

[ ] Disconnect appliances

[ ] Defrost refrigerator and freezer

**Pack and clearly label box of moving-day essentials**

[ ] Scissors

[ ] Measuring tape

[ ] Band-Aids

[ ] Cell phone charger

[ ] Paper towels

[ ] Surface/glass cleaner

[ ] Paper plates, cups, and utensils (enough for at least one day)

[ ] Extension cords

[ ] Flashlight and spare batteries

[ ] Hammer

[ ] Nails

[ ] Screwdriver

[ ] Light bulbs

[ ] iPod and clock radio

## Moving Day

[ ] Dress for moving day. Wear pants and keep two sets of keys (new and old), markers, and cell phone on you at all times

[ ] Set aside boxes you will be moving yourself to avoid confusion

[ ] Be sure someone is on location to direct movers

[ ] Note all utility meter readings

[ ] Lock doors and confirm all windows are closed before departure

## Delivery Day

[ ] Be at delivery location upon movers' arrival

[ ] Check your belongings carefully and note on the inventory paperwork any damaged items

[ ] On an interstate move, be prepared to pay the driver before your possessions are unloaded

[ ] Supervise unloading and unpacking

[ ] Be prepared to pay your mover with cash, certified check, or traveler's checks unless other arrangements have been made in advance

# [✈] Our Trip Planner

### Airline 1

**Frequent Flyer Number** _____

**Website and Phone** _____

_____

_____

### Airline 2

**Frequent Flyer Number** _____

**Website and Phone** _____

_____

_____

### Airline 3

**Frequent Flyer Number** _____

**Website and Phone** _____

_____

_____

**Hotel Program** _____

**Number** _____

**Website** _____

_____

_____

**Hotel Program** _____

**Number** _____

**Website** _____

_____

_____

### Other Travel-Related Memberships

_____

_____

**AAA Number** _____

**Travel Agency** _____

**Contact Info** _____

_____

_____

### Online Travel Planning Site Account

_____

_____

_____

_____

### Online Travel Planning Site Account

_____

_____

_____

_____

### Online Travel Planning Site Account

_____

_____

_____

_____

## Our Dates to Remember

Remembering birthdays, anniversaries, and the like is harder now that you're doing it for two. Keep track here, and use this to mark up your calendar when you get it each year. You'll never again miss an important event.

**Her Mother's Birthday** _____

**Her Father's Birthday** _____

**Her Parents' Anniversary** _____

**Her Maternal Grandmother's Birthday** _____

**Her Maternal Grandfather's Birthday** _____

**Her Maternal Grandparents' Anniversary** _____

**Her Paternal Grandmother's Birthday** _____

**Her Paternal Grandfather's Birthday** _____

**Her Paternal Grandparents' Anniversary** _____

**Her Siblings' Birthdays** _____

_____

_____

**His Mother's Birthday** _____

**His Father's Birthday** _____

**His Parents' Anniversary** _____

**His Maternal Grandmother's Birthday** _____

**His Maternal Grandfather's Birthday** _____

**His Maternal Grandparents' Anniversary** _____

**His Paternal Grandmother's Birthday** _____

**His Paternal Grandfather's Birthday** _____

**His Paternal Grandparents' Anniversary** _____

**His Siblings' Birthdays** _____

_____

_____

# Our Dates to Remember (continued)

### January

_____
_____
_____
_____
_____
_____
_____
_____
_____

### April

___ _____
___ _____
___ _____
___ _____
___ _____
___ _____
___ _____
___ _____
___ _____

### February

_____
_____
_____
_____
_____
_____
_____
_____
_____
_____

### May

___ _____
___ _____
___ _____
___ _____
___ _____
___ _____
___ _____
___ _____
___ _____

### March

_____
_____
_____
_____
_____
_____
_____
_____

### June

___ _____
___ _____
___ _____
___ _____
___ _____
___ _____
___ _____
___ _____

July

August

September

October

November

December

# Gifts We've Given

| Who | Occasion | Gift | Thank-You Sent |
|-----|----------|------|:---:|
| | | | [ ] |
| | | | [ ] |
| | | | [ ] |
| | | | [ ] |
| | | | [ ] |
| | | | [ ] |
| | | | [ ] |
| | | | [ ] |
| | | | [ ] |
| | | | [ ] |
| | | | [ ] |
| | | | [ ] |
| | | | [ ] |
| | | | [ ] |
| | | | [ ] |
| | | | [ ] |
| | | | [ ] |
| | | | [ ] |

# Gifts We've Received

| Who | Occasion | Gift | Thank-You Sent |
|---|---|---|---|
| | | | [ ] |
| | | | [ ] |
| | | | [ ] |
| | | | [ ] |
| | | | [ ] |
| | | | [ ] |
| | | | [ ] |
| | | | [ ] |
| | | | [ ] |
| | | | [ ] |
| | | | [ ] |
| | | | [ ] |
| | | | [ ] |
| | | | [ ] |
| | | | [ ] |
| | | | [ ] |
| | | | [ ] |

# Our Wish List

Keep a list of the top twenty things you'd like to do in your life together. Include places you'd love to visit, skills you hope to learn, goals you'd like to accomplish.

1. _____

2. _____

3. _____

4. _____

5. _____

6. _____

7. _____

8. _____

9. _____

10. _____

11. _____

12. _____

13. _____

14. _____

15. _____

16. _____

17. _____

18. _____

19. _____

20. _____

# Our Anniversaries

## First Anniversary

We gave (paper):_____

How we celebrated:

_____
_____
_____

## Second Anniversary

We gave (cotton):_____

How we celebrated:

_____
_____
_____

## Third Anniversary

We gave (leather):_____

How we celebrated:

_____
_____
_____

## Fourth Anniversary

We gave (flowers):_____

How we celebrated:

_____
_____
_____

## Fifth Anniversary

We gave (wood):_____

How we celebrated:

_____
_____
_____

## Sixth Anniversary

We gave (iron):_____

How we celebrated:

_____
_____
_____

## Seventh Anniversary

We gave (wool):_____

How we celebrated:

_____
_____
_____

## Eighth Anniversary

We gave (bronze):_____

How we celebrated:

_____
_____
_____

## Ninth Anniversary

We gave (pottery):_____

How we celebrated:

_____
_____
_____

## Tenth Anniversary

We gave (tin):_____

How we celebrated:

_____
_____
_____

# [acknowledgments]

To my right hand, Rosie Amodio, and The Nest team—Kathleen Murray, Amy Keith, Katie Herrick, Alonna Friedman, Laura Gilbert, Celeste Perron, Meredith Gray, Kristen Hawley, Linda DiProperzio, Christine Heslin, and illustrator Jason O'Malley—your talent, enthusiasm, and dedication never fail to floor me. Thank you for every long hour that you contributed to this project. As you all know, it would not be a reality without you.

To my editor, Pam Krauss, and her team at Clarkson Potter: You added so much to this book and to the evolution of The Nest overall. Thank you for bringing The Nest alive on bookshelves and for taking such care to perfect this first product.

To my fabulous agent and great friend, Chris Tomasino: Thank you for making this series happen and for always offering to assist me in meeting the latest challenge.

To my DH, cofounder, and partner in crime, David Liu: I've enjoyed learning so many of the lessons in these pages with you. Thank you for being my better half.

To my kids, Havana and Cairo: Thank you for being so fun and so funny.

And finally, to The Nesties: Thank you. You constantly amaze and amuse us with your honesty, loyalty, and excitement about your lives. It is your posts, your questions, and your conversations that inspire us. You are The Nest.

# INDEX

646.78
RONEY

Roney, Carley
[The nest] newlywed handbook:
an owner's manual for modern
married life
R0104801637

SANDL OF HINGS

Atlanta-Fulton Public Library

AUG          2012